Monsoon Season

An Autobiography

Willliam Q. Wu, M.D.

Introduction by: Leonard Woodcock

UniStar Publishing Inc.
Las Vegas, Nevada

UniStar Publishing, Inc.
P.O. Box 27740
Las Vegas, NV 89126
(801) 233-9319

Front Cover Art   Lana Ferris
Marketing & Publishing Consultant   Paul Berger
                                          Clipper International Inc.

Library of Congress Catalog Card Number: 96-60262
ISBN Number: 1-885854-01-03
10 9 8 7 6 5 4 3 2

Printed in the United States of America

Dedicated to:

My wife, Cecile M. Franking Wu,
My sons, William Franking Wu and Christopher Nelson Wu,
And to the memory of Christina A. Helm,
All of whom have enriched my life.

Acknowledgements:

Special thanks in preparing this memoir are due to my wife and sons, each of whom helped out, and to Leonard Woodcock.

Foreword
by Leonard Woodcock
Former U.S. Ambassador to China

I first met Dr. Wu in 1978 when he visited China with a group of American physicians. We met again in 1982 at the University of Michigan where I was teaching, an institution in which we have a common bond. When he invited me to write this foreword I readily accepted but then took overly long in doing the job. I was puzzled to find a theme to relate to this uncomplicated, personal, and remarkable narration. Then one day it came to me that much of the story of China, more than is true of any other nation, is simple, personal, and familial.

It was my great good fortune to be sent by President Jimmy Carter to China in July 1977 as America's envoy to the most populous on earth.

Twenty-eight years before, a civil war on the mainland of China had ended in the overwhelming triumph of the Chinese Communists and the retreat of the Nationalists (Guomindang) to the island of Taiwan.

The July week in 1977 which saw my coming to Beijing for the first time also witnessed the return to political power for the third time of China's paramount leader, Deng Xiaoping. This watershed event marked China's emergence from the trauma of the Cultural Revolution into a period of modernization, with foreign involvement, but based essentially on Chinese self-reliance, modes, and traditions.

The full emergence of Deng Xiaoping as China's political leader in late 1978 introduced a decade in which the Chinese people enjoyed the greatest stability, peace, and prosperity in 150 years. By the end of the decade, however, that great achievement was marred by the tragic events in Tiananmen Square when passive resistance by the authorities to seven weeks of student demonstrations for greater reforms was suddenly succeeded by extreme official violence, bringing on the Chinese regime the denunciation and sanctions of the developed world.

External events may have influenced this shift: Gorbachev's "new

v

political thinking" unleashed a growing "people power" in Eastern Europe, culminating in May, 1989, with civilians helping Hungarian soldiers tear down the barbed wire fence between Hungary and Austria, forever breaching the Iron Curtain. For months, as communist regimes crumbled in Eastern Europe and the Soviet Union itself, China's future hung in the balance. Another critical turning point may have been engineered by Deng Xiaoping on his trip to Shenzhen during Chinese New Year of 1992 when he issued his clarion call for renewed economic reform and continued opening to the outside world.

China has resumed its economic progress and the rising living standards of its people, making it more likely that a more humane governance can be achieved in a Chinese way.

China's is the longest-lived, continuing civilization and culture in our world. There had been retreat from the glory days when China was the most developed of all nations. From the shameful Opium Wars of 1840-42 perpetrated by Britain, China had been assailed by stronger powers and had seen its society torn by civil wars and chaos.

The attraction of China for her former sons and daughters is not a political one in the narrow sense but an understandable pride in a China which, after more than one hundred years of turmoil attended by foreign humiliation and domination, is once more standing on her own two feet. Well before the Opium Wars, Napoleon had said of that eventuality: "When China rises, the world will tremble ...." That fear, I think, is not consistent with the genius of the Chinese people.

It is probably idle to speak in historical terms of the genius of a people, as it is to speak of the affinity of the Chinese and American peoples. Yet these are facts which do not explain themselves in other ways.

Dr. Wu's attractive story is one aspect of that affinity.

PROLOGUE

I was born in Toisan, a district of Guangdong Province in China. Once named Sunning, it lies on a plateau and its southern boundary touches the South China Sea, a portion of the Pacific Ocean. The port city of Guangzhou, or Canton, lies to the east. The British Crown Colony of Hong Kong, the gateway of southern China, stands southeast of Guangzhou.

The influences that brought me to America started in the nineteenth century. At that time, the sea-going trade in Guangzhou attracted many people from Toisan, which was overcrowded and unable to feed all its population. When word of the California gold rush reached the impoverished district, its people eagerly took ship for America if they could. When successful adventurers began to send money back to Toisan, their relatives and friends also wanted to go. As the gold boom receded, they found other occupations. In the 1860s, the Central Pacific Railroad of California began hiring Chinese workers. They too later found other occupations and one man returned to build the first privately owned railroad in China, in Toisan.

The city of Toisan held the local government. It had jurisdiction over the many villages, each of which belonged to a specific clan, such as Chen, Wong, and Ng — the last pronounced "Wu" in Mandarin. The clans had semi-official governing bodies of their own, so many of their internal problems were solved within the clan. Each clan also had elected representation in the legislature of the prefecture. The system was nominally democratic after the Revolution of 1911 under Dr. Sun Yat-sen, but corruption remained a problem. The clans also established their own primary and high schools, usually locating the high schools in Toisan City.

Some of the emigrants from Toisan travelled abroad and were successful enough to return wealthy. Others succeeded in their endeavors and remained where they were, while of course most were not so fortunate. The descendants of emigrants from Toisan to the United States became ethnic Americans.

I first left home for America as a child in 1923; twelve years later, I journeyed back to my village for the first time.

Chapter One

I set sail for China on May 4, 1935.

At that time, I had just taken a leave from the University of Michigan Medical School. A few months earlier, my father in China had sent a telegram saying that my third sister, Bijin, had died at the age of nineteen. Too distraught to finish the semester, I had arranged to go home to my family back in our peasant village.

I took the train from Ann Arbor, Michigan, to Seattle, still upset by my decision to leave school in mid-term. It felt like an admission of failure, even under the pressure of a tragedy. The purpose of my trip was to help me recover emotionally.

As I stepped off the train in Seattle, wondering how to find my ship, a stranger came up to me.

"Are you going to China?"

"Yes, sir."

"I'm George Wong, a travel agent. What's your name?"

"I'm Bill Wu."

"I'm pleased to meet you. I see you aren't one of my clients, but if you have no commitments, I'll be glad to help you."

"Thank you. I'd appreciate it." By his speech and manner, I knew he had been born in the United States, obviously of Chinese descent.

"What is your field?"

"I'm a medical student."

"Ah. Congratulations." His manner became even more considerate. "You have tickets for your trip already?"

"Yes. I'm scheduled to board the S.S. Empress of Canada, sailing tomorrow out of Vancouver."

"All right. We have to move fast, but we can make it."

We met three more clients waiting for him at the exit of the train

1

station. He dropped them off at his place of business and then escorted me to the Canadian Pacific Co. It owned the fleet of Empress ships and could sell me a ticket for the overnight ferry to Vancouver.

At the pier, American immigration officers checked my papers and found everything in order.

"You still have about an hour and a half before the ferry sails," said Mr. Wong. "Let's get something to eat first."

He took me to a restaurant where we had a fine Chinese dinner. I could not have found as good a place on my own. When we finished, I offered to pay my share.

"No, this is my treat. You students don't have any money, anyway, and I'm glad to have your company."

When I offered to pay for his services, he refused again and laughed. "When you become a big shot, then you can remember me."

"I may never become a big shot, but I'll always remember you."

We returned to the pier, where we shook hands and he pressed his business card into my palm.

The ferry sailed at eight P.M. Already fatigued from the train trip, I went to bed early and slept well. At dawn, the ferry docked, and after a brief immigration check at the pier, all the passengers were guided to the gangplanks of the <u>Empress of Canada</u>.

The stewards directed us to our cabins. Though I was a third class passenger, who would normally travel in a large dormitory-like room in the lowest level, they took me to a very nice double cabin just to the side of the second-class dining room. The ship had only eight such cabins. I learned later that I received this consideration entirely because of Mr. Wong.

Just before the ship sailed, everyone went to the top deck to wave and throw streamers. I joined them, though of course no one on the dock knew me. Afterward, I returned to my cabin and met my roommate.

He and all our neighbors in the other seven cabins were Chinese students. Three were coeds attending the University of Wisconsin and the rest came from various parts of Canada, including a student from McGill University in Montreal. I felt very fortunate to be among a group of students near my age and I suspected that Mr. Wong had arranged this, too.

Thinking of him, I took out his business card and looked at it. On the back he had written, "When you arrive in Hong Kong, show this to the travel agent there."

As the time for dinner approached, I explored the nearby area of the ship. I walked around alone, learning my way. At one point, an opening door almost struck me.

"I'm sorry," said a young, pretty Chinese woman.

"That's all right; no harm done."

She spoke excellent English, and we struck up a conversation. I suggested that we explore the ship together. We were both shy as we learned our way around, and I did not ask her any personal questions. During our walk, we only talked about the ship; we did not even exchange names. By the time we located the dining area, dinner had begun. The ship served Chinese food, since most of the third-class passengers were Chinese. We sat down together to eat.

The square tables seated eight and as we sat down with six men, we finally introduced ourselves. She was Grace Sun, a graduate student from the University of Toronto who originally came from Beijing. Though I had learned some Mandarin from my fraternity brothers in Alpha Lambda who came from northern China, I could not converse with her in her dialect, so we continued to speak English together.

Our table mates were all older businessmen from Toisan, the district in Guangdong Province where I was born. They spoke either broken English or Toisanese. Grace did not understand Toisanese, so I translated for her when one of them said something interesting.

After dinner, Grace and I walked along the promenade deck. We later learned that third-class passengers were not allowed there, but no one stopped us. I invited her down to meet my roommate and the other shipmates in our secluded section.

After a while one of the other young women spoke up. "I don't have a roommate. If Grace doesn't mind the upper bunk, perhaps we could move her here."

Grace thanked her but hesitated for fear of intruding. Everyone assured her that she was welcome. The next day, we contacted the Chinese steward in charge. He had no objection, so Grace joined us.

To our surprise, just before dinner time, one of the attendants informed us that if we did not mind waiting a little, we did not have to go to the dining room to eat. They would serve us in our quarters. We were glad to have the convenience and privacy for meals, but all of us were surprised at this special treatment.

As we became more acquainted with the Chinese stewards and service staff, we learned that they considered us the new intelligentsia of China. In the 1930s, China suffered both from civil war between the Communists and Nationalists and also from the invasion of Manchuria by Japan. The Chinese stewards and staff members felt that we Chinese college students studying in the U.S. and Canada would someday contribute to building a better and stronger China.

During their leisure time, they would come and play cards and checkers with us. They also told stories about their lives, many of which were very interesting and some of which were quite sad. At other times, when we were not interrupted by safety drills, we would read or nap. One fellow had a guitar, and he played while the others sang.

I liked Grace a lot, and we quickly established a comfortable rapport. Though we had just met, our new friends in this group assumed by our manner that we were old friends. As the days went by, we spent most of our time together, and our friendship grew closer. Yet we had not really confided anything personal in each other.

We went to the movies on Tuesday evenings and to church on Sunday. On other occasions, we used the promenade deck as though we belonged there. In the afternoon, we usually sat on deck chairs and gazed toward the horizon, ignoring the areas marked for shuffleboard and deck tennis.

Early one evening, I asked timidly, "Would you mind telling me more about yourself?"

"You probably don't want to know much about me." She smiled slightly. "If you promise not to laugh, I'll tell you all you want to know."

"I promise."

Grace told me she had been born and raised in Beijing. As an only child, she had been lovingly spoiled by her parents. After middle school in Beijing, she had taken entrance examinations at Qilu University at Zhinan, in Shandong Province. She had majored in sociology there and had engaged in many extracurricular activities. Reluctantly, she added, "I was elected queen during my senior year." She blushed a little, a feminine touch that made her more beautiful than ever.

Suddenly the horn blew for a safety drill and we ran back to fetch our life jackets and take our assigned stations. During the drill, we just made sure we did what we were supposed to do. When the interruption ended, we found a cozy little spot at the foot of a staircase and continued our conversation.

She told me that while at Qilu, she had had many boyfriends, especially after she had been elected queen.

"I don't doubt it."

"Don't laugh," she said seriously. "Since I was very close to my parents, I promised them that no matter what happened, I would let them choose a husband for me. I know this is old-fashioned in this day and age, but I wanted them to be happy."

I nodded, anticipating what she would say next.

"Three years ago, before I left for Canada, I was engaged to a high school teacher who was picked out by my parents. Now that I have my Master's degree in sociology, I'm on my way home to marry him. That's my story, and I hope you enjoyed it."

I could tell from the sound of her voice that she was unhappy; for that matter, I was disappointed to learn that she was engaged. However, I understood. I had left my home and everyone I knew at the age of eleven because my family had felt it would be good for me to grow up and be educated in the United States. In the same way, she was allowing her parents to make this decision for her. She had the same devotion to family duty that I had. I respected her more for the fact that she did not want to hurt her parents by going back on her promise.

While we had talked, the hour had grown later. Now the beautiful sunset shone down on us. We returned to our quarters and found

5

the rest of our group eating dinner.

"You'd better hurry before it's all gone," someone called. "It's especially good tonight!"

We joined them. Afterward, we read until someone suggested poker. As usual, we played penny ante just for fun, until nine-thirty when one of the stewards brought a bowl of noodles for each of us. Grace and I did not talk about personal matters again that night.

Either the Pacific was unusually calm on this trip or I had outgrown the seasickness I had experienced crossing to the U.S. as a child. Perhaps the quarters, at a higher level of the ship than the ones I had used before, made the biggest difference. The companionship of friends with mutual interests created a pleasant, protective atmosphere. Now, most important of all, I had a lovely female companion with whom I could discuss anything from personal thoughts to world events.

As time passed, our friends began making teasing remarks, saying, "You two certainly make a nice couple."

Grace did not tell the rest of our companions that she was engaged. The teasing embarrassed us, but it was also fun. The attention made us feel even closer.

On another afternoon, after playing shuffleboard, Grace and I sat in a couple of deck chairs watching the sky. The sun hid behind a thick cumulus cloud while other clouds filled the wide horizon. Colors changed so fast and often that it looked as though rainbows were piled up on each other. We looked at the magnificent view for a while and then Grace turned to me.

"It's your turn to tell me about yourself," she said quietly.

I explained that I was a medical student in Ann Arbor, Michigan, and how my third sister, Bijin, had died either from a ruptured appendix or perhaps a ruptured tubal pregnancy. She had been married only a year. When I had left the village, she had been just a baby and yet this news upset me more than that of my grandmother's death. My grandmother had lived out her full life, but the death of a nineteen-year-old seemed unfair and unnatural.

Because of this news, I could not concentrate on my studies. My grades had faltered. The Dean's office had called me in for an explanation.

I told Dr. Arthur Curtis, secretary of the medical school, about my sister's death. His tone was sympathetic, but he told me to take some time off and go home if it would help; otherwise, I wasn't going to make it. I came away with a feeling of relief, since I really did not know how to deal with the situation. This semester was already a failure, but I had to avoid repeating the problem.

After all these years away from home, I still had a sealed letter my father had given me when we parted. He had told me to keep it and open it when I faced a serious problem. For the first time since then, I felt really unhappy. I finally chose to open it for the advice he had said it contained.

My father quoted Confucius: "The chief glory in life does not lie in never failing, but in rising every time you fall."

It was an inspirational message, but it was irrelevant to the occasion. I hoped that going home would ease my sense of loss. In any case, I had been gone since the age of eleven, and I wanted to see my family again.

Grace listened sympathetically, nodding.

I added to Grace that I had taken a train across the country to Seattle, and that I looked forward to seeing much of China on my trip. Some day, when I finished medical school, I wanted to work at PUMC — Peking Union Medical College, created by the Rockefeller Foundation in 1923. "Peking" was English for Beijing in those days.

"PUMC!" Grace sat up excitedly. "That's where I'm going to work when I get home. I'm going to be the Director of their Social Services Department."

"How nice — congratulations!"

"I wish you were finished with school now so we could go back there and work together."

"Yes, wouldn't it be great?" Privately, I wasn't so sure, since she would be getting married soon.

"During this trip home, are you planning to visit Beijing, too?"

"Yes, I am."

"I have a suggestion. Why don't you join me and go there directly? I would be glad to show you Beijing. I'll take you to see your friends and PUMC."

I liked the idea. My frat brother Paul Kwan had graduated from Michigan three years ahead of me and was now doing his surgical residency in Beijing. He had often urged me to join him.

In addition, I had agreed to look up Han Tu, or Ruby Han, a student at Yenjing University. She was a fianceé of Raymond Huang, a fraternity roommate of mine, and she was planning to join him soon. Before I had left Michigan, he had requested that I accompany her back to the U.S. when I returned.

Grace's suggestion was enticing. However, it necessitated a change in my itinerary. I would have to disembark at Kobe, Japan, and take a smaller Japanese ship to Tanku, the port of the Chinese city Tianjin. I did not know if this could be arranged, but the purser told me it could be done with a slight additional charge, so I made the arrangements.

That evening, Grace and I took a short walk. She was pleased that I had changed my plans to come with her. We sat down near the game room and looked at each other silently for a moment.

"Kiss me," she whispered suddenly.

I did. She seemed almost to faint, and I was a little scared. Fortunately, she came around. I was glad no one was nearby. Though I wanted to kiss her again, I said that we should get back. That was the first real kiss I had ever given to a young lady, and the experience left me a little shaken.

We walked back to our quarters arm in arm, in a quiet mood of delight. By the time we returned to our respective cabins, the others had already gone to sleep. However, I had not forgotten that Grace was engaged.

Chapter Two

I had to write home to inform my parents of my new itinerary. The letter would be mailed from Japan, since the Empress line of ships did not stop in Hawaii. We followed a course northward along the west coast of the U.S. and Canada, then passed westward just south of the Aleutian Islands before turning southwest to Japan.

The remainder of this leg of our voyage passed quickly in Grace's company. Soon the ship sailed into the Inland Sea of Japan. It was a beautiful waterway among the islands on the way to Kobe. As I watched the scenery, though, I began to get anxious, wondering if I had made the right decision.

When I looked at Grace again, I forgot my doubts. Prolonging my time with her would be wonderful, even if she was engaged. As the ship pulled up to the pier, we had our suitcases with us, ready to go ashore. The freight handlers would transfer the larger trunks.

Grace and I carefully walked down the gangplank carrying our bags. As soon as we were on land, a Canadian missionary couple, Dr. and Mrs. Noyes, greeted Grace warmly. She introduced me shyly as a student shipmate who was also going to Beijing.

I had the feeling that they were suspicious of our relationship. However, they did not object outright to my presence. They were kind enough to take us to lunch. Then we went to the ship company office to confirm the new reservations that the purser had made for me by wireless.

Everything was in order. However, our ship for China, the S.S. Choan Maru, was not sailing until noon the next day. That meant we had to have lodging for the night. Dr. and Mrs. Noyes lived on the other side of Kobe and could not put us up if we were to catch the ship by sailing time the next day. Instead, they took us to a small but very nice Japanese hotel with a garden in the middle. They made sure that I had a room across the garden from Grace.

As soon as they had left, however, Grace came to my room. She told me that she was afraid to be so far away from me. Flattered, I took her back to the reception desk and asked if two rooms close to each other were available.

The man at the desk spoke perfect English. "There is no problem." He winked. "I'll give you two new rooms directly facing each other across the corridor."

"Thank you," I said. His unaccented speech made me curious. "By the way, where did you learn to speak such good English?"

"I was born in Hawaii." He smiled, amused by our request. "Have a good rest and a good night."

I helped Grace move her luggage and then shifted mine to my new room.

"Come here," she said. "Let's make some plans for tomorrow."

We sat down in a couple of chairs, but they were small and uncomfortable. Instead of remaining in them, we moved to the sofa, and without a word, Grace lay down and rested her head in my lap. I was startled, but made her comfortable. She looked up with tears in her eyes.

I kissed her lightly and she rose up to put her arms around my neck. We held each other for a moment, and then she began to sob.

"I don't know what I am going to do," she said. "I think I've fallen in love with you."

"You mustn't. Your life is all mapped out for you." After a moment, I added, "My feelings for you are the same. But I've constantly reminded myself that I shouldn't create any new complications in your life. In a few days, you'll be home and that will probably change everything."

She fell asleep in my lap. I carried her to her bed quietly and returned to my room. Tired after the long day, I went right to bed.

I had visited Japan once before, when I first journeyed to the United States as a boy to join my Uncle Howard in the Chinatown of Philadelphia. On the way, my ship had docked in Yokohama, Japan. All the passengers went ashore in the evening after Japanese immigration officers finally finished checking the passenger list. I went ashore with Cousin Feng Chiu, a grown relative who accompanied me on the trip. They all seemed to know where to go.

We each rode a rickshaw to a nice little house where everyone had to remove his shoes before entering on a mat-covered floor. The smell of perfume choked me. The kimono-clad, heavily made-up young women came out and one by one took the passengers upstairs. At first I thought it was a restaurant, but I finally realized it was a brothel. I had heard of them.

One of the girls, realizing that I was just a boy, came out to entertain me. She tried to talk with gestures, and put a stool near a little stove for me to sit on. Then she gave me a cup of tea. While I drank it, she sang a song to me. Pleasant and understanding, she kept me company while I waited.

As I thought of my previous visit to Japan, I fell asleep.

In the middle of the night, I was awakened by a knock on the door. A glance at my watch showed me it was around four A.M. I opened the door with the safety chain still attached and saw Grace, wearing a robe over her nightgown.

"I've been awake more than an hour," she said. "I took a hot bath and changed into my nightclothes, but I've been lying awake feeling lonesome and sad. I hope you don't mind my waking you up, but I need your company. Please come over."

I put a robe on over my pajamas and walked across the hall, closing her door behind me. When I entered the room, Grace was already back in bed. She gestured for me to lie down beside her. I took off my robe and joined her.

"What irony," I thought to myself. "I'm here in a Japanese inn without knowing a single soul, in bed with a beautiful young woman for the first time in my life, and I'm only worrying about interfering with her marriage plans."

Grace whispered, "Please kiss me."

We kissed and fondled each other gently.

After a moment, she said softly, "Why don't you do it to me?"

I was stunned and remained quiet.

"Is anything wrong?"

"Please don't be angry, but listen to what I have to say."

11

She nodded.

"Ever since we met, I've dreamed of a chance to be alone with you like this. But after learning about your impending marriage, I suppress a fantasy every time it surfaces in my mind. Now the fantasy has become a reality, but I still don't want to hurt you or leave you with any guilt. I've stuck to my principles and tonight I've had the acid test. I hope you understand."

She smiled. "I think you're a fool not to take advantage of an opportunity that you may never have again. Moreover, I should feel insulted and angry at being rejected. But I've always considered you a gentleman. You're courteous and pleasant to everyone, charming and intelligent. I've never been afraid of you. Yet it's those attributes of a gentleman that I admired, that led to love."

Actually, I wasn't as certain as I had sounded. Still, if I really cared about her, ruining her marriage would be very selfish. She knew that, of course; both of us had our sense of family duty.

I was very glad she was not angry at being turned down.

The next morning, we rose early and took rickshaws to the pier. We did not talk about the night before. Our need to board the ship gave us an excuse to keep busy.

The S.S. Choan Maru was about a third of the size of the Empress of Canada. It had only two classes of passenger. Since we could not afford first class, we traveled general class. Instead of staterooms, we slept in an open ward with wooden beds lining each side. The beds held thin mattresses covered with reed mats. Though about twenty beds lined each wall, low partitions separated a small space for each occupant.

All the other passengers in our class were Japanese. They seemed to be businessmen or traders. Though they watched us curiously, their manner remained polite.

Fortunately, Grace received the first space on the starboard side, so that her left was against a wall, and my bed was on her right. I slipped off the partition separating Grace and me. This aroused even more curiosity among the others.

Since the ward offered no privacy, all of us slept in our clothes.

The two bathrooms had one entrance, with a center wall inside separating the male and female facilities. We did have access to an open deck for sunlight and fresh air. Sometimes when most people were outside, individuals would change clothes quickly.

Neither Grace nor I liked the food, which was unfamiliar to us. They served fish at every meal, in a sort of buffet on two long tables. These held sashimi, rolls of rice wrapped in seaweed, and sushi in different styles. Pickled vegetables and roots and broth with bits of fish floating in it completed the selections. Some of the Japanese had their own eating utensils, but the ship provided bowls, plates, spoons, and disposable chopsticks. We ate only when very hungry.

Although Grace and I were actually sleeping right next to each other, we had no privacy for any romance, even of a modest sort. At night, a dim light exposed the entire sleeping deck to the many watchful passengers. We could only hold hands as we went to sleep.

During the day, we walked around the open deck or sat on the wooden benches, as there were no deck chairs. Since we could not speak Japanese, and the other passengers could not speak English, we made no friends. We only smiled and nodded to them, usually receiving bows in return. Reading, walking, sunning, and napping consumed our three-day crossing.

As before, the time passed quickly. At times we wished it would last longer, since at the end of the trip we would be permanently separated. We said very little, but all of it was meaningful. Despite the quiet, we felt very close.

Finally the ship docked at Tangku. After gathering our luggage, we took an English lorry to the Tianjin railroad station. About noon, we boarded the train for Beijing.

Two hours later, we stepped off the train at Beijing. I was nervous and uneasy, and sensed that Grace was, too. Her parents and her fiancé were waiting for her at the exit.

Grace embraced her mother and both of them cried. Then she shook hands with her father and fiancé warmly. They were both in their sixties, handsome, with an easy, friendly manner. I stood by, embarrassed when they noticed me.

Finally Grace took my hand, continuing to speak in Mandarin.

13

Though I was not fluent in the national language, I was able to understand the gist of what she said. She explained I was a medical student in the United States, originally from Guangdong Province. She added that I had come to Beijing to visit friends and to look over PUMC with the idea of working there in the future.

"Since he does not speak Mandarin well enough to get around, I told him we could help him locate his friends and perhaps we could also show him some of the scenery and historical sights in Beijing."

At last, all three of my new hosts smiled and nodded, offering their hands.

"Oh, by the way, Mr. Wu was a great help to me throughout the entire voyage," said Grace, as we all shook hands. "Nearly all the third-class passengers and stewards were Cantonese but we were able to speak English to each other. I owe him much gratitude."

Her mother suggested that Mr. Shen, her fiancé, help me find lodging. He and I both agreed. Grace and her family took rickshaws home.

Mr. Shen and I took rickshaws to the PUMC area at my request. He spoke a small amount of English. Our conversation remained polite but stilted, since I could not tell him anything of substance about my trip with Grace. He located a small inn with about twenty rooms, charging only five Chinese dollars, or yuan, a day. It was nicely kept, though dusty when the windows were open.

With my limited Mandarin, I thanked Mr. Shen and told him I would get along fine as soon as I contacted Dr. Paul Kwan. That should be no problem. He assured me that he and Grace would check with me and take me out to lunch or dinner soon, then left.

So I knew I would see Grace again, but I doubted I would see her alone. For now, I tried not to think about her. After unpacking and washing up in the bathroom down the hall, I ventured out for a haircut.

The barbers knew I had come from elsewhere by my clothes and my clumsy Mandarin. I was able to tell them that I wanted a haircut and a shampoo. They all listened politely, nodding and smiling, probably amused at my accent.

When they finished, adding a little hair oil, they charged me only one yuan. Since I had no small change, I gave the barber another yuan for a tip. He was quite surprised and probably thought I was stupid for over tipping so much. In any case, he bowed constantly as I left the shop.

Next, I wanted to look up Paul Kwan and get my mind off Grace completely. As I walked from the barber shop to Wang Fu Jiang Street, and headed for PUMC, I thought about my first arrival at the University of Michigan. I had stepped off the train as a stranger in town, but that hadn't lasted long at all.

The moment I looked around the small train station in Ann Arbor, I saw some Chinese students. One of them came up to me and asked, "Are you a new student? A few of us are here to meet and help new arrivals."

"Yes, I am."

"As soon as you get all your luggage, we'll help you find a place to stay."

They met one other new Chinese student, as well. We went from the train station to 1402 Hill Street, the house of the international Chinese fraternity, Alpha Lambda. One of its activities was to assist Chinese students anywhere in the world, without any coercion for them to pledge their frat. In fact, they offered to help me locate a place of lodging elsewhere.

"Is there a place for me to stay here?" I asked. "At least until I get my bearings?"

"Of course," said Peter Lim, one of the fellows who had met me at the train station. "I'm not sure when the rest of the students will return. In any case, don't worry. I'll help you get settled."

That gave me a great deal of reassurance. In a short time, I was startled to learn that Peter not only came from Toisan, but had even attended the same grade school as I. That made me feel more at home. As it turned out, I did not have to move, either.

Later, I chose to join the fraternity. I liked the purpose and principles of the fraternity. It had no political affiliation, but promoted friendship and fellowship among its members. Also, it provided social, financial, and scholastic help to members when necessary. This was exactly the kind of environment I had been looking for, as well, with Chinese students who intended to return to China someday to work.

It had a mundane advantage, too; I learned to cook there.

Alpha Lambda had a preponderance of engineering students in different areas, including Chen Fu Hua, who became a friend. An outstanding architectural student, W.P. Li, had won a fellowship to study in Rome. Another student did graduate work in bacteriology under Frederick G. Novy, dean of the medical school, and one of the few remaining students of the German scientist, Robert Koch, who had discovered the tuberculosis bacillus. The only medical student in the fraternity was Paul Kwan.

Paul acted as my big brother. He gave me much valuable information in my preparation for medical school. With his advice and my determination, I earned an acceptance after three years of college.

When I reached PUMC, I entered a large compound shaped in a square, with entrances on every side. Two entrances led to the medical college and two to the hospital. Inside the compound, crosswalks connected the school and hospital, while shrubbery and flowers adorned the central courtyard. The architecture was externally patterned after imperial palaces, and internally designed for Western efficiency. The decor combined cultural influences from both; the roof was made of traditional Chinese tiles of gold and green, while the hospital lobby had marble columns.

I knew that prominent Americans chaired most of the departments, except for a few Chinese who had been educated in America or Europe. An American woman directed the nursing school. PUMC, with its original financing from the Rockefeller Foundation, was regarded as the finest medical complex in East Asia at that time.

The information desk paged Paul Kwan for me. Luckily, he was not scrubbed for surgery. Paul was amazed to see me and pumped my hand eagerly.

"When did you get here? How did you get here? Why didn't you write first?"

I explained as he led me to the house officers' quarters.

"I'm off tonight," he said. "We'll go out to dinner tonight unless you have other engagements."

I accepted, and waited in his quarters until he finished his shift at five o'clock. He showered quickly and changed from his white uniform into street clothes. "There's a nice little restaurant nearby," he said. "Let's walk."

"Fine. I'm still getting rid of my sea legs."

At the restaurant, Paul did the ordering. "This is not the Cantonese food we're used to," he cautioned. "But I've become accustomed to the local cuisine, and it's not bad."

Paul told me about his experiences at PUMC. His first year had been difficult, with a language problem since the patients spoke Mandarin. Now that he had mastered the dialect, he was very happy. He told me that the training program was excellent and that his colleagues were all friendly and cooperative.

"It would be a fine place for you to come after your graduation. However, you have to work very hard here, especially in the surgical service. I haven't seen my family in the three years that I've been here. Perhaps I'll take a couple of weeks off this year and pay them a visit."

When dinner was served, we had fish, mutton, vegetable dishes, and soup. This northern Chinese cuisine definitely was strange to me. However, it seemed like gourmet food after the daily diet of raw fish on shipboard.

Paul asked about some of our old frat brothers and the medical school, particularly the faculty. I told him that the important professors he knew were almost all still there. Bob Bartlett, one of his closest friends in medical school, had advanced to the rank of instructor of surgery under Dr. Frederick A. Coller, the Chairman of the Department of Surgery at Michigan.

Following Dinner, Paul showed me a few sights and then walked with me back to my hotel.

"How long will you be in Beijing? I'd like to show you around more, but I'm pretty much tied down at the hospital. But if you get bored, you can always come to my quarters or spend some time in the library."

I explained that I had a few other friends to see, one of them being a frat brother who was now a professor of economics at the University of Beijing. I told him that I also had to look up a Ruby Han at Yenjing University.

"I understand. But before you leave town, I would like to take you to an excellent production of 'Camille.'"

I accepted and Paul said he would be in touch with me about it later.

When I returned to my room, I found a note under my door from Grace. It read, "I was here to see how you were getting along, but you were out. I'll be here tomorrow morning about nine-thirty to take you to see some of the city or visit your friends, as I promised. My fiancé is in school, so I am free. Please wait for me."

Chapter Three

During the evening, I had distracted myself from thinking about her, but now I was excited by the thought of seeing her alone again. In fact, I could hardly sleep that night. The next morning, I got up early, washed, and dressed, then had to wait for her. When I met her in the lobby, I could hardly keep from giving her a kiss and a hug, but Chinese custom would frown on it. Since no visitors of the opposite sex were allowed in the hotel rooms, taking her there was out of the question.

We held hands timidly as we left the hotel. I told her that I had already spent a day at PUMC and had had a very pleasant reunion with Paul Kwan.

"He'll take me to see the play 'Camille' one evening," I said. "Otherwise, I have no other engagements except to say goodbye to him before I leave town."

"Good." Grace smiled happily. "Today, I would like to show you Beijing. We'll start with Beihai Park, where there's a beautiful historic white pagoda, and a pond full of gorgeous water lilies. It also has the Bridge of Perfect Wisdom. Then we'll go see the Palace Museum, better known as the 'Forbidden City.'"

We took rickshaws to Beihai. The park was as beautiful as she had described, but I was more interested in her than in the park. All I could think about was how much I wanted to be with her and how little time we had left. I glanced at her periodically and she would lower her eyes momentarily before looking up as though she was about to say something. Instead of speaking, though, she just smiled and squeezed my hand.

Later, except for a general impression of the place, I hardly remembered anything about it — certainly not much history.

Before we went over to the Palace Museum, we stopped at a small shop for noodles. It was time to bring the situation out into the open. I asked about her parents and Mr. Shen.

"They're fine," she said slowly. "I have the feeling that my mother knows something is bothering me. She didn't ask about you, but she did ask if I was feeling well. She thought I might be tired from the trip. I told her that I was just thinking about my coming marriage."

"I see."

"Mr. Shen ... is not as handsome or as charming as you," she said with a little smile. "He's honest and dependable, though, and he'll take good care of me. He has a good job and when I start to work, we'll do well."

"Not many people could say that," I said. "I wish you happiness, too —"

"I'm happy at this minute," she interrupted. "I'm happy when I'm with you, but it's only temporary. Soon you'll be gone, I suppose forever."

I couldn't argue with that. We dropped the subject. Then we left the restaurant and took a bus to the Palace Museum.

This was an imposing city within the city of Beijing itself. Once called the Forbidden City, it had been the palace grounds of Chinese emperors for centuries. A high, thick wall stood around it with guard towers at every corner, and a moat encircled the wall. These defenses surrounded several large palaces and many smaller buildings, numbering in the thousands.

Grace explained that the Yuan, Ming, and Qing Dynasty emperors had constructed these protected grounds for their own residence and government buildings, beginning with Kublai Khan. Beautiful marble, brought from various parts of China, adorned many of the structures. The beauty of the Palace Museum and the history told by the guides began to draw us out, and we became very talkative.

Late in the afternoon, I suggested that she return home, lest her parents or Mr. Shen suspect the intimacy of our relationship. She agreed, and we took rickshaws back to the street leading to my hotel. As I hopped out, she called to me.

"I'll be over again the same time tomorrow morning!"

I spent the evening alone. However, I had enjoyed Grace's company all day and looked forward to her returning in the morning. This time, I slept better.

In the morning, I waited for Grace in the lobby. She arrived dressed western-style. Still self-conscious in public, we shook hands, and walked out together.

"I haven't had breakfast yet," I said. "I'm hungry."

Grace was more relaxed and casual today. "Poor boy. I'll take you to a Cantonese place down the street and get you some of your native food."

We went to the Canton Flavor Shop. Everything looked familiar and tasty. I ordered a bowl of congee — soft-cooked rice with chopped pork — and a dish of doughnut twists, as well as tea. Grace had already eaten, and ordered only tea.

When we had finished, Grace grabbed the check and paid it. "You are a guest in Bejing and we don't want you to spend any money while you're here. In fact, my mother gave me extra money to entertain you. I was surprised, but she must like you, too. And if you're free Saturday evening, the day before you leave, you are invited to have dinner at our home."

I was pleased. "Thank you. I will."

We left the restaurant hand in hand.

"First we'll stop by the Temple of Heaven," said Grace. "Then we'll take a bus to the Summer Palace. This afternoon, I'll go with you to Yenjing University to look for your friend."

"That sounds fine."

Once again, as we began to see the sights, I hardly listened to the detailed descriptions given by our guides. I concentrated on Grace, and the only historical facts I learned at our first stop were that the ornate Temple of Heaven had been built without even a single nail and that the emperors went there annually to pray for a good harvest. Everything else they said missed me completely.

The trip to the Summer Palace by bus took about twenty minutes. I was surprised to find the front entrance quite small. Once inside, we could see many palaces, temples, and pagodas on Longevity Hill to the right. Kunming Lake lay on the left, with its famous Seventeen-Arch Bridge in the distance. Covered walkways held a thousand paintings.

We walked down to the elaborately carved Marble Boat, at permanent anchor in one corner of the lake. In the nineteenth century, the Dowager Empress had used naval appropriations to build the entire Summer Palace for her personal enjoyment and comfort. The Marble Boat symbolized the navy she was supposed to have built.

At one o'clock in the afternoon, we stopped at a vendor's stand for a snack and then took three buses to reach Yenjing University. Beijing was still a walled city in those years and we left through the west gate toward Yenjing in the suburbs. We went directly to the administration building and found the information desk.

After some searching, the university staff located Ruby Han, who had just finished her afternoon classes. They brought her to the information desk. Ruby's straight black hair was artificially curled in the contemporary western fashion. She had a warm and sometimes impish smile. Her face was more long than round, with high cheekbones. She was quite attractive, though Grace seemed more feminine in feature and carriage.

She did not know who I was until I explained my friendship with Raymond Huang, her fiancé in Michigan. I told her he wanted me to take her back to the U.S.

When Ruby understood, she became very excited and invited Grace and me to the reception room of her dormitory. She served tea and crackers and introduced me to some of her friends. I could tell she was curious about my relationship with Grace, but she did not ask.

Ruby did ask where I was staying, and she invited us both on a picnic to the Great Wall that Saturday. That was the night of "Camille." I told Ruby I would be occupied that evening.

"Then I'll show you more of Beijing during the day," she said. "I'll come and get you at nine A.M." She looked at Grace, who shook her head.

"No, thank you. I'm a native of Beijing," said Grace. "The two of us are shipmate friends, and I've also been showing him around."

I was not surprised that Grace declined the Saturday trip. Mr. Shen would be off work and of course expected to spend time with her. When we decided to leave, Ruby escorted us to the bus and waved goodbye.

On the bus, Grace was quiet.

"Are you all right?" I asked.

"I shouldn't feel this way, but I'm jealous. As the Chinese say, you must have a life of 'peach blossoms'— always surrounded by pretty girls."

"On the contrary. You belong to someone else. And when Ruby gets to America, she'll marry someone else, too."

"Well, I'm not worried. You'll find others better than any you've met yet. Besides, after having met you and having shared the moments we have, I shall always feel that a little part of me always belongs to you."

"You shouldn't feel that way," I said. "Your future should be solidly with Mr. Shen."

"But he's so stupid!"

I had nothing to add to that. The rest of the long ride was uneventful. Gradually, we both dozed off and awoke just before my stop. Grace and I squeezed hands lightly and I got off the bus.

Chapter Four

Another message waited for me at the hotel. It was from Paul, telling me to dress and join him at PUMC for an Alpha Lambda dinner. It was to be given in my honor, since I was President of the Ann Arbor chapter. Surprised, I hurried over to meet him.

I was awed by the group to whom he introduced me. They were all distinguished, and older than I. Some of the men had brought their wives, bringing the total to about thirty people. Paul introduced me to most of them and I circulated, introducing myself to the rest. The men were all professionals, such as professors, doctors, accountants, and government officials.

The guests asked about frat activities in the U.S. and particularly in Ann Arbor. After some toasts, we settled down to a delicious dinner in a large, private dining room. I thanked them for their hospitality and gave a brief report on the fraternity chapters in America. I told them that we would strive to measure up to the standards of accomplishment demonstrated here at the dinner. Their encouraging response honored me.

On the way home, I stopped at PUMC for a moment with Paul. We talked for a while, and he reminded me that he had tickets for "Camille" the next evening. Then I returned to my hotel.

The next morning, Grace arrived as usual and took me to breakfast again. "Beijing has many more places of interest," she said. "Still, I don't want to wear you out."

"I had a pretty good evening last night." I told her a little about my dinner the night before.

"You must be a popular person to have so many friends even here in Beijing."

I laughed and shook my head. "Except for Paul, I just met them. So what are we going to do today?"

"Since this is the last day we can be alone, why don't we find a

24

nice outdoor spot to enjoy the sunshine and good weather?"

"That sounds good."

"Coal Hill overlooks the Palace Museum and the greater part of Beijing. It's an interesting view. What do you think?"

"You're still my guide. It's your home city, so I'll just follow you."

By the time we had climbed up Coal Hill, the day had grown warm. We shed our jackets and walked around in the breeze, looking at the gorgeous view. For a moment, Grace dropped behind me. When I turned, she was opening a handkerchief wrapped around a box of food.

"You did plan a picnic! I'm glad." I sat down beside her.

Grace had brought chicken, hard boiled eggs marinated in soy sauce, and apples. We chatted casually. I still felt very close to her, but I was afraid to develop any further emotional involvement.

At one point I asked, "How long have you known Mr. Shen? I was wondering how your parents happened to select him."

"That's not an interesting story," she said plainly. "I'm more interested in your future. I wonder what it'll be like twenty years from now. You have a romantic personality and you're compassionate, concerned, and caring about people. I'm certain you'll be a great physician. I'm also envious of your wife, whoever she may be."

"Well, life is unpredictable. But if one follows the basic virtues, such as honesty, compassion, concern, and support for others, life should be happy." Then I realized I was preaching. That was the way my father talked sometimes. "I'm sorry."

"Don't be sorry; just continue. I like listening to you talk. I think you'll be the kind of person I envision you will be. Maybe twenty years from now, we'll meet again and see whether our predictions are correct." Then she saddened. "You know we'll never see each other again. Life can be so cruel sometimes. Why shouldn't we share life together, instead of following what's already ordained?"

I just shook my head. "Just think positively. Try to forget the currents that may rock the boat."

"Whatever you say, I believe. I also wish you nothing but the best. I've resigned myself to my future as long as my parents are

25

happy."

I nodded. The subject kept leading us to a dead end. Besides, the sun had lowered in the sky.

Grace remained quiet.

"I'm afraid I have to return to my hotel," I said finally. "I have to meet Paul in the hospital cafeteria for dinner before we go to 'Camille.'"

We gathered our belongings and started down Coal Hill.

"I have to go shopping tomorrow," said Grace. "I won't be able to see you."

"That's all right. I've been lucky to see you so much already."

"I wish it was more."

"Don't forget that I'm having dinner with your family on Saturday."

We took rickshaws back to town, and parted.

I hurried home to change and dress. "Camille" was the first western play I had ever seen presented in Chinese. Knowing the story, I could follow it even in Mandarin. It was well done. Two of the actors were father and daughter in real life.

Afterward, I thanked Paul for a pleasant evening. I also explained that I would not be able to see him before I left Beijing on Sunday. We shook hands and he said he expected to see me back in two or three years. He would not be able to see me off, since he would be on call at the hospital.

I had enjoyed my visit with him, but all my thoughts now were of Grace.

I had Friday to myself. I spent it writing letters and telegrams to friends. Also, I sent my family my arrival date in Hong Kong. Since I was in north China, I felt that I might as well visit as many places as I could on my way south. I wrote to friends in Tianjin, Zhinan, Nanjing, and Shanghai. That much of the trip would be made by rail; from Shanghai, I would take a boat to Hong Kong. With these arrangements made, I felt better about lingering in Beijing as long as I had.

Ruby called that afternoon to invite me to a Beijing opera at seven o'clock that night. I accepted and agreed to meet her in my hotel lobby. She arrived at six-thirty, dressed in western clothes, more slender than Grace and quite attractive in an athletic way. Going by rickshaw, we arrived at the theater just minutes before the opera began.

We each had a program detailing the opera, but the cacophonous music was so loud and the singing so high and nasal in falsetto that I could hardly stand it. I suffered through the performance and when it was over, I told Ruby that it would be hard for me to get used to the ear-piercing sounds. She told me that it was traditional for anyone from the south to attend at least one Beijing opera when they visited here. I thanked her, glad that my obligatory experience with this tradition had ended. She escorted me back to my hotel, promising to come for me tomorrow morning at ten.

When Ruby arrived the following day, Beijing was already bustling. Neither of us had eaten breakfast yet, so she took me down the main thoroughfare to a large restaurant. During breakfast, she asked me where I would like to go.

"Actually, I've seen most of the tourist spots now," I said. "I'd like to visit your school again and see more of the campus. Also, I'd like to see the University of Beijing and Qinghua University. That's the one built with the indemnity fund that China paid the United States after the Boxer Rebellion."

"Fine." Ruby seemed pleased. "You can meet more of my friends and classmates."

We rode the bus. It was a beautiful, sunny day and if I had not been committed to dinner with Grace's family, I would have taken a trip out to see the Great Wall. However, that involved an all-day excursion.

Ruby took me to the reception room of her dormitory. It had table tennis, card tables, and tea available at all times. Several of Ruby's friends came by and I was surprised to find that, like Ruby, they spoke English and Cantonese with barely discernible accents, in addition to their native Mandarin.

Her friends all asked about her fiancé, especially because they had heard recently that he had been seeing a Chinese American woman. I knew nothing about that, but assured them that casual dating was an

27

accepted custom in the United States. Of course, they may have known more about it than I did.

After we had some tea, about six of us toured the campus. We visited some laboratories, including the Harvard Institute for research. These labs all had recent equipment. The library was large and held many volumes, but the library at the University of Beijing remained without peer in China. I was particularly intrigued by the water tower at Yenjing University, built in the style of a pagoda.

We visited Qinghua University next. It was located outside the west gate of the city on a very pleasant campus. We did not get much of a tour, since none of our group located anyone we knew there. Most of the students there were at the graduate level.

The original campus of the University of Beijing lay inside the city wall. The buildings were old but in good repair. This university stressed literature and the arts and its library contained many first editions, some dating back centuries. In China, this was considered the seat of learning, centered around its library. Many great students and professors had emerged from Beijing University.

Ruby suggested that we take a general bus tour of the city. We did, and I was tired by late afternoon. Ruby was still full of energy, however.

As soon as Ruby left for her dorm late that day, I returned to my hotel room to get ready for dinner. Grace and Mr. Shen both met me in the lobby. I was amused by the hotel manager's reaction, as he seemed puzzled by the variety of my companions.

We took rickshaws, with Mr. Shen's leading the way. Grace's followed him, and she frequently turned to see if mine was still behind them. After about fifteen minutes, we turned off the main street and got out to walk. We took several steps down a narrow passageway called a hu tung and then turned first right, then immediately left.

The house, a solemn gray, was quite handsome. Its exterior had been made of sliding wooden walls, designed in Japanese-style panels. The front door folded open on both sides.

When we entered, we had to step over a small bar used to anchor the doors when locked. The furniture inside was traditional carved rosewood. I sat in a rosewood chair and found a high, square stand next to me that held teacups. As soon as I sat, a servant filled one for me.

Grace's parents sat down with Mr. Shen, Grace, and me. Her parents told her, acting as interpreter, to tell me not to feel uncomfortable even though we could not speak directly. Both gestured for me to drink tea and have some of their homemade cookies, which I did.

Mr. Shen engaged me in some conversation in his limited English. With Grace's help, we communicated fairly well. Everyone had a good laugh at our efforts.

We moved to a large, round table for dinner. I sat between Grace and her mother. To start, her father offered me a toast to welcome me to Beijing.

I asked Grace to explain to her father that I was allergic to alcohol, and to permit me to use tea instead. He refused, and so I just touched my lips to the glass, and he was happy. I had no physical tolerance for alcohol.

For dinner, we had dishes of chicken, pork, fish, and mutton in addition to vegetable soup. Mrs. Sun constantly gave me more food and told Grace to help me, also. Because of the language difficulty, we talked very little, but I felt comfortable. After dinner, we retired to the parlor.

"Excuse us," Grace said suddenly. "I just want to show Mr. Wu the other side of the house."

Everyone nodded, and she led me out of the room. Around a corner, she gave me a tender kiss and a loving embrace. I enjoyed it, but was afraid that someone would discover us. She slipped an envelope into my pocket and whispered, "Don't open it until you get home."

We returned to the parlor. Shortly thereafter, I begged my leave because of my scheduled rail departure at ten A.M. I had hoped that Grace alone would escort me back to the hotel, but Mr. Shen offered to come as well. I thanked Grace's parents heartily and the three of us took rickshaws to my hotel.

When they dropped me off, Mr. Shen said, "Tomorrow morning we'll see you at the sta—"

"I'll come by," Grace interrupted. "I'll be here early enough to take you there."

Mr. Shen said nothing more, and they left.

As soon as I got into my room, I tore open the envelope. I found a snapshot of her inside, on the back of which she had written, "To Quokan, a real gentleman, who has helped protect me and has given me much loving care. Our journey was made more pleasant and we developed a close and endearing friendship that I will cherish all my life. May your future be happy and boundless. Grace Sun."

Her gift moved me, but the feeling was bittersweet. I put it away carefully. It would be a special souvenir after I left Beijing.

The next morning, Grace arrived early, as she had promised. She had to wait for me in the lobby, since I was still packing. I finished hurriedly and joined her.

"You haven't had breakfast yet, have you?" Grace asked. "Let's go down to that little place again."

"All right," I said, with a shrug. "I ate so much last night that I still don't feel hungry." I could hardly believe that our last day together had arrived.

She took me to a small restaurant, and I ate a light breakfast. She watched me with tears in her eyes and I had difficulty holding mine back, as well. As we left, we held hands.

"We'll see each other again," Grace said, squeezing my hand.

Her parents and Mr. Shen greeted us at the station. Naturally, Grace and I had to keep up a reserved façade. Ruby and two of her schoolmates had also come.

"Write and tell me when you plan to be in Hong Kong," said Ruby. "I'll meet you there for our trip to America."

The time had come for me to leave. I shook hands with everyone and bade them farewell. Grace winked, and let a tear drop. I boarded the train and, as it pulled away, I watched them as long as I could.

This was the saddest parting I had experienced since I had first left home as a child. I had fallen in love for the first time. Grace and I had grown nearly inseparable and now I was leaving her to a man who meant nothing to her. She had told me she loved me, as far back as the Japanese inn in Kobe.

We had had a whirlwind romance across the Pacific. I was tempted to jump off the train at the next stop and hurry back for her.

It was like being caught up in the sweep of a monsoon.

I reminded myself that I was in the middle of medical school. Even more to the point, I had taken the trip home because I had been failing to keep up my grades in medical school. Besides, going back to Grace wouldn't change the fact that she was engaged.

A deeper involvement with Grace almost certainly would have destroyed my career. Even so, the temptation to take that chance was great. The feeling of emptiness and loss was, too.

Chapter Five

Grace's devotion to family duty reminded me of the first time I had heard of America. I had been a child of six, living in Ping On Village in the district of Toisan. Monsoon season had arrived.

Explosive thunder rumbled across the sky toward the west. Flashing bolts of lightning filled the low-hanging clouds with brilliant gold. Then the rains fell.

I watched the gray deluge for three days as it flooded our village in southern China and swelled the mountain streams which poured down the lush, green slopes to the east, filling the rice paddies around the village. The villagers worried that the torrent might break through the earthen embankments around the rice paddies and engulf their homes.

Fortunately, the downpour stopped as suddenly as it had come.

After the rains, the clouds vanished and tiny stars twinkled in the night sky. Nearly everyone in the small village came out to enjoy the fresh air as a crescent moon emerged over the eastern mountains.

I heard the adults bewail the hardships of life. Like peasants and farmers everywhere, they had just seen nature destroy their crops. Helpless, they spoke of destiny and destruction, and the cruelty of fate.

On this evening in the summer of 1918, my paternal grandfather reclined in a bamboo chair on an earthen terrace at the edge of the village.

Grandfather spoke up loudly over the complaints of the others. "But now, the monsoon is over. We must look ahead."

I sat at the foot of his chair.

"Quokan," Grandfather said, using my Chinese name. "Look at the new moon rising above the mountains. Beyond them is an ocean. Across that ocean is the New World, known as America. Someday, you will go there."

32

I looked into the dark sky, past the new moon.

"The New World is completely different from our own. People there speak a strange language. I believe they do not have monsoons. True, there are difficulties in life anywhere, but I think in America, you could overcome anything. They have many schools, carriages drawn by horses, engines that pull linked cars that run on long parallel tracks. They have factories that make machines and even cars that can run on streets. It is a fascinating place. Besides, there are unlimited opportunities, especially for the young."

He gazed over the moonlit silhouette of the mountains, reminiscing about the years he had spent in America.

"Oh, I forgot to tell you about the people there. They are taller than most of us and have pale complexions, with different colors of hair. Some of them even have golden hair! Their eyes are different colors, too. However, the most distinguishing feature is their prominent noses. Some of them are friendly, but many used to make fun of us, perhaps because our attire was strange to them. But, you, as a young man, could learn to speak and read their language, and you could go to school and become a scholar like your father. No monsoons ...."

Eventually, he fell asleep, leaving me to imagine what America must be like. It sounded like a fairy tale. Meanwhile, the moon rose quite a distance above the eastern horizon. I woke him so we could go back into the house and go to bed.

My grandfather went to America in the late nineteenth century and remained for ten years. In San Francisco, he sold ceramic and porcelain ware. He did not make a fortune, but he fulfilled his dream of providing the family in Toisan with a brick house and sending my father and uncle to the best schools available.

That night, my grandfather had given me his vision of my future. In a more direct way, Grace's parents had arranged their vision of her future for her, also with her welfare in mind. Like her, I had commitments to others.

I took the train to Zhinan and tried to concentrate on my upcoming plans. In Zhinan, I made arrangements to visit Eugene Chan, who was now Professor and Chairman of the Department of Ophthalmology at Qilu University Medical School. I had first met him during his seven years at Johns Hopkins, when he had recommended the University of Michigan Medical School to me; since then, he had returned to China and was probably the best American-trained Chinese ophthalmologist in China. He had built his department at Qilu, and now it rivaled even that of PUMC.

Once I had arrived at Qilu University, I was able to reach him. We talked for some time. He warned me of a problem I had not known.

"If you plan to return to China to work, you must have the courage to fight with some of the older foreigners here. They have headed some departments in China for many years and will not relinquish them to better-trained Chinese. Originally, they were supposed to turn their responsibilities over to qualified Chinese when people of our generation received modern educations."

Eugene went on to give me an example that had occurred when he had first returned to China. At that time, he had applied for a position in Ophthalmology at PUMC. Dr. Peter Kronfelt, the department head, had offered him the same rank of assistant professor that he had held at Johns Hopkins. Eugene had been insulted and discouraged. Fortunately, his reception at Qilu University had been much better. As a result, he had made his department famous and had begun publishing the Chinese Journal of Ophthalmology there.

"Foreign dominance in Chinese medical institutions should be ending soon," he said. "But we have to fight for it every inch of the way. When you return, you'll meet similar obstacles, but stand up to them. Michigan is a great school, and you'll receive an excellent education there. In fact, you should feel that it's second to none."

I stayed with him until I left for Tianjin. When we parted, he shook my hand. "I expect to see you back in a couple of years. Good luck."

In Tianjin, I was met by Peter Lim, another Michigan Alpha Lambda frat brother. He took me to the home of his in-laws, who were one of the richest families I had ever met. His father-in-law was President of the Bank of China in Tianjin and also president of a coal company. Three generations lived in one huge, multi-level building. The head of the house owned an automobile as well as several custom-built rickshaws. The staff included a chauffeur, a dispatcher, and several rickshaw pullers. They and the other servants lived in a separate house on the grounds away from the mansion. I found the large gap between rich and poor here enlightening.

I accepted their invitation to remain overnight and had time to visit Nankai University, another famous institution, before I left Tianjin.

Next, I stopped in Shanghai, where I was met by frat brother Bob Suez. His father had been a Chinese diplomat in South America. Bob was born there, and his surname, "Shi" in Chinese, had become Suez. I spotted him easily at the station, as he stood much taller than the others around him. He had made a reservation for me at the Hotel Metropole, and took me there.

Bob was always sincere and willing to help a friend, but he could also be brusk. "How long will you be in Shanghai?" he asked. "What do you want to do?"

"I'll be here only two days at most. All I want to do is visit a couple of hospitals and see a few friends, such as yourself."

"I'll see what I can do. See you tomorrow."

Bob entered the hotel coffee shop the next morning while I was having breakfast. "I think I have your program arranged for you. Since one of my uncles is Minister of Health, I had his office call the Red Cross Hospital and St. John's Hospital for visits during the day. This evening, a small fraternity group will have dinner with you."

"That's great," I said. "You certainly are efficient."

"If you only want a general tour of the hospitals, I'll go with you."

"Yes, that's fine."

We took a taxi to the Red Cross Hospital where we enjoyed a quick tour. The hospital was generally satisfactory and sanitary, but the patients were too crowded. Since it had no special point of interest, we did not stay long.

"Actually, I don't know anyone at St. John's," I told Bob. "Why don't we skip it?"

"All right. Let's go look around the French Concession and the International Settlement."

We did. These areas of the city had been owned by foreign

powers for many years, and were filled with European architecture. It was a foreign enclave, outside of Chinese governmental jurisdiction.

"What's wrong?" Bob asked, as we walked through the streets.

"This whole area disturbs me. I've just returned from a foreign country to see China. In the midst of our largest city, foreign powers have taken over our territory, and are doing as they please with their own laws to govern themselves here."

"I know. But someday this will be ours again. Please cheer up!"

Bob and I returned to the hotel for afternoon tea and a nap. He remained with me all day, and in the evening took me to the fraternity dinner. About twenty members of the local chapter were present. From Ann Arbor, I knew Benjamin King, Chester Ma, and Y.C. Mar. The others were strangers, but of course as fraternity brothers, everyone was friendly and talkative. Bob introduced me as president of my chapter and I gave another report on the fraternity in Michigan. They told me about their own chapter here in Shanghai. It numbered about one hundred fifty members, though only about fifty attended meetings. Most of them were professionals. Counted by occupation, engineers and businessmen were the most numerous, but the chapter also had architects and physicians. Bob was an automotive engineer.

Early the next morning, Bob arrived at the Metropole dressed up and carrying a suitcase. "I am going with you to Nanjing," he announced.

"You don't have to do that for my sake. The family of Chen Fu Hua is expecting me."

"I have projects there and I travel between the two cities frequently."

"Well, it's kind of you to come." I felt he was intruding, but of course I could not stop him from boarding a public train, and he had been hospitable in his own way.

We got on the train, which was ferried to Puko before journeying to Nanjing. The trip only took about two hours. Bob knew the city well and took me to the hotel where he usually stayed. Since I did not know Chen Fu Hua's family, I had written them and told them not to meet me at the station. At the hotel, which was fairly new and western in architecture, Bob helped me contact the Chens. They invited us both to dinner that night.

Nanjing was now the capital of China and the Chens sent a government car to pick us up. We arrived at a rather new house, western in architecture with some Chinese features. It had a large garden surrounded by a high wall.

Mrs. Chen was of average height, kind and radiating warmth. However, we again had a problem communicating because of the difference in our spoken dialects. The man of the house was a Mr. Wei, Secretary-General for the current Nationalist Government under President Lin Senn. However, he was not the father of the family, for everyone addressed him as "Uncle." He may have been a stepfather or Mrs. Chen's brother, but I never found out.

Mr. Wei was very much a gentleman of the old school. He greeted me by shaking hands and bowing slightly at the same time. Then we all sat down for tea. A shy young lady who spoke a few words of English asked about her brother, Chen Fu Hua. Named Edith in English, she was quite attractive, wearing a flowery Chinese gown and glasses. I told her that her brother was fine.

The conversation became stilted. I was quite annoyed that Bob had not been more sensitive, since he was really in the way. At that point, Mr. Wei pointedly asked him why he had come.
Bob replied somewhat sheepishly. "Chen Fu Hua, Bill Wu, and I were friends when we studied in the U.S. I'm accompanying Bill here in Nanjing because I have business here, and friends to visit." However, Bob did not take the hint to leave.

Dinner that first night was a banquet. We had shark's fin soup, roast duck, a special chicken dish, and an unusual fish that was a Nanjing delicacy. I sat next to Mrs. Chen, who kept piling food on my plate with the serving chopsticks. Occasionally Edith, at her mother's command, added more. They served Bob similarly, and we were both full quite soon. For dessert, we shared fruit and tea.

Before we left, Mr. Wei told us that he had made a car and chauffeur available to us while we were in Nanjing. He suggested that if Bob knew the city well, he should show me the sights in the car. We accepted.

When the car arrived at the hotel the next morning, we found

Edith waiting for us as well.

"My mother felt it would be discourteous if no one from our family accompanied you," she said.

I was very pleased to have her company. She sat between Bob and me in the back seat of the car and we conversed in a mixture of English and Mandarin. I told her more about her brother's life at Michigan.

During the ride, we viewed the Golden Purple Mountain, where the tomb of the first Ming emperor is located. We also climbed up more than three hundred steps to the mausoleum of Dr. Sun Yatsen, founder of the Chinese republic. We later visited the Five Continent Park and the Old Bell Tower.

The Chens had also arranged for me to see the Central Hospital. Modern, well-equipped, and well-staffed, it was run by the government, and accepted all government staffers as patients. Many doctors on the hospital staff had been educated in the U.S. Our guide was an orthopedist who was a friend of the Chen family.

When we took Edith home, she invited us to dinner again. I was too embarrassed to accept so soon after the previous night, but we did go inside. We thanked Mrs. Chen again for her kind hospitality and thanked Mr. Wei for his thoughtfulness in providing the car.

On another evening, we did have dinner at the Chen's again. That night, Edith said to me in English, "President Lin Senn is leaving in a gunboat for Lu Shan, up the Yangzi River, for a vacation. During the past few years, we have been invited to go along with him. We have already arranged for you to join us, if you wish. Lu Shan is a gorgeous, idyllic spot in the summer. It is cool and the mountain itself is majestic. Many foreigners and government officials spend their summers there. And it would be an experience to sail on China's largest river." This was an unusual opportunity for me. I was tempted to accept. Yet if I did, I would have less time at home, and I did not want to forget the real purpose of my trip. Apparently, Edith could see my hesitation.

"I'm sorry to cause you any inconvenience in your plans. My mother and I thought that if you had the time, you would come with us."

"You're very kind. I'll check my itinerary and let you know tomorrow."

After much soul-searching, I reluctantly informed the Chens that my family was anxiously awaiting my return, and that I had to decline their kind invitation. Missing the chance to meet the president, and sail on the Yangzi River, disappointed me, but I was happy that the Chens had been so hospitable.

Mr. Lin Senn had the title of President of China, but he had no real clout. Jiang Jieshi (Chiang Kaishek) was at the peak of his power, controlling the military. Officially, he was Chairman of the Military Affairs Committee, from which the foreign press derived the title "Generalissimo" for him.

At that time, Nanjing had the appearance of a new and modern capital. Construction was underway everywhere, for schools, hospitals, and housing. The city had an optimism, hoping that this government might finally unify China and eliminate centuries of foreign influence on its way to becoming a truly democratic republic, as Sun Yatsen had intended. I left Nanjing elated over the possibilities.

Bob remained in Nanjing. Relieved to leave him behind, I said goodbye and returned to Shanghai in order to catch a ship for Hong Kong. When I reached Shanghai, I learned that the S.S. Empress of Japan was sailing late and I was able to board without spending another night in the city. Though smaller than the S.S. Empress of Canada, I found this ship designed similarly and therefore familiar. The ship set sail amidst the usual farewells and excitement.

I finally realized, then, that I was about to go home.

Chapter Six

I was in the first grade the year of that monsoon, and I was very close to my sister Xinyue, meaning New Moon, who was only two years older than I. We played together as we were growing up and our father taught us to read, write, and recite the "Three Character Classic." This was sort of a ditty. Both my sister and I could recite the whole book before I started school.

Unfortunately, at that time the region had no schools for girls, and my sister could not attend until several years later. However, Father taught us at home, believing that both boys and girls should be educated. Many villagers were envious because he insisted that we become an educated family.

My father was one of the last Imperial scholars of the Qing, or Manchu, Dynasty. During the first decade of the century, in his early twenties, he had gone to Guangzhou and successfully passed the rigorous, three-day examinations for Imperial Scholars.

He had attained the rank of Juren, or Imperial Scholar, through these examinations. When this news reached us, all thirteen villages of the Wu Clan celebrated. The crackle, smoke, and smell of fireworks accompanied beaten gongs, singing, and lion dances. My mother's eyes gleamed with joyous pride. I was told that after I was born, my grandmother looked from my father, who was six feet tall and handsome, to me, as she basked in reflected and projected glory.

Although not rich, we now belonged to a privileged class. A beautifully carved wooden plaque, painted red and gold, hung above the front entrance of our house proclaiming my father an Imperial Scholar. He was revered by thousands of clansmen bearing the name of Wu, or in our local dialect, Ng.

At the same time, his responsibilities to them also increased. My father was already a poet, but now immediately became an official at large, who advised people as a lawyer, taught school from the

40

primary to the college level, and helped his clansmen in ceremonies such as weddings and funerals. He also arbitrated disputes. As a boy, I had already sensed his importance and I enjoyed going places with my father. As the eldest son of the family, I was nicknamed "Crown Prince" by some of our relatives in a good-natured way — and sarcastically by others, who resented our family's prestige.

My grandfather's story about the New World stayed with me. However, my father could not leave the village because of his responsibilities to the community. I dreamed of someday getting to this distant land, but it was only a dream.

When I started school, I was uneasy, but Grandmother said, "Don't worry. I'll take you to school and I'll go back and bring you home every day. We'll have a good time talking about what you learn. You see, I've never been to school. You will have new things to tell me. You'll be my teacher." Though not educated, she was wise and affectionate.

The school lay about two miles away, held in three ancestral temples centrally located among the thirteen villages of the clan. Every morning after breakfast, my grandmother would carry me piggyback part of the way to school. After school, she would wait for me with a tangerine, plum, pear, or banana, depending on the season. This continued until I was too heavy for her. When I first started, she would allay my fears about school. She sang as I bounced on her back and I loved her attention.

A couple of years passed this way. I felt frequently that I was closer to my grandmother than to my mother. During my early childhood, I slept with my grandmother, later moving to another bed in the room when I grew older. I loved my tiny mother no less, but she had bound feet. They were considered attractive in traditional society, but made walking any distance difficult for her. Grandmother had normal feet.

Besides school, I would go with Grandmother to markets. We went to sweep the graves of our ancestors each year, on Qing Ming, a Chinese memorial day in the spring. Xinyue stayed home and helped with chores and with younger siblings as they were born. Two more sisters followed me, then two brothers. The third sister, Bijin, meaning Pure Jade, was the next baby and I adored her.

Once I asked, "Grandma, why aren't your feet bound?"

"I came from a hardworking peasant family and they needed me to be able to walk and work."

"I'm glad, because I'm happy when I go places with you."

Grandmother lived only three houses down from our main house, but she seldom interfered with the household activities of either of her two daughters-in-law, my mother and my aunt. All of us always ate our meals together. My uncle, who later took the English name Howard, lived with his wife and young son on the other side of the main house. He left for America when I was eight years old.

In the custom of Chinese society at the time, the youngest married woman in the household did most of the cooking. That responsibility fell to my aunt. She was good at it and frequently made meat dumplings or fragrant dishes that she knew I liked. Mother and Xinyue also helped.

Every evening, I was eager to cooperate when they said, "Quokan, call Grandmother to eat." She would hold my hand as we walked to the main house. In her gentle voice, she might remind me of some little courtesy, always adding, "Just follow your father's example."

She never bragged about it, but she knew she was the mother of an Imperial Scholar. She had a quiet pride, and radiated warmth. This attracted young people. In the evenings, they would gather in her small sitting room, to listen to tales she told or sometimes just to visit and share their own stories. However, she suffered from coughing spells. When she said, "I can't keep up with you young people; I have to go to bed," everyone would leave.

At the age of eight, I graduated from the clan primary school to another one in Toisan City, where my father had an office. All the students lived and ate together in this boarding school, but only two meals were served. Each evening we would go out or someone would bring back to the dormitory bowls of hot noodles, won ton soup, or rice with sausage. At first, I desperately missed the daily walks to the village school with Grandmother by piggyback and felt very lonely.

Gradually, I started making friends. I learned to play table tennis, volleyball, and soccer. When we had no soccer ball, we squeezed newspapers into a small spherical shape and wrapped it tightly with string. The outer layer was made of rags tied tightly around the newspaper. It was tough on our toes, but good enough.

Teaching the three R's was not much different from that in western schools, except that we read out loud and recited literary classics frequently. Especially in the beginning, I was very homesick. My understanding father made arrangements to get me home by train on the weekends. After four stops, Grandmother and Xinyue would be waiting at the station on Friday afternoons. I jumped off the train and ran to them so we would walk home hand in hand.

Each weekend, Mother sat near the door to welcome me and my aunt always prepared some favorite delicacy for me. Mother and Xinyue just sat there and watched me eat while Grandmother returned to her house to rest and prepare my bed. Such weekends were pure joy, and school became more fun. I settled into a routine that I enjoyed.

Suddenly, in January 1923, my uncle sent word that he had made all the arrangements for me to go to America to continue my education. Jubilation reigned throughout the village, but I was torn. My dream was coming true, but it meant leaving home — my grandmother, parents, brothers and sisters — my childhood. It was all happening too quickly.

Father decided that I didn't need to go to school in Toisan City any more. He said that I should spend the rest of my time at home with my family. I was relieved, since this helped me get used to the change coming in my life.

Everyone in the family doted on me in anticipation of my leaving, but I could not imagine what my new life would be like. At home, I had always been a dutiful son, though many people in the village said teasingly or otherwise that I was also spoiled as the scholar's eldest son. Leaving the village for Philadelphia represented a family duty, since my family had made the decision for me. Accepting this decision impressed upon me the importance of fulfilling my duty, at the expense of what I preferred.

❖

In 1920, Uncle Howard had contracted to teach Chinese to Chinese Americans in San Francisco. He had taught there two years, then went into business in Philadelphia. By 1923 he was able to sponsor me to come to the United States. Apparently, my grandfather, father, and uncle had been planning this without my knowledge.

My father quoted the old sages: "A young man's future lies in the four corners of the earth." He also explained that in the New World, I would find a whole new world of science, in addition to that of literature and the arts. I understood only part of what he said, but I believed him because he was my father and he was an Imperial Scholar. In fact, he was one of the last such scholars, since the examination system had ended with Dr. Sun Yatsen's revolution in 1911, overthrowing the Qing Dynasty.

My mother was a strong woman of small size. She had a kind heart and her love for my brothers, sisters, and me was greater than for herself. While she wanted me to do what Father wanted, she felt that I was too young to leave home to enter a world of which she had very little understanding.

"To send him away when he has hardly grown into boyhood makes my heart jump. Not only that; he'll be among total strangers who may not be nice to him." She sobbed, and over and over she muttered, "His father knows best about this, but I am not happy."

In February 1923, at age eleven, I left home for America. I would be accompanied by one of the Wu clansmen who had come back to China to build a new house for his family. He was returning to America to earn more money.

The morning I left, the whole village came out to say farewell. Some of them transported my luggage by wheelbarrow to the local railroad depot of the small railroad. Since the owner of the small, hundred-mile railroad through the mountains had been a classmate of my father's in college, he gave us first-class tickets as a farewell gift. My mother was crying and could hardly say anything audible. My aunt, sisters, younger brother, and grandmother wept also. Grandfather had died the year before, but I thought of him and his words to me after the monsoon.

At the last minute, my mother gave me a reassuring hug and then planted a kiss in my right palm. She folded my fingers and said, "This is for you to keep forever. It is a symbol of my love and good wishes."

My grandmother said something I could not actually understand, but I sensed the meaning — that we would not see each other again. I burst into tears. Two years after I left home, she died. .

I cried all the way to the railroad station, and on the train. My father escorted me to the British Crown Colony of Hong Kong via Guangzhou. He patted me off and on but said very little.

At the end of the train ride, we moved to a houseboat large enough to accommodate forty people with sleeping facilities. It had to be pulled by a smaller steamboat. Worn out by all the tension and the sorrow of farewell, I cried myself to sleep in my bed on the boat.

The next morning I had cried myself out. Exhausted, I followed my father in a daze. We reached Guangzhou that day and stopped at a nice hotel where my father often stayed. Then we took another train to Kowloon, the mainland portion of Hong Kong.

I was still thinking about my mother, and looked at my palm off and on for the kiss she had placed there. Then I stared at the passing scenes out of the windows, but they meant very little to me, for my heart was still at home. My father read the newspaper periodically and left me alone with my thoughts. I choked and coughed from the coal smoke whenever the train passed through a tunnel, but I didn't cry any more.

On arriving at the Kowloon terminal near the Star Ferry pier, some of my father's friends and clansmen met us. They all greeted us warmly and congratulated me on going to "Gum San," or "Mountain of Gold, " as they called America. Since they were in a festive mood, we took the ferry across Hong Kong Bay to Hong Kong Island. During the next several days, we stayed in a small hotel. I had my inoculations, including my smallpox vaccination, and at last received final clearance. Throughout the ordeal, I was silent and fearful, already feeling isolated from my family, friends, and clansmen.

I hardly noticed when "Cousin" Feng Chiu located us. He was the clansman who would accompany me on board ship and then across the United States to my destination in Philadelphia. I had never met him before.

Two days later, the necessary travel details had been completed.

We tied identification tags on the luggage and separated those I would need for daily use from the large steamer trunk that would remain unopened until I arrived. It contained other clothing, gifts, and some Chinese books that my father provided for me to read later on so I wouldn't forget either to speak or write the Chinese language.

The ship was to set sail at two o'clock in the afternoon. We had an early tea lunch with a few close friends, sharing many varieties of meat dumplings, custard tarts, marinated chicken wings, taro balls filled with chopped beef, noodles, and fried rice with ham and Chinese sausage. It was a very fancy lunch, but I was too nervous and upset to eat much. My father had arranged to have the luggage sent ahead, except for the small handbag I was to carry with me on board.

The importance of the day called for special clothing. I wore my school uniform. It was somewhat military in appearance, but I was proud of it. Besides, my passport picture had been taken in it. My father wore a gray woolen suit, western style, while the others who would stay behind wore warm Chinese clothes in the February chill. Cousin Feng Chiu wore a dark blue suit which he had brought from America. My father had hired a car to take the three of us to the pier, while his friends took the tram.

At the pier, I was surprised that some other family friends had also come. They probably pleased my father by coming; it hardly mattered to me. I was hanging on to my father's arm as he talked to the others.

The S.S. President McKinley was docked in the middle of the harbor.

Father said, "Go thank your friends and relatives for coming, and bid them farewell."

I bowed to them all, and nearly everyone gave me a small red envelope with "lucky money" in it, a custom that wishes health, wealth, and general success upon the recipient. They are usually given to children or young married people at birthdays, farewells, and particularly at New Year. I collected many of them, but they meant very little; I was simply going through the motions. With this little ceremony over, I returned to Father's side. He held my right hand with his left, then reached into an inside pocket of his jacket. Then he

46

pulled out an envelope with a red streak down the middle with my name written on it.

"My son, it has been very difficult for me to say much to you about the plans that were made for you to go to America. Your mother and I have thought about this many times. In our hearts, we want you to stay home and grow older before we send you away. But opportunities do not come frequently and your uncle has provided a big one for you. We feel that you should take it and meet the challenge that it offers. When you feel homesick or when things become difficult, just read what I have in the envelope for you. It may help. We are proud of you and we know you'll do great things."

Just then, a loudspeaker blared out. "Please listen carefully for your names to be called. Then step into the tender which will take you to the <u>S.S. President Mckinley</u>."

We listened attentively, but it was not until the third tender that I was able to board. My father squeezed me tightly and lovingly and for the first time I noticed that he was trying to hold back his tears. That made me burst out crying, as he said goodbye.

Then I boarded the tender.

Chapter Seven

Thoughts of my childhood farewell did not burden me, however, as the S.S. Empress of Japan pulled away from Shanghai. As most of the passengers milled about the top deck, I walked among them, suddenly feeling a more recent void. The similarity of this ship to the Empress of Canada brought back tender memories that Grace and I had shared, and now she was gone.

Until now, I had remained busy enough to distract myself from too many thoughts of Grace. Now that was impossible. On shipboard, the memories overwhelmed me.

I was in no mood to make friends. Instead of mingling, I returned to my cabin, thinking only of Grace and the experiences we had shared. I daydreamed until I fell asleep.

The gong for dinner woke me up. I joined the other passengers, mostly Chinese again, for Chinese food. The next table was entirely occupied by one large Chinese family that had a young black son who spoke Chinese with the rest of them.

Looking over the rest of the dining area, I saw no unattached young women. My companions at my table were all pleasant older men from Toisan. I remained polite, but was not talkative.

After dinner, I went up to the open deck and sat on one of the few deck chairs there. An American woman came by and said, "Good evening."

"Good evening. It's nice up here." I started to rise and offer her the chair, but she spotted another nearby.

"Don't get up, please. I'll bring the other one over."

After conversing a few moments, I learned that she was a Christian missionary named Mrs. Johnson.

"Are you a Christian?" she asked bluntly.

I hesitated. "I am trying to be one."

"What do you mean by that? You either are one or you are not. If you have been reborn through baptism, then you are one."

"Don't be cross with me," I said. "According to your definition, I'm a Christian, because I was baptized by immersion. However, just going through the rituals does not make one a Christian. To me, Christianity is a religious ideal. To be a Christian, therefore, one has to think, act practice, and live toward that ideal. I am still far from reaching that ideal. That's why I said I was trying to be a Christian."

Apparently, Mrs. Johnson had never had anyone discuss Christianity with her in this fashion.

"I understand your point of view, Mr. Wu, but I'm not sure that I agree with you completely. You're an intelligent young man and you're a thinking person. I'm certain that whatever field you pursue, you'll succeed."

"Thank you."

Other passengers began coming up on deck, either to breathe the fresh air or to pollute it by smoking.

Mrs. Johnson rose and said, "I certainly enjoyed this little discussion with you. I think I'll turn in. Good night."

I bade her good night and returned to my own cabin shortly thereafter. However, I had trouble going to sleep. I felt guilty for taking so long to get home. At the same time, I was simply anxious about returning after such a long time.

The next day I still did not feel sociable, so I spent the morning sorting odds and ends in my luggage. After walking around some, I spent most of the day reading a new version of a classic Chinese novel, The Romance of the Three Kingdoms, in Chinese.

At dinner that evening, I learned that the large family seated near me were named Lee. They had lived in Trinidad for many years, where they had adopted their black son. I spoke to him briefly and found his Chinese as good as mine.

Later, I realized that the difference in our color was forgotten by both of us as we conversed. I found myself thinking that if everyone in the world spoke the same language, many misunderstandings would be avoided. In any case, I enjoyed seeing a family which embraced a difference in color as a beauty and not as a problem.

Despite that pleasant interlude, I still did not feel very sociable. This leg of the trip offered very little. I finished <u>The Three Kingdoms</u> before I went to sleep the second night.

The next noon, everyone prepared to disembark. As the ship neared the pier, I started jumping up behind the crowd of passengers at the rail, trying to see the people waiting for us. I spotted my father, at six feet tall, towering over the friends and relatives around him.

Despite all the interesting people I had met, and all the places I had been, the feeling of coming home at last was extraordinary. I experienced a quick memory of the sadness, fear, and uncertainty of my leaving; then I was absorbed by the happiness of finally landing. In the press of people, I waved, but my father and his companions couldn't see me until I was on the gangplank.

They all came forward, then, and I grabbed my father around his waist. He squeezed me tightly, and I began shedding tears without any embarrassment. His friends picked up my luggage.

We were told, then, that all passengers had to go through immigration and customs. It took some time, but I had no problems. At last I rejoined my family outside.

"We'll take a bus to our hotel," said my father. "Then we will have lunch."

During lunch, everyone questioned me. I told them what I could about life in the U.S. and my trip back home. After lunch, we went to the railroad station and managed to get tickets for the morning train to Guangzhou. From there, we would catch an overnight boat ride to the small port of Jiangmen, and then take the Toisan train back up to the district.

The next day, from the local train, I began to recognize certain landmarks and buildings. People worked in the fields and water buffaloes pulled plows, just as I remembered. Other farmers worked on irrigation canals. Nothing had been modernized or otherwise changed since I had left, but the farms appeared luxuriant, telling me the rain had been plentiful. Soon the train pulled into Toisan City.

Reaching Toisan City was an even greater thrill than arriving in Hong Kong. Each step brought me closer to home. My anxiety and excitement increased the nearer I came to seeing my mother again.

We got off the train at West Station in Toisan City. My father took us to eat there. I experienced an even greater feeling of being home from the local cuisine.

"When are we going to get home?" I asked.

"Don't worry, son. I know you are anxious to get home, but I have to stop at my office here to get something. Then we will take the bus home."

"The bus?"

"Yes. Four years ago, a group of local merchants organized a bus company that would serve the surrounding market places, like Sijiu, near our village. Since I am currently Chairman of the Prefecture's legislative council, I was involved in convincing the city to pay half the expense of a new road, while the bus company paid the other half. Now we have good bus service in the area."

"I see."

"They made me Chairman of the Board of the bus company. I opposed giving passes to company officers and allowing their family members a discount. Since I was outvoted, though, I ride for free and our family members ride for half-fare."

The mayor owned the only automobile in Toisan City. He had made it available to my father out of courtesy for the day. However, my father did not want to abuse the privilege, so he dispatched the chauffeur back to the mayor's office with a note of thanks as soon as we reached the bus station.

The road took us directly to the village, though the bus stopped at Sijiu, the market, on the way. Finally the bus pulled up to the entrance to the village patio. Everyone in the little village came out to greet us. The most excited of all was one of my contemporaries who happened to be a deaf-mute. He came out smiling and gesturing. Somehow, he and I had always had a natural understanding of each other. As a child, when I had come home to the village from school in Toisan City, he had always come out to greet me before running to my family and announcing my arrival with his gestures. After all these years, his enthusiasm remained. I grabbed his right hand and shook it vigorously. Children surrounded us, all of them born after I had left.

Then my mother came through the crowd, with two of my sisters and my four brothers. My second brother, Kwok Git, had reached adulthood by now but the others were still young. They grabbed my hands and my clothes, but I gave my mother a hug and kissed her on both cheeks. She cried with happiness.

"You haven't had dinner yet," said my mother. "Your aunt has everything prepared, so have something to eat right away."

The excitement began to die down as my mother escorted me to my aunt and her two children. We ate quietly, with little to say.

"How long was the trip?" my mother asked. "Did you get seasick?"

"No. I seem to have outgrown seasickness." Since none of them had travelled overseas, I explained that the Pacific was a very wide ocean, and the ship took sixteen days to cross it. Also, I told them that I had had a chance to visit Beijing and some other cities in the hope of finding a good place to work in the future. Neither of my parents seemed to hear anything I said, nor did they say much. It had been so long since I had been there that all they did was sit and watch me happily.

I had brought a few presents with me. After dinner, I gave them to my mother to distribute, including a bracelet for my mother and a fountain pen for my father. They were both pleased with them. Then, because the hour had grown late, my mother told me that the old bed in my grandmother's house had been prepared for me if I wanted to sleep there. I accepted and suggested that Kwok Git, my second brother, join me in the house. We felt awkward together at first, but soon became reacquainted. He kept me company in my sleeping quarters and we were inseparable for much of my visit.

Grandmother's house stood only three houses away in the tightly-spaced buildings of the village. I got there by following the old narrow passage between buildings. My grandmother was long gone now, of course, having passed away three years after I left home, but the house brought back my childhood memories.

Everything had been cleaned out except the bed, a chair, and a chest of drawers. An oil lamp also remained. Another family lived on the other side of the duplex. It was completely familiar, and I felt at home.

Strangely enough, the place suddenly reminded me of my first sexual experience. When I was eight years old, Qin Xiu, a girl of seventeen or eighteen, lived with her mother on the other side of the duplex, opposite my grandmother. She offered to babysit for me occasionally, and my mother accepted. I had thought it would be fun to sleep with someone again, as I had as a younger child.

One night, after my grandmother was fast asleep, I felt Qin Xiu rolling me over. She had her pajama top open and she put her left nipple into my mouth. Then she rolled me over on top of her. She played with me until I had an erection, and then inserted my penis into her. I was fully awake by then, but I felt no special sensation. She held me there for some time and I eventually fell asleep on top of her. Later she rolled me onto my back again.

From time to time, she had me repeat these nocturnal activities. Though I was too young to enjoy sex, I became interested in the female body. When she aroused me, I played with her breasts and pelvic area, even though it was too dark for me to even see them. I was glad that this period occurred before my puberty. She was pretty, but certainly bold. Several years later, at age twenty, she got married. Once she told me quietly, "When you grow up, remember what I have taught you."

My mother and my aunt had planned a big dinner for the next day. The purpose of the event was to pay respects to our ancestors, to the spirit of my departed third sister, and to celebrate my safe journey home. After the ceremony to the spirits, we sat down about noon for a big dinner. Close relatives joined our immediate family. The group occupied two entire tables, seating about ten people each.

My family intended the dinner to be a happy celebration for the family. Also, of course, the occasion welcomed me home. Yet I could hardly feel happy with the feeling of sadness still pervading the house over Bijin's death.

Later, I told my father that I wished to have a quiet memorial service for my third sister, just for the immediate family.

"All right," he said. "However, let's wait a little while, since you will be here for some time. And don't be too disturbed, for life depends on fate. Things are decided by heaven more than we think. Try to have a good time with your brothers and sisters, and get to know them again."

I had brought home a portable Victrola and both Chinese and English records. I asked my older sister to supervise the Victrola, especially to prevent having the records scratched. Whenever she played this little machine, a small crowd of children from all over the village gathered around to listen.

In the meantime, my father resumed working in his office in Toisan City. Since I had gone to primary school there for a while, I wanted to see some of my former teachers and schoolmates who might still be there. Mother thought it would be a good idea, perhaps just to get me out of the house.

As I had as a child, I walked to the railroad station at Sijiu and boarded the noon train. I got off at the East Station, near the east gate of the city wall. However, the wall had been leveled a few years before. On top of its base, a road had been built that now encircled the city.

I explored, and found that I could hardly recognize some parts of the city because of changes. Curious to see how much I could remember, I walked a great deal. After a while, I tried to find my father's office without asking anyone and succeeded.

My father happened to be in. "Why didn't you let me know you were coming? I just had lunch with two of your former teachers."

"I didn't plan ahead. I didn't know I'd be coming, actually."

"Well, perhaps we can locate some of the others and go out to dinner with them. I am sure they would be glad to see you."

Since my father had no telephone, he sent a messenger with notes to my former history teacher and calligraphy teacher. Obviously, Toisan City still had not become completely modernized. Both of my former teachers accepted.

At dinner, they asked me about life in the United States — its schools and people, its way of life, and its rumored wealth. I told them what I knew, as truthfully as possible. Of course, conveying an impression of any substance was difficult if not impossible.

My teachers were also glad that I had not forgotten my Chinese.

"That is one thing we don't want him to forget," said my father. "He will learn English and American literature as long as he goes to school in America, but it will be easy to forget his native language, and especially the teachings of the old sages. I'll continue to supply him with books that he can read from time to time." My father had done this throughout the years. Every two months, I had had to write him a book report. It was difficult, but I eventually realized his wisdom. To this day, I still remember my Chinese.

As one of the few remaining Imperial Scholars, my father apparently realized that the kind of profound literary achievements he had attained would be gradually de-emphasized, and might eventually vanish. He wanted me, as a child, to retain as much Chinese culture and literary background as possible, though he knew it would make my learning English more difficult. He had always believed that it would be more natural and easy for me to continue my Chinese and add English in the U.S., rather than stop Chinese and then try to start again when I was older. I had rebelled inwardly as a child against this, but I never disobeyed my father.

All the way through high school in Philadelphia, I had continued to study Chinese. At that point, he felt I was no longer in danger of forgetting it, but I still wrote home to him once a month. Years later, after he died, I continued to write home to my mother and brothers.

Because of my father's insistence that I keep and develop my Chinese, I had learned to speak in several dialects as well as to read and write it. It became especially useful in trips to Taiwan, China, and Hong Kong. I now appreciate my father's farsightedness more than he ever hoped.

That day in Toisan City, after my father and I finished dinner, we returned to his office. He also kept sleeping quarters there and I lay down to sleep. My father remained awake to work before going to bed. This experience was also nostalgic for me, since I had often stayed there as a boy.

The room I slept in had a square window. A single piece of porcelain had been set into the metal frame, shaped so that it formed both a full square border and also a pattern running across the middle. It required no glass. As a child, I used to sit there for hours watching people going by or birds flying above the treetops. In the summer, an outside screen blocked out mosquitoes, but it was not necessary now. Besides, both my father's four-poster and my smaller bed had their own mosquito nets.

At noon the next day, as usual, he had a tea lunch with a few of his friends. This was a sort of tradition, dating back as far as I could remember whenever he was in Toisan City. During these lunches, he and his friends would discuss current events, gossip, and exchange literary opinions. Personally, I always enjoyed the variety of steamed, boiled, and fried dumplings that came with the tea.

I asked my father if he knew where any of my old schoolmates had gone.

"Well, they are all grown up now, of course, as you are. Some have probably gone to America, Canada, or the South Seas, depending on where they might have relatives. The rest may be working here or in Guangzhou. I have little contact with them."

"Do you know where Chu Ching is?"

"Chu Ching, that rascal? He has been a troublemaker all his life. I have rescued him from many difficulties, but he has never shown any appreciation. I don't know what he is up to now, but let's not talk about him."

I nodded. Chu Ching certainly had been a troublemaker. A few years older than I, he had lived next door. In any group of boys, he was always the ringleader. One day he knocked at our door and asked me to play. When I came outside, he said, "I have something good for you to see."

I followed him to a thick grove of bamboo where he had three girls lying on the ground with their pants off. Startled, I looked at them momentarily and then got scared and ran home. None of them was much older than I was, and only one had any pubic hair. How Chu Ching talked them into this, I never learned. I was terrified that my parents might find out, but fortunately they never did.

When my father and I returned to his office after lunch, the mail had arrived. It included a wedding invitation for me from Beijing. I was stunned, though I had known it was inevitable. Grace's wedding invitation arrived alone, without a letter.

My father was surprised and curious. For years, it was he who had received invitations to various functions. Perhaps this was the first time that he realized I had really grown up and had my own circle of friends.

"I met this young lady on board ship," I said casually. "She was going home to get married."

I did not even consider returning to Beijing for the wedding. That was the last communication between Grace and myself. I secretly wished her well, but I did not respond.

Chapter Eight

Since I had been in Toisan City for several days, I decided to take the train back to the village. I continued to get more acquainted with my siblings. Gradually, we grew more comfortable with each other.

One of our village games was shuttlecock. In our version, the "cock" was made by inserting several chicken feathers through the square hole in a coin, and then tying them together. We then kicked it around in a circle with the inside of the foot. We also played catch with a small ball; Kwok Git enjoyed this in particular.

Everyone was intrigued with my Kodak camera. Photography had become well developed in China by this time, but my camera was a new type to them, opening and closing like a bellows. Also, the villages always remained behind advances in the cities.

Toisan City, for instance, had electricity but no telephones. The villagers lagged behind Toisan City, and still used lanterns, candles, and flashlights for illumination. On special occasions, Coleman lamps would light the village homes, but ordinarily villagers used only small oil lamps with wicks. Studying under these conditions had been taxing to the eyes.

During this time at home, I retraced much of my boyhood grounds. By the end of my first month back, my father had selected a special day for a memorial service in honor of Bijin. Some of my sadness had lessened, making the memorial gathering more relaxed and pleasant than my welcome-home dinner.

However, when the Taoist priest performing the ceremony began to chant, he brought out tears from many of us. He placed incense in front of Bijin's picture on the small altar and lit a little oil lamp with it. Then everyone in the family, starting with my father, walked to the altar, bowed, and then went to sit down again. Afterward, the priest chanted again briefly and blessed all of us. I felt satisfied, finally, that I had paid Bijin proper respects. Because she had been a baby when I left, I really had not known her very well, but I had still cared about her very much.

Two weeks later, I asked my father if I could go to visit Bijin's burial place in the country.

"Of course," he said. "But you must realize that the cemetery is about five miles away, and walking is the only way to reach it."

"That's all right," I said. "I just need someone to show me the way."

Xinyue, my older sister, volunteered to take me. Kwok Git wished to go but was unable to get the time. He warned me that the trip would be strenuous and time-consuming.

We left on a bright day, with a southwestern breeze. It was a little warm, but we didn't mind. First, we followed one of the main roads leaving the village. Then we took a branch road leading up into some hills. My sister led all the way.

Finally we arrived at the cemetery and found the mound of earth over Bijin's remains. I bowed and placed some flowers we had picked to put on her grave. She had been such a lovable girl when I had last seen her. I cried a little, then pulled myself together.

On the way home, my older sister and I held hands. We were still young enough to recapture some of our old childhood feeling, and this excursion brought it back.

Time passed quickly in the village. The summer raced on, and the rice paddies turned golden brown. By August, all the farmers from the villages in the area came out to harvest the rice with their sickles. After they harvested the grain, it was threshed into a large wooden container. Then the stalks were gathered into shocks and spread out to dry.

As a child, I used to walk along the village patio this time of year, smelling the newly-reaped rice being cooked. Everyone teased me then about looking for fresh rice to eat. At the time, my mother had been embarrassed, since I appeared to be begging for rice. Now, after all these years, I found myself walking along the village patio once more at this time of year, and again, everyone in the houses along it welcomed me.

Now that August had arrived, I had to concern myself with returning to school. I had to clear my health certificate and reentry permit at the American Consulate. Fortunately, I was able to get a spot on the <u>S.S. Empress of Canada</u>, leaving August 15. This would get me back to the U.S. by the first week of September. I wrote immediately to Ruby Han, telling her to meet me on August 14 at my Hong Kong address.

Since I would need twenty-four hours to get from Toisan to Hong Kong, I told my parents that I would have to leave the village on August 12. My siblings were disappointed, but my parents realized that the time for my departure was coming. I said that there was no need for my father to accompany me to Hong Kong again. They agreed, though my mother would have preferred that he do so.

The day before I left, my mother held a farewell dinner for me. It was also an occasion to pay respects to our ancestors and to pray for their protection during my journey. We honored Bijin once more as well.

After the dinner, everyone helped me pack. My father asked one of my cousins to help transport my luggage to the train station. I took my leave the next morning.

I embraced Xinyue. She was engaged to be married soon.

"Quokan," she said, "you take care of yourself. The next time we see each other, I'll be part of a new family." Tears began to run down her cheeks.

"Ai Dei," I said, addressing her as "older sister," "I'll always cherish our childhood fun. I know you'll be happy with your new family. Take good care of yourself."

I gave Kwok Git a special squeeze and shook hands with my father. He put his arm around my shoulder and patted me gently. My mother was crying, and kissed my left palm this time.

"You have my love and blessing in both palms now. Just keep well, study hard, and we'll see each other again when you've reached your goals."

I kissed her on both cheeks and hugged her. As I started away, everyone followed me onto the village patio and waved to myself and a cousin, who was pushing my luggage in a light wheelbarrow. When we reached the road, I turned back to wave again. I also wanted to absorb the local scenery one last time — the size and shape of the hills and higher mountains, including one that resembled a teapot with a spout.

The rice fields were dry now, with shocks of straw standing in rows like soldiers at attention. We crossed the stone bridge into Sijiu, the market center, and walked through it to the train depot. My cousin helped me load my luggage onto the train. I thanked him and boarded the train, which blew its whistle as we left.

This time, leaving home was much easier. As a boy, the many unknowns ahead had been frightening. As an adult, leaving again was sad, but necessary. My parents also knew that I could take care of myself now. Still, as the train passed through the prefecture and stopped at Toisan City for passengers, I saw many more places that brought back fond memories. After we had picked up passengers, mail, and freight at the city's east and west stations, we proceeded beyond the area I had known as a boy. I was on my way once again.

❖

The train made many more stops and also made the ferry crossing once again. At Beijie, I took the overnight ferry to Guangzhou. The water was calm, but in the middle of the night, I was awakened by gunfire.

"Stay down everyone!" someone shouted. "Stay down!"

Another exchange of gunfire followed. A group of passengers had huddled along a wall near me. All of us were nervous.

"River pirates," one of them whispered.

The gunfire stopped, and soon a bell sounded an "all clear." All the passengers relaxed and some said that this was a common occurrence. Fortunately, our ferry crew had been prepared to fight off the bandits. Dawn arrived across the still water, and an hour later we docked.

On the pier I hired two rickshaws, one for myself and one for my luggage. I reached the Guangzhou-Kowloon railroad station just in time to catch the morning train to Kowloon. Three hours and several tunnels later, the train arrived at the main station near the edge of Hong Kong Bay. From there, I took a taxi to the Hong Kong Inn, only a few blocks away.

61

When I registered, the clerk handed me a note from Ruby, informing me that she was already in Hong Kong with a former schoolmate. They would meet me here that evening. Since the time was now early afternoon, I left my belongings in the room and went out to find a cheaper lunch than the hotel offered.

That evening, I waited for Ruby and her friend in the small lobby of the hotel. When they arrived, Ruby looked prettier than I remembered. I suggested that we go out to eat.

"All right," said Ruby. "I must tell you that Raymond told me that everything between us should be dutch."

"That will be fine." I had no money to spare anyway. We went to a medium-priced restaurant and had an excellent dinner.

During dinner, I asked Ruby about her travel documents. Her friend spoke up and explained that everything was in order. By the end of the evening, I felt as though Ruby and I were old friends already. When we parted, I asked her to come by at mid-morning to confirm our tickets and cabin assignments.

The next morning, Ruby and I walked to the Star Ferry, about three blocks away, and rode to Hong Kong Island. At the Canadian Pacific Company, I showed the clerk our tickets and also the business card of George Wong, the travel agent I had chanced across in Seattle.

The man at the desk looked up. "You are friends of Mr. George Wong?"

"Yes, sir."

"Please have a seat and let me check your reservations." When he returned, he smiled pleasantly. "You are lucky. I have been able to change your cabins to better ones. Bon voyage, and give my regards to George."

This time, of course, I knew what he meant by "better cabins." I thanked him profusely and we left. However, I didn't tell him I didn't expect to see George Wong again.

Ruby did not say a word. She had no idea what was happening. I told her that a few second-class cabins were sold to special third-class passengers. She thought I really had pull somewhere, and I let her think so.

We took the Star Ferry back to the Kowloon side, where she

caught a bus back to her friend's place. I walked back to the hotel, rested, and had dinner out alone. From there, I almost went to a movie, but decided to go back to my room and re-organize my luggage instead. Satisfied that I was ready for another trans-Pacific voyage, I went to sleep.

Ruby and her friend arrived late the next morning. We had an early lunch in the hotel and then took a taxi for the pier in time for the noon sailing. After we had our larger pieces of luggage checked, we both took one suitcase on board.

Since I knew where the cabins were this time, I needed no help from the stewards. When we reached our special cabins, some of them recognized me from the trip over.

"Going back so soon?" One of them was surprised. He pointed to Ruby. "Is that your new wife?"

Ruby blushed. "No."

Another steward said in a low voice, "That guy's lucky. He brought one beauty coming and has another going."

"We're schoolmates," I said. "We have to return in time to register for the fall."

It did not matter to them, and I was not sure if they believed me. In any case, I decided that no further explanation was necessary. They did not bring up the subject again.

Soon, the others booked in these special cabins appeared. One was Morris Newman, who had been a student in Russia. The others were all Chinese-Canadians. In addition to a Mr. F.L. Lee, there were Herbert Kwan and his two sisters, Lilly and Margaret, and a pair of brothers, Paul and Matthew Chen. The last two were products of the Hong Kong school system and were both on their way to M.I.T.

As soon as we were introduced, we all climbed up to the open top deck for the farewell. We joined the other passengers to wave, throw streamers, and yell goodbye as the ship pulled away from the pier. The whistle blew loud and clear, announcing that we were on our way.

Chapter Nine

I couldn't help but remember my first trip across the Pacific. After saying farewell to my father, I had boarded a tender that would carry me to the ship. I watched our friends gather around Father as the tender pulled away from shore.

The other people who were on the tender attempted to console me: "Young man, not many boys of your age have the opportunity of going to America. You'll like it there. We'll help you. Don't be afraid."

The ocean breeze was blowing across the bay, causing the tender to rock. I began to feel dizzy as the tender stopped at the lower end of the gangplank leading to the ship. When I climbed up to the deck, I was relieved to see Cousin Feng Chiu, who had boarded from an earlier tender. He took me to his tourist-class cabin. It faced the promenade and seemed very comfortable to me. He then led me to my place, which was one class below on a lower deck.

This deck was barely above water level, and the ocean constantly splashed against the tightly-closed portholes. Instead of small cabins, as I had expected, the entire deck was like a large, open hospital ward without partitions between the beds. Most of the passengers' belongings were placed under the beds.

Practically all the passengers were older men, and I found no one near my age. I was disappointed and discouraged in this gloomy atmosphere. Then I got up into my bed without changing clothes, since I was very tired. I fell asleep quickly.

After a couple of hours, the man next to me awakened me for dinner. When I rose, I was seasick, and couldn't get to the dinner table. I vomited several times and the same man helped me and told me to stay in bed. He also reassured me that when I felt better he would get me something to eat.

I slept through the night until breakfast, when I had to go to the bathroom anyway. Now I felt better, but still unsteady, as the steamer was tossed by the mighty ocean. I ate breakfast carefully and sparingly. However, the best position for me was back in bed again. This was my daily routine until we reached Shanghai for more passengers and freight.

This twenty-four hour stopover was a welcome respite for me. As soon as the boat docked, my seasickness ended and I followed the others to the next deck for fresh air and a view of the beautiful skyline and the famous <u>Bund</u>. Snow flurries happened to appear and I was intrigued. It was the first snow I had ever seen.

The ship's purser made an announcement. "Anyone with proper documents may go ashore, but you must be back on board before we set sail, exactly twenty-four hours from now. Two o'clock sharp. Have a good time ashore."

In the meantime, I had located Cousin Feng Chiu. Visiting among passengers in different classes was discouraged, so we had not seen each other since we had boarded. We disembarked together and looked around.

Very few of the passengers had friends or relatives in Shanghai. Like the others, we just got on land to stretch our sea-legs and to admire the <u>Bund</u>. With its flowers and trees, it meandered along the shoreline of the Huangpu River as it cut across the city. Then something dawned on me as I gazed at the foreign gunboats, destroyers, and merchant ships sailing or docked along the river. Only a few old wooden junks flew the Chinese flag. For the first time in my young life, I realized that China was largely controlled by foreign powers.

I persuaded Cousin Feng Chiu to find a restaurant before we returned to the ship. He told me that he had other things to do, but that we were not far from the ship, which was in fact still in sight. We did have a good meal before I walked back to the ship myself.

The ship was practically deserted except for some of the sailors and stewards on duty. Since many of the service people were Chinese, we chatted and they showed me parts of the ship. Then I went up to the open deck. At one point I was tired and fell asleep on one of the deck chairs.

Around sundown, I returned to my bed. Most of the passengers remained ashore. The empty ship seemed eerie and made me uneasy. However, the calmness of the anchored ship gave me a restful night.

Only a few people came to breakfast, but I enjoyed it this time. I went up to the next deck again for more sunshine. The flurries of snow had stopped. I considered going ashore again, but I was afraid of getting lost.

By lunchtime, most of the passengers had returned. Shortly afterwards, the whistle blew and the S.S. President McKinley set sail toward Japan. I had suffered on the first leg of the journey and knew that more was to come.

No matter how hard I tried to remain steady, I was overwhelmed by the tossing waves that I could see through the portholes. One minute the entire ocean nearly pushed the ship over sideways, and the next minute the blue sky appeared through the same window. My equilibrium couldn't stand this incessant assault, so my seasickness returned more violently than ever.

About four days later, we reached Yokohama, Japan. This was another welcome break. As soon as the ship docked, all the passengers prepared to go ashore. Finally, in early evening Japanese immigration officers finished checking the passenger list and allowed us to leave the ship. I found Cousin Feng Chiu again and we went ashore with the others. They all seemed to know where to go.

We each rode a rickshaw to a nice little house where everyone had to remove his shoes before entering on a mat-covered floor. The smell of perfume choked me. The kimono-clad, heavily made-up young women came out and one by one took the passengers upstairs. At first I thought it was a restaurant, but I eventually realized it was a brothel. I had heard of them.

One of the girls, realizing that I was just a boy, came out to entertain me. She tried to talk with gestures, and put a stool near a little stove for me to sit on. Then she brought me a cup of tea. She sang a song to me, and remained pleasant and understanding while I waited.

Then Cousin Feng Chiu and the others filed out, having gotten rid of their "ship's poison." We walked about three blocks to a Chinese restaurant for a big dinner. Afterward, the others were ready to explore the town. I felt out of place, so I took a rickshaw back to the ship.

I got back about nine o'clock. Once again, I walked around the upper deck and viewed the night lights of the city and its port. The sight was pretty, but I was still lonely. I went back to bed with a quiet stomach in the motionless ship.

When I woke up, the ship still lay calm. Most of my immediate shipmates had not returned. I was glad I could eat breakfast without being nauseated and afterward, I walked around the rows of beds. Several people were playing blackjack with small stakes.

After we departed from Yokohama, most of the entertainment was mahjong or fantan. Mahjong has some similarity to gin rummy. Fantan is simple but vicious. It consists of a square board with a pile of buttons in the middle. The bettors put their stakes along one of the four sides or at one of the four corners. Then the buttons are counted off four at a time. The winning number is the remainder, which could be four or less. If one's stake is at the corner of sides one and two, and two is the winning number, one wins the equivalent of the bet. However, if one's stake is along side two, the payoff is three times the value of the bet. On shipboard, the sudden rocking of the ship frequently tossed the buttons and mahjong tiles in all directions.

As the trip neared its end, my seasickness abated somewhat, though the ship's movement made reading and writing difficult. Still, I was able to keep some food down and visit with some of the men. They were all very kind and encouraging, and they told me not to gamble but allowed me to watch.

Ruby and I sailed from Hong Kong on a pleasant summer day. The ocean breeze up on deck made the scene even more comfortable. Still, Ruby seemed uneasy.

"Is everything all right?" I asked.

"Yes." She said nothing else.

"Let's walk around the deck once," I suggested. "Then we'll go back down to our quarters, okay?"

"All right."

After our stroll, we joined the others in our special section. I did not want to pair off with Ruby as I had done with Grace, but this was hard to avoid. Ruby felt that I was there to advise and escort her and I did not wish her to feel rejected. She was attractive and pleasant, and any young man would be pleased with her company. I simply did not want to risk getting involved, as I had done with Grace.

Ruby and I chatted with the small group and tried to get better acquainted. The Chen brothers, in particular, enjoyed playing cards, chess, and checkers. The Kwan sisters had gone to China to visit their grandparents, who were in their eighties. Lilly was studying education; Margaret, fine arts. Their brother Herbert had just graduated from the University of Toronto in electrical engineering and had visited China before taking a job in Canada. L.P. Lee was going to Canada for the first time to start graduate school in chemistry.

One evening, L.P. Lee asked Ruby to take a walk with him on the promenade deck. She looked at me, apparently for permission. I smiled approval. Shortly thereafter, Lilly asked if I would accompany her on deck for a cigarette. I told her that I did not smoke, but that I would be glad to keep her company.

We found two empty deck chairs and sat down. The breeze carried her smoke away from me and we talked casually, about her life in Canada and her trip to China. Ruby and L.P. Lee joined us for a while and then went on their way. I was glad that I felt no jealousy regarding Ruby.

Lilly and I returned to the cabins before L.P. and Ruby. Someone jokingly suggested that I go check on them, but they returned soon. The matter was dropped.

Since the stewards again brought us food in our cabins, we did not concern ourselves with meal times. We gradually fell into daily routines. Also, we began to meet other Chinese passengers in tourist class. Several of them were physicians. Two were going to Michigan for postgraduate work in thoracic surgery and one was going to the Mayo Clinic for further work in ophthalmology.

We had quite a group of intellectuals. Sometimes we discussed world politics, especially involving China and the U.S. On other occasions, we talked about each other's fields of interest.

Perhaps we discussed Japan most often, as it had been an enemy of China for many years and had occupied Manchuria in 1931. From what we could tell on the surface, the Nationalist (Guomindang) government appeared to be doing a good job. Chiang Kaishek (Jiang Jieshi) was gradually winning support from people both in China and overseas. However, his government showed evidence of too much nepotism and corruption, and he had not fully unified China yet. Four major warlords remained independent of him, including Zhang Xueliang, the Young Marshal, and Feng Yuxiang, the Christian General. The Communists had been sent into hiding and at that time did not appear to be a significant power. Of course, later events would prove how limited our understanding of China's political and social evolution really was at that time.

One such gloomy conversation was interrupted when someone shouted, "Look over there! Are those whales?"

We looked, but could not tell for sure. No one had binoculars, but the water in one certain area seemed to be more agitated than the rest of the ocean that day.

Then the whistle blew for a safety drill, and we lost the chance to watch.

Ruby had not been part of the group talking right before the safety drill. After the drill ended, I decided to see how she was. She greeted me in her cabin.

"Where have you been?" Ruby asked.

"Why? I've been talking on the open deck with some people. Is something wrong?"

"Well, not exactly. Mr. Lee is becoming attentive and he is occupying too much of my time." She spoke hesitantly. "I don't want to get too attached to him."

"Well, I'd say, just tell him the truth — that you're engaged and expect to get married shortly after you reach the United States." I figured that would put him off, since Grace had given me her version of it.

Ruby frowned. "I think we told you in Beijing that some friends say Raymond has been dating a pretty American-born Chinese girl. I would hate to get there and find that he has no interest in me."

"When I left Ann Arbor, Raymond was only talking about you. He wasn't seeing anyone else as far as I know."

That was true, but I'm not sure that she was completely reassured.

"In any case," I added, "as far as L.P. Lee is concerned, you can keep your distance."

"I need your help," she said.

I began escorting her more often. At one point, I hinted to L.P. that Ruby was engaged. He was surprised, but not very concerned. I added that any problem between the two of them was their business, not mine. He understood that I had discussed the matter with Ruby.

Shipboard life settled into a routine. One afternoon, when I returned to my cabin to look for a book, I found all the cabin doors open. No one seemed to be around, but when I knocked at Ruby's cabin, she sat up in the top bunk.

"Hello," she said pensively.

"Hello. Are you taking a nap?"

"I was trying to, but I couldn't sleep. I'm just resting."

I stood by the door and we talked. She was still worrying about what would happen to her in America. I tried to explain that her imagination was probably a greater culprit than anything she would actually meet.

"Actually," she said, "I really don't know that much about you. Yet I feel comfortable with you, talking about personal matters. Perhaps it's from what Raymond wrote. I agree with him, that you're a courteous and considerate gentleman. I also want to add that you're quite eloquent in both English and Cantonese. In fact, I like listening to you talk."

"You've just given me an idea," I said.

"What's that?"

"For some time, I've been wanting to learn Mandarin. My fraternity brothers tried to teach me, but it was always random and irregular — we were too busy with our regular studies. Since we still have a few days before we arrive, perhaps you could give me some regular lessons."

"I'd be happy to. When do you want to start?"

70

"Tomorrow. You take your nap now."

That seemed like a good idea, in fact. I went to take a nap myself. The Pacific had been calm nearly all through the trip and the journey was comfortable.

I rose early the next morning and ate a good breakfast in the dining room while my companions were still asleep. Since I was in the mood to break my routine, I then went up to the open deck to enjoy the early mist and sunshine. Most of the older Chinese businessmen congregated in a certain section. They were Cantonese, and since I spoke their dialect, I joined them.

They welcomed me, and I found that a few of them were Wu clansmen who knew my father. They seemed pleased to meet me, especially after I told them I was studying medicine. I said goodbye after a while, and as I walked away, I overheard someone say, "He's just like his father — a real gentleman and a scholar. Someday he'll bring honor to our clan."

I hoped they were right.

At mid-morning, I returned to my quarters. Ruby had already eaten breakfast. We walked around until we found a secluded corner in which to sit. Ruby had already written a list of common vocabulary, including the tone for each word. Mandarin has four tones, and each word has one of the four assigned to it. She illustrated these by using four different words that had the same basic pronunciation, but different tones. This was the most difficult part of learning Mandarin, since it required good pronunciation and clear enunciation. I practiced repeating words with Ruby until noon.

We broke for lunch. Afterward, most people took a nap. "Let's go again, Bill!" Ruby called.

"So soon?"

"There's a lot to learn, if you're serious."

"Of course I am!"

We returned to our quiet spot and I continued repeating the words after her until I had the correct pronunciation of every word on the list. Then she forced a new list of characters on me.

"You're a tough teacher," I said.

"That's the only way to learn."

71

"Okay. I asked for it, didn't I?"

"Not exactly. I just want you to be as eloquent in Mandarin as you are in the other languages that you know. I want to play a little part in helping you to do this, since there is nothing else I can do to show my appreciation for your company." Ruby looked away as she spoke.

Every day, we spent two hours in the morning and two hours in the afternoon at my lessons. The rest of the time, we socialized as usual with our companions. L.P. Lee continued to be friendly, but obviously was disappointed to find so much of Ruby's time occupied.

Once, as Ruby and I passed by, someone called out, "Where have you been hiding?"

"We've been studying," I shouted back.

Our Mandarin lessons continued for another week before we reached Vancouver. During that time I learned a great deal, but my speech was still not fluent. On the last day before we arrived at our destination, we had no lesson.

"I've enjoyed these sessions with you," said Ruby. "I've gotten to know you better. But you're a gentleman and I'll always remember that. I really don't know how to thank you for taking such good care of me on this trip. I hope you know how I feel."

"It's been fun for me," I assured her. "And you've taught me almost to speak Mandarin. I thank you for it."

The S.S. Empress of Canada sailed majestically into the port of Vancouver. Our small group stuck together even as we descended the gangplank. On land, the Kwans and L.P. Lee were home. The Chen brothers met friends. Mr. Newman, like Ruby and myself, was not met. He was on his way to New york.

The families of L.P. Lee and the Kwans met them on the pier. Both invited Mr. Newman, Ruby, and me to go home with them for a short visit since we had several hours before our ferry left for Seattle. However, we declined in order to avoid disrupting their family reunions.

The three of us then took a taxi on a brief tour of Vancouver. We got out at Chinatown, where we were amazed to find such a large

72

colony. After exploring a little, we found a fine restaurant for dinner. Ruby and I spoke to Mr. Newman more that evening than we had at any time during the voyage. He was a bookworm, and had remained alone most of the time on shipboard.

After dinner, we returned to the pier for the trip to Seattle. The ferry was docked next to the huge <u>S.S. Empress of Canada</u>, which dwarfed it. We retired to our own cabins on the ferry as we sailed past the city lights and harbor traffic. I awoke at dawn and by the time I got outside, Ruby and Mr. Newman were already on deck to debark in Seattle.

Ruby had to go to a separate inspection line, since she was arriving in the U.S. for the first time. Much to our surprise, then, Raymond Huang and some of his former Yenjing University friends appeared. Of course, most of their attention was focused on Ruby. Following the initial excitement, Raymond turned to me and thanked me profusely for looking after his fiancée during the trip. Before we parted, Ruby shook hands with me and wiped tears away. "Thanks again," she said.

I turned to Raymond. "I'll see you back in Ann Arbor in about ten days."

They were driving to San Francisco, and left to get on the road. It was still quite early in the morning. For my own journey, I had to find a train for Philadelphia.

Chapter Ten

I first landed in Seattle when I was eleven years old, and away from my family for the first time. All the passengers gathered our belongings and filed out under the scrutiny of immigration officers. I was nervous, but Cousin Feng Chiu had been to America before and walked down the gangplank with great ease. He had already told me that I would have to stay in the immigration detention house until certain procedures were cleared. Preparing me for it in advance helped, since the building was something of a prison.

Like the other immigrants, I had to remain in the detention house until I was interviewed; for me, the wait lasted ten days. Cousin Feng Chiu came to call several times, which helped. I had nothing to do, but at least I was no longer seasick all the time. Finally I was interviewed and scheduled for release in two days.

Then I developed the mumps. Feverish and weak, I was sent to a Japanese American hospital — for some reason. Anyway, the doctors there were very kind and reassured me that I would join my relatives as soon as I was well.

Cousin Feng Chiu visited me several times in the hospital. When I recovered, he came to get me. He was calm and businesslike, but I didn't know where we were going.

First we went to Seattle's small Chinatown, where he took me to a store. I was surprised to learn that everyone there knew who I was, namely, the eldest son of the well-known Imperial Scholar. The owner of the store and the employees were all Wu clansmen.

The store's facade was that of an import-export firm, but it had other functions as well. One of the most important was to provide aid to Chinese immigrants who had just arrived and also to those wishing to return to China for a visit, such as Cousin Feng Chiu, since they required certain papers.

One section of the store was partitioned into a small dormitory sufficient to house ten people. Board could be provided for people like us, waiting for transportation elsewhere. It was crowded, but fortunately, we stayed only one night.

The next day, we left for the Great Northern Railroad station. My uncle had arranged everything with Cousin Feng Chiu's assistance. We were going right on to Philadelphia.

The coming journey from Seattle to Philadelphia filled me with anxiety. I wanted to reach Uncle Howard's home, and yet I was worried about starting a new life with a relative who was really a stranger. Even before he had left home several years earlier, I had hardly known him.

Cousin Feng Chiu and I were escorted to the railroad station by several employees from the store. Just before we boarded, I started to bow to them in farewell, and was told that from now on, I should only use handshakes. We all shook hands, then Cousin Feng Chiu and I boarded the train.

The trip would take several days. Once we were underway, I looked out the window of the sleeping car at the scenery. I was awed by the magnificence of Mount Rainier. Its snow-covered peak seemed so near, despite the obvious distance. Fascinated, I gazed at it until it was out of sight.

The sleeper interested me from the beginning because it had upper and lower bunks. I chose the upper deck because I enjoyed climbing up and down and I could dress and undress lying down. At night, it made a little nook for me.

I was unaccustomed to the motion of the train, but I slept out of sheer fatigue. Since the rocking of the train was different from that of the ship, I had no more motion sickness. This allowed me to enjoy the trip and the sights.

During the daytime, I was intrigued by the great scenery of the mountains. I watched them continually from my seat. We were able to buy sandwiches without going to the dining car and Cousin Feng Chiu had brought Chinese snacks with him.

On certain curves, I could see both the locomotive and the caboose. I saw wild deer drinking at a mountain stream. Wild horses and goats with horns and goatees stopped to watch the train. Day after day, we traveled through mountain passes near snow-capped ranges.

As beautiful as the sights were, even these became monotonous after a while. We played cards and checkers to pass the time, but I was not interested in them. I was thinking more about what was to become of me.

Finally we reached Chicago, a huge city reminiscent of Shanghai. All we did was change trains there, boarding one on the Pennsylvania Railroad bound for Philadelphia. This was our last leg.

The weather remained cold the entire trip. It snowed frequently. When the Alleghenies came into view, they were covered with snow. Our route carried us through Pittsburgh, where the Allegheny River met the Monongahela to form the Ohio. The factory chimneys spewed out black smoke all across the skyline to form dark clouds hanging perpetually over the city. As the train entered the city limits, I saw many dilapidated houses and shanties. I turned to Cousin Feng Chiu.

"Look at those shacks," I said. "People are in there, because smoke is coming out of some of them. I thought there were no poor people in the United States."

"They are bums," he said.

I didn't know what bums were, and he could not explain it to my satisfaction.

While riding at night, waiting to fall asleep, I thought frequently of pleasant past experiences. In particular, I thought of my baby sister, Bijin. I had a sweet memory of her and a special attachment to her. She was so tiny and cute, and much too young to understand that I was leaving on such a big trip. The upper berth also reminded me of a tree house that a neighbor had built for his children near one of the farms where I had played. I usually fell asleep reminiscing this way.

I would have liked to see the dining car, but we did not. At mealtime, Cousin Feng Chiu requested a small table from the porters which fit between our two seats. He carried various kinds of sandwiches, but the best food was chicken wings and drumsticks that had been fried Chinese style. We also had chunks of deep fried fish, hard boiled eggs, almond cakes, and fruit.

He was a quiet man, not well educated but with experience in the United States. We sat in silence most of the time, since he made little small talk and did not spend much time playing cards or other games with me. For me, the monotony of the trip was sometimes broken when American kids would approach me and invite me to join them. I knew little English, and we communicated poorly. Still, I was pleased to find them kind and considerate.

About an hour before we reached Philadelphia, Cousin Feng Chiu spoke to me seriously. "Quokan, I am not an educated man, as your father is. I am sorry that I could not make this trip more interesting to you by telling stories or pointing out famous towns and landmarks we have seen. I have no knowledge of the geography of the United States. I had no opportunity to go to school, as you have. When I came here, I was too old, anyway."

""If I were alone, I'd be scared here. You've done more for me than you know. My father wouldn't have had you take care of me on this trip if he didn't think you were a good man."

He seemed touched. "Your uncle is an educated man too, but he has been somewhat aloof toward me and some others who didn't go as far in school as he did, back in China. However, all of us here are just trying to support our families and educate our children. Because of his attitude, he and I have not been very close, although we have been clansmen in Philadelphia for several years. He has been a president of the Philadelphia chapter of the Guomindang and a member of the Hip Sing Tong, as well as the Association of Wu Clansmen. His education makes him a respected man. I am sure he will take good care of you. So don't worry. Be a good boy and grow up to be like your father."

I liked learning about his feelings toward Uncle Howard and his respect for my father, since it explained where he stood.

Just before we got off the train, he added, "Your uncle's home is not far from my store. Come see me some time. I am interested in your progress, too."

I was glad to hear that, and promised that I would see him after I got settled. Then the conductor called out, "Broad Street Station. End of the line." We gathered our luggage and clumsily got off the

77

train with it.

In the station, I looked excitedly for Uncle Howard, but he was not there. I was disappointed, but Cousin Feng Chiu explained that it was a weekday and he could not leave his work. Cousin Feng Chiu took me in a taxi to Uncle Howard's place of business.

My uncle had a three-story house, in which the ground floor had been converted to a restaurant with a capacity of about twenty-five. We arrived in mid-afternoon and only a few customers were inside. Uncle Howard appeared strange, after my not seeing him for so long.

He shook hands with me. "I am glad you are here. I have been waiting for some time for you to arrive." He pointed to a chair at one of the tables for me and also invited Cousin Feng Chiu to stay for tea.

Uncle Howard and I both thanked him for his kindness and help to me during the trip. When Cousin Feng Chiu had finished his tea, he said that he was anxious to get home. We said goodbye, and he took a streetcar from the corner of South Sixth Street.

The conversation with Uncle Howard continued to be strained. He mentioned that he would find some Chinese who spoke good English to help enroll me in Vare School, a few blocks away. "You can walk back and forth, even for lunch."

The kitchen in the restaurant was managed by another clansman working as a cook. A black woman named Lily was the dishwasher. They had apparently heard I was coming, and both were pleasant. Lily shook hands with me and said, "You look just as we thought — a nice-looking boy. Welcome to the United States. Hope you'll like it here."

The cook smiled. "My hands are wet and greasy, so I won't shake hands. I've heard about you for a long time. Your uncle is a fine man; don't worry, he'll take good care of you." He pointed to a table and chair in the kitchen. "I have just fixed a small bowl of won ton and noodles for you. Sit over there and enjoy it."

I thanked him and sat down, still feeling awkward and uncomfortable.

"Any time you want something to eat, just come in and tell me. I'll fix it for you." He winked.

My uncle then showed me to my room, up on the third floor. It was a nice little room with a brass bed. The mattress was soft and comfortable. He told me that Lily had prepared it for me in the morning. There were two chairs and a small table with a lamp, in addition to a light in the middle of the ceiling. The walls were papered, and the paper looked new. When I looked out the window I could see houses across the street and the streetcars as they passed on the tracks in the middle of the street.

"This is your room, and you'll have to keep it clean yourself. If there are things you need, ask me." He went back downstairs.

He had spoken sternly, suggesting to me that in this new environment I would take care of myself more than I had been accustomed to at home. For the first time, I pulled out the envelope my father had handed me when I left Hong Kong. I did not open it; just looking at it gave me strength. I said to myself, "I'll show him I'm not as spoiled as he thinks."

Like my father, Uncle Howard was six feet in height, huskily built, and strong in appearance. His hair was thick and parted in the middle with just a tinge of gray at the temples. He had worked hard to get where he was and he wanted to impress upon me that great opportunities waited here if one worked hard enough. Uncle Howard meant well in arranging my coming and staying with him, but he radiated very little warmth when I needed it the most.

In fact, this never changed. I observed over the years that he was envious of the accolades and respect that my father, his older brother, received for being an Imperial Scholar. Perhaps this caused part of his reserve toward me.

From this time on, I was no longer spoiled but I still had duties to fulfill. It was an abrupt change. I cried myself to sleep every night.

❖

Medical school registration began at the beginning of the second week of September. I returned to Ann Arbor just in time to enroll for my second year. Most of my courses were still basic. They included pathology, pharmacology, and biological chemistry. These were the foundations of medical training, but simply listening to lectures and pursuing laboratory studies remained tedious and uninteresting. We had to wait until our junior year before we saw our first patient.

Medicine has always been a demanding study and profession. In addition to having a strong medical education, a physician should be a well-rounded individual, versed in literature and the arts as well as in science. This places an even greater burden on the medical student. Finally, this field requires the ability to face life and death without personal and emotional involvement.

I thought a great deal about these issues before I entered medical school. During my second year, I became certain that medicine was my field and I never wavered, though the going became rough at times. Persevering through four years of medical school was a test of everyone's physical and intellectual stamina.

My third and fourth years involved clinical study, which made them much more interesting than the first two. Each morning, we attended four hours of lecture, followed by medical and surgical sections in the afternoon. Each student was assigned to a specific patient.

In the medical section, each student began by getting acquainted with the patient. Then we had to review the patient's medical history. This gave us the chief medical complaint of the patient. The student then proceeded to examine the patient from head to foot, paying special attention to that part of the body causing the main complaint. We recorded our impressions after the examination, which included a blood test. The student performed both the physical examination and blood count of the red and white cells.

A professor led ward rounds every day with an entourage that included his own staff members, residents, interns, and medical students. The professor began each discussion by asking a medical student to present a patient's history and the student's own findings. The interns and residents supplemented this information with their findings and impressions before the professor conducted his examination. Then, when differences of opinion arose, the group would discuss them to reach the correct conclusions.

Dr. William Osler, a Canadian, had started bedside teaching decades earlier. He said that studying medicine without seeing patients was like learning to be a sailor without ever going to sea. Bedside teaching has been common practice ever since.

Students in the surgical sections followed a similar routine, but occasionally we had the opportunity to observe surgery either in an amphitheater or by scrubbing up and joining the operating team. A student had no function in a crowd of interns and residents, but he was able to get a close look at surgical technique.

I gained a big boost in morale from these experiences. Being part of a team making daily rounds, and having my first contacts with patients, made me feel like I was closer to being a physician. Then in my senior year, I became responsible to the intern in the same way the intern reported to the resident, and so on up the ladder. Some diseases required sophisticated tests which I now performed.

During this time, I saw one patient with meningitis who ran a high fever. Restless, semi-conscious, and sensitive to light, he kept his eyes closed and pulled on the bed clothing incessantly, despite a stiff neck. The intern on this case taught me how to do a spinal tap, an essential diagnostic test for this disease.

One of the most unforgettable patients I encountered as a student was a man who had trichinosis. He was admitted to the hospital with fever, diarrhea, and hard and painful muscles. In this case, questioning him helped reveal a potentially difficult diagnosis. The usual cause of the disease was eating undercooked pork that was infested with the tiny worm, trichina spiralis. The patient's history revealed that he had attended a picnic where a fresh shoulder of pork had been roasted. He had apparently eaten meat near the bone that was not well cooked. The living parasites passed from the pork to his intestinal wall, where they burrowed and multiplied, causing acute myositis in the muscles. The patient's blood count showed increased white cells with characteristic eosiniphilia, which appeared as orange-red granules under a microscope. A muscle biopsy, a small piece of excised tissue viewed under a microscope, showed the worm within the muscle tissue.

Trichinosis has no specific treatment. Some patients die during its acute stage and others recover. This disease impressed me so much that forever after I was very careful when eating pork.

Another part of our training included the procedure for examining the ear, nose, and throat. Placement of the doctor's head light, use of the laryngeal mirror, and positioning of the patient's head were stressed. We learned to use the nasal speculum for inspecting the nose and the otoscope for the auditory canal. During one of our clinical demonstrations in this area, I asked the instructor, Dr. Frank Lathrop, if he would examine me for a chronic history of epistaxis, or nose bleeding. I had had this problem since childhood and had seen numerous physicians over the years in China as well as in America. The problem persisted, though, and in fact the nasal bleeding might start suddenly at any time — during class, while walking on the street, and in my sleep.

We made an appointment for eleven the next morning. During his examination, I followed his procedure mentally. First he inserted the nasal speculum into my right nostril, adjusted his light, and tilted my chin upward a bit.

"Everything is fine here," he said. Then he cleaned the speculum with an alcohol sponge and repeated the procedure. "There it is," he said almost immediately. "I see a chronic ulcer deep on the medial side on the bony portion of the septum. You probably had a fall on your nose as a child. It's deep and in an unusual place. That's why no one else saw it."

Dr. Lathrop cauterized it twice and the abnormal bleeding came to an end. More than any other consideration, this experience convinced me to take up a specialty. After suffering through the nose bleeds throughout my life up to that time, and seeing many generalists who failed to diagnose it, a specialist had solved it in minutes.

We became more conversant with special tests, more involved with patient care, and better at interpreting X-rays. Those in the surgical services scrubbed for operations more frequently. We asked more intelligent questions overall, and found ourselves giving better answers to problems. Our final obstacles to getting the M.D. degree were writing a thesis, writing final examinations, and passing an oral examination before a board of five faculty members.

Chapter Eleven

When I returned to Ann Arbor from China in September, 1935, I had to make up some unfinished classes in addition to keeping up with my new studies. From that perspective, the road ahead seemed endless. Despite the commitment required by medical school, however, it was still not quite my entire life. The personal side of my life gave me some respite from my responsibilities and I needed it.

The Chinese Students Club held its first meeting of the year two weeks into the season. Since I had been active in the organization before, I went to see how it was getting along and how many new students had come from China. As soon as I arrived at Lane Hall, one of my friends told me that someone was looking for me. I went up to the auditorium and found about a hundred people there. C.K. Yang, a frat brother, enthusiastically brought a pretty, young woman to meet me.

"Bill, this is Miss Franking. She's very interested in China. You should have all the latest information for her."

He turned to her. "Bill has just returned from China. He'll give you all the dope. I'll leave you alone; see you later."

Miss Franking and I talked briefly and then sat down when the president called the meeting to order. Ruby and Raymond were sitting a few rows away and apparently had been watching us. They smiled and waved.

During the meeting, the host asked all the new members to introduce themselves. About thirty were present. Miss Franking introduced herself as an Ann Arbor native and a freshman; her first name was Cecile. Many people, including myself, were curious about her presence there.

Actually, she created a sensation. She was very attractive; her face possessed some Caucasian features with a touch of Asian influence, and she was slender and well-proportioned with pretty legs.

When the meeting began to drag, I asked if I could escort her home, unless someone else had brought her.

She smiled. "No one brought me."

We sneaked out quietly and I walked her home. On the way, she explained that her father had been one of the first seven Chinese students to study at the University of Michigan. She now had a scholarship to attend school here. The evening was pleasantly cool, with the sky clear and the Big Dipper prominent. We passed Ann Arbor High, her alma mater, on the way to her house.

"Here we are," she announced.

I came up onto the porch with her and asked timidly, "May I see you again?"

"Yes, I would like to talk to you more about China. We didn't have much of an opportunity this evening."

"That's true. May I have your phone number so I can ask when you'll be free?"

"Of course." She gave it to me and we shook hands. "Good night."

I was elated; I liked her, and I had spent enough time taking care of other people's women.

October 10, known to the Chinese as "Double Ten," was the national holiday of the Republic of China, celebrating the overthrow of the Manchu Dynasty. It occurred about two weeks after I met Cecile Franking, and I was looking for an opportunity to see her again. I called to invite her to a dinner celebration of Double Ten. She was very pleasant and cordial, but said she had another engagement. I was dejected, but went to the dinner with a group of fraternity brothers, including Raymond and Ruby.

I never called a girl for a date after I had been refused, either out of false pride or fear of humiliation. Though I was very interested in Miss Franking, I didn't call her again. I saw her walking to class carrying her books, sometimes with friends. My heart accelerated slightly when I saw her, but I avoided crossing her path.

❖

I had first adjusted to new social situations when I started school as a child in Philadelphia. Another cousin came by my uncle's restaurant to take me on my first day. When the school authorities learned that I spoke hardly any English, they put me in a class with European immigrants, including Poles, Italians, Lithuanians, and Jews from several countries. I was the only Asian and the youngest in a group of about thirty. As such, I was the object of much curiosity.

Miss Esther Cohen, the teacher, got everyone's attention again and continued teaching. After class, she told me to bring a certain type of notebook and pencils next time. She also told me not to be afraid of my classmates, that they were just curious about me.

In Miss Cohen's class, I continued to be uneasy because my classmates looked strange to me and, in turn, they would look at me periodically and smile to themselves and each other. Some of them made faces at me. Whenever the teacher noticed this, she would simply say, "Class, pay attention to what I'm writing on the blackboard," or ask a question of someone looking at me.

As time went on, some of the girls tried talking to me during recess. Then two or three boys invited me to play ball with them between classes. My discomfort shrank as I learned more English. Curiously, a pair of Italian boys first wanted me to play with them. I wondered, "Did Marco Polo have anything to do with this?"

When I walked from school back to Uncle Howard's, I was subjected to stares, racial slurs, and other names which I did not understand. I realized they were insults by their tone. This continued daily as long as I went to Vare School.

Miss Cohen called me "William." When she addressed me in class, she would ask, "Do you know the answer, William?" At first I was puzzled. Later I learned that she thought "Wu" was "Wm."
When I had first enrolled, I had written my name down Chinese style, with the surname first and the personal name second: Wu Quokan. My first name has been "William" ever since.

After I had passed one semester, Miss Cohen felt my English was sufficient for me to enroll in one of the regular grades. I started in third grade and was promoted to the sixth in a few months. I had studied some math, geography, and drawing in China. Only the English held me back.

The sixth grade teacher was Miss Christina Helm, who was in

her middle thirties. With brown hair and a fair complexion, she was pleasant-looking, and a friend of Miss Cohen as well as a colleague. She had been trained as a teacher at the Philadelphia Normal School.

Miss Helm lived across the street from school, in the same building where her father operated a pharmacy. One day after school, she took me home and introduced me to her family. Then she explained that my other subjects were satisfactory, but my English remained below standard. Out of personal interest and concern, she volunteered to tutor me in English two hours after school each day.

My Uncle Howard wasn't very happy about this, since he had me working at his restaurant every day after school. I pointed out that my purpose in coming to the United States was to be educated. How could I make any advancement with poor English? When I told him that I would work later hours, he finally agreed.

With the aid of Miss Helm's tutoring, my school work improved steadily. Working after hours was tiring, however. By the time I got to my homework, I was often half asleep already. I only had Sundays off, when Uncle Howard gave me three dollars either to go to a movie or visit a park.

I became a part of the Helm household and they always invited me to Sunday dinner. Also on Sundays, I often went to Chinatown, where I made a few friends my age. Gradually, I became accustomed to the new routine.

In Chinatown, I made a close friend named Yee Hoy. He had come from China about two years ago and had learned that the First Baptist Church held an English class open to anyone. It was followed by a Sunday School class for Chinatown residents. I didn't know much about Sunday school, but I was interested in the English class.

I joined the English class that Yee Hoy attended and later the Sunday School class. We continued for several years, during which I practiced my English and gained some understanding of Christianity. Finally, Yee Hoy and I were baptized. Although I was not entirely clear as to what I was doing, I was certain that it was something good. Later, I joined the church and, from the sermons and Bible classes, I began to understand Christianity better.

Mr. Cromwell, a retired musician from the Philadelphia Orchestra, taught Sunday School. He was fine and kind, except for his strange request that I promise not to see any more movies. That was my main source of entertainment, and I learned more English from them as well. I could not agree to this.

My father was a Buddhist, but when I told him I had been converted to Christianity, he wrote back and congratulated me on being mature enough to choose my own religion. I was surprised but pleased. The Helms, being of German origin, belonged to a Lutheran church to which they had taken me on occasion. They were somewhat disappointed when I became a Baptist, but after their initial surprise, they never mentioned it again. As a courtesy, I occasionally asked to go to church with them. They did not seem to mind Baptists, they were strongly anti-Catholic, a quality I could not understand at the time.

By the time I had been in Philadelphia for five years, I was sixteen. Uncle Howard said, "Now that things have been pretty well arranged for your education and your work in the restaurant, I'm planning a trip home. It's been eight years since I left."

"Everyone at home was looking forward to your coming back," I said. "But did you know that when you return, your immediate family expects you will build a new house for them? That's the custom of men returning from the United States."

"I know. I'm not sure that I can manage that, but I'll go back for a visit anyway."

I knew from my own observation that Uncle Howard had an adequate income. Except for my school supplies and a few clothes, he spent virtually nothing on me. By my estimation, he should have made enough to build more than one house back in China. Still, I believed him when he said he might not have the money. I later learned that he was an inveterate gambler.

In fact, I also suspected that he spent much of his money on a white woman who often stopped into the restaurant. She always sat at a corner table, and Uncle Howard would sit and talk to her when business was light. This woman, who was never introduced to me, had a pleasant appearance, with dark hair and large brown eyes. Her clothes were good, but she wore more make-up than average. She always smiled at me and said, "Hello, William." I never knew anything else about her.

Uncle Howard left for China in 1928. Prior to his departure, he sold his restaurant. I did not feel this was a good idea, but I was in no position to speak up. At least he sold it to a clansman, who kept both Lily and the cook, who had also become a good friend to me. He did me many favors and kindnesses and I called him "Cousin."

I had a special fondness for Lily because she had taught me how to work in the kitchen, washing dishes and silverware. The first time I washed dishes, she laughed very hard; I thought only the insides of the dishes had to be cleaned. At home, I had never been asked to do domestic chores. She also taught me how to make my bed and keep my room tidy.

By the time Uncle Howard left, I was attending Central High School, the outstanding secondary school in Philadelphia at that time. Uncle Howard rented a room for me at the YMCA, but the Helms objected to my staying there. They offered me room and board in their house in exchange for cleaning the house, doing the dishes, and running errands to the wholesale supplier for Mr. Helm's pharmacy. I accepted. The chores varied, and Miss Helm and her mother usually helped clean the house, anyway.

While staying with the Helms, I learned more American customs and manners. At the end of Mr. Helm's workday, I frequently waited for him to close his store. Then, in warm weather, I sat with him on the front steps in the evening to chat.

Mr. Helm used to tell me stories of the World War I era, which had ended about ten years earlier. People would yell obscenities and throw snowballs and rocks at his display windows because of his German descent. He had been born in the United States, and his elder son Robert had been in the armed services fighting for Uncle Sam, but these facts made no difference.

"They upset me, naturally," he said. "But I never argued or fought with them. Mob psychology is vicious and without reason. Its aim is destruction."

I could understand his experience with this. Ever since the first day I had walked out on the streets of South Philadelphia, I had been subjected to name calling, threats, and objects thrown at me. Since I was small in build and often alone, I could not fight my attackers. Instead, I just ran.

During the time I stayed with the Helms, I also began to realize for the first time that Americans, particularly young people, were not all like this. Some of my schoolmates began to call on me and invite me to the movies, to go out around the neighborhood, or to their homes. Joseph Orloff often came by and took me to his house to study. His father was a physician, and very courteous. His mother, too, was kind. She would bring ice cream or cookies to us after we had studied. Joe would escort me home around nine-thirty. I felt more at home in Philadelphia than ever.

One evening, Joe's father asked, "What are you going to be, William?"

"I'm not sure, but I'm thinking about engineering."

"You should study to be a doctor. There is no field like medicine if you like it. I'd like Joe to be a doctor someday."

I agreed with him out loud, but I still wanted to be an engineer.

Jacob Wolf, another schoolmate at Central High, took me to my first football game. It was played at Franklin Field between the University of Pennsylvania and Cornell University. In China, children of all ages played "football," and I expected to see the same game I knew from China — soccer.

The spectacle impressed me. The huge crowd created a dazzle of colorful winter outfits. Male and female cheerleaders performed acrobatics and yells. The marching bands were well drilled, but I did not know the songs they played.

The crowd let out a cheer when the Cornell team came running out onto the field. A louder cheer followed when the home team ran out a moment later. Then the whistle blew and someone kicked the football. After that, I could not follow the action, except to see that people kept piling on top of each other. After a while, someone else kicked the ball and everyone went chasing after it.

I turned to Jake and asked, "When is the game going to start?"

He was startled, but figured out what had confused me. "It's almost half over. I should have explained that this is American football. It's not like soccer."

During halftime, he tried to explain some of the intricacies of the game. I remained confused. Still, I appreciated being initiated into an important American custom and thanked him profusely for taking me. I grew to become an avid football fan.

Chapter Twelve

My senior year at Central High turned out to be the most difficult school year of my life. Although my English had improved a great deal, reading and understanding Shakespeare became a major task. Charles Dickens, Robert Louis Stevenson, and George Eliot were easier, but I still had to look up many new words in my Chinese dictionary. Alexander Pope's couplets were more difficult. My other subjects, such as ancient history, also required a lot of time.

Finally, I graduated with honors, taking Latin and German as foreign languages. The Helms were proud of me. I gained confidence and a belief in diligence and perseverance. That may sound corny, but it was a logical step in my growing up; it was an extension of the family duty I had encountered so abruptly by leaving the village as a child.

Uncle Howard had talked of sending me to an Ivy League school, but he was unable to pay for it. He had spent a great deal of money on his trip back to China even without building a new house for his family there. After he returned to Philadelphia, he had to re-establish his financial standing.

At the same time, the Helms had become more of a family to me than my uncle. They were more realistic, as well, in finding a way for me to start college. One evening we had sort of a family conference.

"William, listen," said Mr. Helm. "You've been with us for some time now and we consider you one of the family. You've been diligent in your studies and you've volunteered to help me and Mrs. Helm without our asking many times. We appreciate this attitude in a young man. As you know, we're not a rich family, but we're a hard-working one, and you've fit in well."

I sat quietly, not sure what he was going to say.

"We'd like to help you pursue your education," he continued. "But we have to pool our resources to do it. Mrs. Helm and I made up our minds a long time ago about this."

Christina spoke up. "I'll contribute to make it a fund, at least sufficient for William to get through college. It should be a loan without interest while he's in school."

I was overwhelmed at this offer and hardly knew what to say. Finally, I said, "I'm very happy. I know you're not rich, but this generosity overcomes me. I don't know how to say 'thank you.'"

Mr. Helm concluded by repeating that this was their decision. "For the details, as to what you want to major in and where you want to go, Chrissie will work that out with you." He and his wife excused themsleves, leaving me with Christina.

"Do you know what you want to study?" Christina asked.

"I think so. For many years, I've thought about studying engineering, especially the branch that deals with mineral industries. I was told when I was a kid that China has many natural resources that need development. That's why I think this might be a good field to go into."

She nodded. "In that case, you might consider Pennsylvania State College. It has a good school of mineral industries and it's located near the Nittany Mountains. My brother Gus went there for mechanical engineering and he has a good job now."

"Well, that sounds good to me." Privately, I was eager to get out of Philadelphia, and State College seemed ideal.

As I considered college, though, an uncomfortable feeling came over me. I had taken several years to adjust to life with Uncle Howard after coming from China, and then I had entered the Helm household, where further adjustment had been necessary. Another move meant another environment to face.

My uncle and the Helms had experienced some jealous moments, but both sides had good intentions. Uncle Howard was frustrated by his financial inability to send me to college. The Helms came to my rescue in a way that neither my uncle nor I had expected, but as much as I was looking forward to going to college in the fall, I was beginning to see life as a series of farewells.

When the day arrived for me to leave, I felt as if I was reliving the experience of leaving my home in China. This was my second home. Even though I had grown older, it was not easy to leave people who had shown me affection, love, and emotional support.

Christina had made the financial arrangements, picked out my clothes for college, and purchased my bus ticket. I had two suitcases to take with me. She and Mrs. Helm would accompany me on the trolley car to the bus station. I said goodbye to Mr. Helm before we left.

"We'll miss you, William," he said, shaking my hand. "Good luck to you." He slipped me twenty dollars.

Trolley car #9 took a circuitous trip through the city. We arrived at the bus station with twenty minutes to spare. Mrs. Helm and Christina waited with me, but I was unhappy.

"Please don't feel bad," said Christina. "You'll be coming back for Thanksgiving and Christmas. Time will pass quickly and we'll see you again soon. Just study hard, as we know you will."

Just before I got on the bus, they each gave me a big hug and a kiss on the cheek. I held back my tears, just as they did.

From the bus, I watched the scenic route to State College. Just outside Philadelphia, we passed through forested areas still green with the late-summer foliage. When we started up into higher elevations, autumn leaves appeared. About a half hour before we were due to arrive, we entered the majestic Nittany Mountains. I liked the country; my early childhood in the rural peasant village had never completely left me. The terrain of middle Pennsylvania facinated me after my years in the heart of Philadelphia.

My basic freshman load included math, physics, organic chemistry, English, and a foreign language. I chose Spanish. All of my instructors were male except in Spanish class, which was taught by a young woman.

I did well in the first semester, despite all the new faces and new surroundings. When Thanksgiving came, I returned to Philadelphia for the first time to join the Helms. I did not see my uncle, who was in New York at the time. Still, I was glad to be back for the holiday. As usual, Mrs. Helm prepared the turkey, with the help of Christina and Gus's wife.

Thanksgiving vacation was fun, but short. When the time came for me to go, I told everyone that I could find own my way now. It was snowing, and I set off for the train station alone to take the long trip back to State College. The snow continued to fall for most of the journey, creating beautiful mountain scenery.

School began again the following Monday. Walking through the snow to classes was fun at first, but quickly became monotonous as the severity of winter wore on. Yet the Nittany Mountains overshadowed us with a gorgeous backdrop all winter long.

Classes became more tense and serious as the semester progressed. Final exams would take place after the Christmas break. Students also talked about finding ways to get home, and local stores put up their Christmas decorations.

My roommate, Hollis Shoemaker, offered me a ride to his hometown of Lancaster, from where I could take a shorter bus ride to Philadelphia.

During this vacation I had the time to visit Joe Orloff, Jake Wolf, and a few other high school friends. Yee Hoy treated me to a good dinner in Chinatown one Sunday afternoon.

"I envy you for the opportunity of going to college," he said. "I had hoped to do the same, but my father became ill and I had to take over his laundry."

"I'm sorry to hear about your father."

"I don't really regret missing college. I'm the oldest, and I have to earn a living to support the family that's still in China. The doctor has already informed that my father will not make it. He has heart disease."

"I'm very sorry." I shook hands with him. Certainly, I understood his dedication to his family duty; it paralleled my own.

As I rode the trolley home, I realized how fortunate I was. If not for the Helms, I might have been in a similar position, perhaps working for Uncle Howard. Realizing this, I appreciated the holiday much more. I helped decorate the Christmas tree as I had many other times on Christmas Eve. Our Christmas dinner featured turkey with all the usual trimmings and it tasted better than ever.

I tried to study during the vacation, but was simply unable to do so. As soon as I returned to the campus, I settled down to work hard. I managed to do reasonably well in final exams and entered the second semester without any problems. The courses in the new semester were mainly continuations of the previous ones and all went smoothly.

The big difference for this semester was that I went out for the soccer team.

Coach Munro was also one of my math instructors. He was a Scot who asked, "Have you played the game before?"

"Not since grade school, when I was in China."

"Never mind. We'll teach you."

I went out to the practice field three times a week after classes. In an intramural game one day, I was put in as a substitute at outside forward. I made a goal with my left foot, despite being right-footed. That impressed Coach Munro and I played in every game the rest of the season. At the end, I received my numerals, 1934, representing my class year. If I had been on the varsity, I would have lettered.

In the fall, I returned to college with a new enthusiasm. I had spent several enjoyable weeks in a summer camp and came back to school as a sophomore. Now that the surroundings and the routine were familiar to me, I felt much more comfortable.

Now I had a course in surveying, required by my major. This involved field trips twice a week, with heavy equipment. Unfortunately, the leader of my five-man team was the varsity quarterback, named Snyder. He acted as though he were king, and the rest of the team worshipped him — except for me.

He seemed to sense my attitude. He grew mean and ordered me, the smallest member of the team, to carry the transom, our heaviest piece of equipment, each trip. His speech was salted with four-letter words and frequent spitting. Some of the words I understood; the rest I could guess. The others spoke in a similar way.

"Hey, Wu!" he would yell. "Set that damn thing up and let's get to work. Get it over there and sight in that direction before I kick your ass to pieces!"

He ordered the others around, but in a less abusive way. I tried in every way to avoid conflicts with him and simply tolerated his treatment. By the end of the year, I had decided that engineering was not for me, perhaps for the wrong reason.

Before I went to Penn State, I had met some students from China who attended the University of Pennsylvania. When I went to State, I hoped to meet more, but the only Asian I met there was a Korean. We became friends, but I was disappointed that there were no other Chinese students. I wanted to meet others who might also wish to return to China and work, possibly together.

I did make friends with American students, some of whom invited me to visit their families on weekends. The first time I hitchhiked, a friend secured a ride for us both in the cab of a coal truck headed for Scranton. The driver was friendly and tried to point out the sights along the way. However, by the time we got out, we were both covered with coal dust that had blown into the cab from the back of the truck. I never hitchhiked again.

Hollis and I moved into a rooming house our second year, but we had to walk down the street to a boarding house for meals. Students from various disciplines ate there. They were all cordial and some were curious about me because they had never met anyone from Asia before. I learned more slang, in particular "spud" and "boarding house reach."

During Christmas vacation that year, I discussed with the Helms my unhappiness with engineering. I was now considering medicine and they remained supportive. Shortly after that, I sent out applications to other institutions, to transfer beginning my junior year. My first choice was the University of Michigan, an excellent university with outstanding professional and graduate schools. Moreover, many Chinese students were pursuing graduate work there. I was overjoyed when I was accepted. Two other institutions accepted me also, but I chose Michigan.

The following summer, the Helms sent me to Johns Hopkins University in Baltimore to make up some of the pre-med classes I would need. I had been accepted there, too, and its medical school was world-renowned. While enjoying my studies at the Homewood campus, I had the opportunity to visit the medical school with the famous "Four Horsemen" on the faculty. They were William Halsted, the father of modern surgery; William Osler, the great clinician who instituted bedside teaching; Howard Kelly, the renowned obstetrician and gynecologist; and William Welch, the unparalleled pathologist of his time. The large painting of these four men was awe-inspiring.

I met Eugene Chan there, a Chinese ophthalmologist on the junior teaching staff who had been trained there. Dr. Chan invited me to dinner the next day and we chatted more along the same lines. I was pleased that his list included Michigan. This reinforced my choice.

Baltimore was hot that summer, but I enjoyed the brief change of locale and obtained good grades in the two courses I took. I also made a few friends among Chinese students living in the same rooming house. They were all graduate students in political science.

My most heartwarming experience came with a Chinese laundry owner. When I first took my clothes to him, he asked, "Are you a student? You look like one."

I told him that I was. As we got acquainted, he told me he had studied under my father in Toisan. We were both excited to find this common bond. All summer, he not only laundered my clothes for free, but even delivered them to my rooming house. Before leaving Baltimore, I went to see him and thanked him for his kindness and generosity.

"It's nothing," he replied. "I wish I could do more. Your father is a great man. I know you will be, too. I wish you luck."

We shook hands and I left. I did not return to Baltimore and I never saw him again. However, the memory of his kindness stayed with me.

In the fall, I had to say goodbye to the Helms once again in Philadelphia. I would go farther away this time, and saying goodbye to loved ones was never easy. Once again, Mrs. Helm and Christina escorted me to the Broad Street Station for a difficult farewell.

I arrived in Ann Arbor, Michigan, the next day. As soon as I stepped off the train, I saw some Chinese students. One of them came up to me and asked, "Are you a new student? A few of us are here to meet and help new arrivals."

"Yes, I am."

"As soon as you get all your luggage, we'll help you find a place to stay."

They met one other new Chinese student, as well. We went from the train station to 1402 Hill Street, the house of the international Chinese fraternity, Alpha Lambda. One of its activities was to assist Chinese students anywhere in the world, without any coercion for them to pledge their frat. In fact, they offered to help me locate a place of lodging elsewhere.

"Is there a place for me to stay here?" I asked. "At least until I get my bearings?"

"Of course," said Peter Lim, one of the fellows who had met me at the train station. "I'm not sure when the rest of the students will return. In any case, don't worry. I'll help you get settled."

That gave me a great deal of reassurance. In a short time, I was startled to learn that Peter not only came from Toisan, but had even attended the same grade school as I. That made me feel more at home. As it turned out, I did not have to move, either.

Later, I chose to join the fraternity. I liked its purpose and principles. It had no political affiliation, but promoted friendship and fellowship among its members. Also, it provided social, financial and scholastic help to members when necessary. This was exactly the kind of environment I had been looking for, as well, with Chinese students who intended to return to China someday to work.

It had a mundane advantage, too; I really learned to cook there.

Chapter Thirteen

Alpha Lambda had a preponderance of engineering students, but they were divided into different areas. They included the aeronautic, civil, chemical, electrical, mechanical, and automotive fields. An outstanding architectural student, W.P. Li, had won a fellowship to study in Rome. Chen Fu Hua studied engineering. Another student did graduate work in bacteriology under Frederick G. Novy, one of the few remaining students of the German scientist, Robert Koch, who had discovered the tuberculosis bacillus. The only medical student in the fraternity was Paul Kwan.

Paul acted as my big brother. He gave me much valuable information in my preparation for medical school. With his advice and my determination, I earned an acceptance after three years of college.

I still lacked a course in scientific German, however, and my admission was contingent on my successful completion of it. Dr. Luther Lee taught that course. He was German in origin and had an M.D. but held his position in the University's Department of Languages rather than in medicine. When I went to see him regarding my predicament, he turned out to be one of the most considerate and compassionate professors I ever met.

Dr. Lee had a stately carriage and large stature, with a resounding laugh. After I explained my situation, he said, "Don't worry, young man. There are a few other graduate students who are taking this course with you. We'll make it as interesting and meaningful as possible."

Under his kind mien, the class worked harder than usual and we learned our German. In the end, we all received an "A." After I had finished my first year of medical school, I happened to see Dr. Lee on State Street, near central campus. I was pleased to tell him that I had survived my first year in medicine, but I saw he had lost much weight and appeared ashen in color. A year later, I was saddened to hear that he had died of cancer of the pancreas.

By that time, I had become President of Alpha Lambda. My closest friends were Peter Lim, Paul Kwan, Bob Suez, Y.C. Mar, and Benjamin King. They were the earliest frat brothers to befriend me and to demonstrate the meaning of the English phrase, "brotherly love," that I had learned in Philadelphia.

These few left through graduation and new students came in to replace them. Following their precedent, we continued to meet Chinese students as they arrived in town year after year. We helped them find lodging and board. Some of the newcomers eventually joined us, while others moved elsewhere.

As President of Alpha Lambda, I was summoned to the office of Dean Bursley, Dean of Student Affairs. He said, "My purpose in calling you in today is that the President of the Inter-Fraternity Council has learned that your frat ranks academically at the top of all the fraternities on campus. However, he noticed that most of your members are in graduate school or professional schools with just a small number of undergraduates. Since the graduate and professional schools grade differently from the colleges, he claims the comparison is unfair."

I was proud of our accomplishment, but I felt the President of the Inter-Fraternity was overly-concerned with this question of rankings. "Dean Bursley, I doubt that any of us ever paid much attention to our ranking among the fraternities."

"In any case, if you agree, we'll prorate the graduate and professional grades to be comparable with the undergraduate system."

"That's fine with us. I'll be interested to see where we really stand."

A week later, I received another call from Dean Bursley's office. When I arrived there again, he greeted me with a big smile. "Congratulations! After all the prorating of grades, the Inter-Fraternity Council finds that you are still ranked on top. Keep up the good work. The University takes pride in your achievements."

In the spring of 1935, I suddenly received a telegram from my father saying that my third sister, Bijin, had died. I was deeply upset and so, in consultation with the secretary of the medical school, I took a leave of absence and planned my first trip home.

I wrote to the Helms and to Uncle Howard, who was now in New York. They both agreed that remaining away from home for twelve years had been long enough, and that with the death of my sister, a trip home might help my mood. So I could make the trip, the Helms and Uncle Howard pooled their resources to give me round-trip tickets by train and boat, plus spending money. I thought I had outgrown homesickness, but it remained instilled in me.

While I remained saddened by my sister's death, I was glad to have the long-awaited opportunity to go home. As a child, I had been homesick many times. I had secretly cried myself to sleep, especially in the first two years I was in the United States.

First I returned from Michigan to Philadelphia to see the Helms. Two days later, I took the same route in reverse that I had traveled before, on the Pennsylvania Railroad from the Broad Street Station in Philadelphia to Chicago, then on the Great Northern Railroad to Seattle. There, I met Mr. George Wong, the travel agent, and of course I found Grace on shipboard out of Vancouver.

Now, back in medical school, my class work became more demanding, especially my lab reports in pharmacology and biochemistry. When Thanksgiving approached, I saw that I would not have the time to visit the Helms or my uncle. Those in my frat who had nowhere to go were invited home for Thanksgiving by American classmates and faculty members. This meant that no one in the frat had to spend the holiday alone, and many of them were able to visit an American home for the first time.

While at Michigan, I had known a number of Chinese graduate students who came to the U.S. to earn a Master's degree in one field or another. This usually took only one year. During that period, they had little time for extracurricular activities.

Some of them traveled as far from Ann Arbor as Detroit, about forty miles away, but no farther. All they learned of the United States before returning to China was the city of Ann Arbor, the University of Michigan, and perhaps a quick look at Detroit. I felt it was a tragedy for them to travel halfway around the world and learn almost nothing about their new environment.

For this reason, I had sometimes invited friends from China to come home with me to Philadelphia. The Helms were very kind and understanding, and welcomed my guests even if they were only passing through the area. My friends, in turn, were able to experience something of American family life and customs. I still believe in the value of this type of personal contact.

One friend, Chen Fu Hua, whose family had hosted Bob Suez and me in Nanjing, obtained his Master's degree in civil engineering in the spring of 1936. He was planning to return to China by way of Europe, and was going straight from Ann Arbor to New York. I persuaded him to stop over in Philadelphia to visit the Helms. He had never visited an American home before.

The Helms were so hospitable that he remained for a week instead of a night, as he had originally planned. Christina showed him the Liberty Bell, Independence Hall, the Betsy Ross House, and the Delaware River. Chen Fu Hua later wrote to me from China expressing his appreciation of their hospitality. He said that he learned more about the American people, history, and society during that week than he had in his first year at Michigan studying engineering. The Helms were pleased and encouraged me to bring more friends home in the future.

During the summer of 1936, I finished making up courses that brought me back on schedule, after falling behind when I had left for China. The summer passed quickly and I had little time left for another trip back to Philadelphia. Christina was just returning home from Europe and we planned a nice family reunion for Mr. and Mrs. Helm after their lonesome summer.

I stayed with the Helms this time for about two weeks. While there, I once again looked up a couple of friends from high school. Joseph Orloff now attended the Temple University Medical School and Jake Wolf, who had graduated from Penn, was managing his father's brewery.

Then I went to New York to visit Uncle Howard. He was operating a curio shop on Pell Street and his financial stituation was gradually improving. Though he was still sorry that he had not been able to help me as much as he had wanted, his morale was better than I had seen for some time. I assured him that the Helms were willing and able to help on a long-term basis. I stayed with him for two days and then returned to Philadelphia.

The Helms, financially, were just an average American family. However, they had more compassion, generosity, and understanding than anyone else I had met. They were glad that I felt at home with them, and shared much with me.

September came again, too soon. I returned to Ann Arbor and was reunited with my frat brothers. Registration had become a familiar routine by now. While other Septembers had been exciting, challenging, or a little frightening, this one was just a case of "back to the salt mines," as the cliché goes.

Chapter Fourteen

As soon as I settled into the new semester, the Chinese national holiday loomed ahead once again. This year I was chairman of the Ticket Committee, in charge of selling tickets to our Double Ten dinner. A week or so before the dinner, I was walking along Washtenaw Avenue toward State Street and saw Miss Franking in the distance, walking toward me on the other side of the street. I hurried across the street.

"Hello." I was excited and timid at the same time. "Would you like to go to the Double Ten dinner?"

"Yes, I would."

I was surprised and elated.

"Call me later," she said, starting to walk again. "I have to get to class."

"I don't know your number," I said. A year had passed since she had given it to me.

She gave me her new number quickly. I wrote it down, suddenly aware that I not only had gotten a date without planning to, but now I had to shell out two dollars for her ticket, as well. I sold myself another ticket.

On the evening of the party, I went to her current address in Camden Court, quite close to our frat house at 1346 Geddes.

Cecile Franking was shiningly pretty, with her black hair curled up from the nape and parted in the middle. She wore a lovely blue dress that fell a few inches below her knees. Since the evening was chilly, she also wore a short wool coat.

We walked only about two blocks to the Michigan League, where the dinner was being held. About two hundred people attended, including some Americans. When the president of the Chinese Students Club finished his opening remarks, we sang the national anthems of both China and the U.S.

Dinner included roast beef as the entree and cake and ice cream for dessert. Professor Raleigh Nelson, Director of the International Student Center, was the guest speaker. He understood the holiday's meaning, and his talk was short but interesting. Dancing followed, but Cecile and I left.

As I walked her home, she told me that she was working as a baby sitter for her room and board where she lived with the George Smith family. They were friends of her American grandparents, with whom she had grown up in Ann Arbor. She seemed to have enjoyed the evening.

"Since we live so close," I said, "we should be able to see each other more often."

"Perhaps."

We shook hands on the porch and I walked home happily.

Halloween approached, and the fraternity decided to follow American custom by holding a Halloween party. I called Cecile and invited her, feeling bold. She accepted without hesitation.

Meanwhile, classes put a greater demand on both my time and energy. Even before Halloween arrived, I had to remind myself that I could not allow my social life to interfere with my studies. Now that I had caught up in school, I didn't want to make any mistakes.

The frat's Halloween party was a success. Somehow, wearing a mask seemed to give people more freedom of action, even to the point of being silly. In this atmosphere, Cecile appeared more relaxed than she had the other night. She mixed well with the rest of the group and on the short walk home, she suggested, "Let's go trick-or-treat."

At the time, I had no idea what the term meant. By the time she had finished explaining it to me, we were standing on her porch. She thanked me for a pleasant evening and I left feeling good, satisfied that we were becoming friends.

A few weeks later, Cecile called me. She invited me to have Thanksgiving dinner with her and the Smith family. I accepted readily.

As usual, most of the frat members had been invited to spend Thanksgiving with American families. Among them, I felt quite smug. I preened for this special occasion.

I walked over shortly after noon. The Smiths greeted me warmly, including their children, Chuck and Betty Lou. Cecile was bright and bouncy as she helped with dinner.

George Smith was a large, tall man who had worked at the anatomy lab in the medical school for many years. He told anecdotes about the various professors with whom he had worked. By this time, of course, I knew some of them. He had a big smile and periodically laughed heartily at some of his own descriptions.

However, he revered Dr. Elizabeth Crosby, a tiny, inconspicuous woman in her early fifties. I had taken a histology class from her, but had not realized then she was world-renowned as a neuroanatomist. Dr. Crosby was loved by both the students and faculty. She was so small that a strong gust of wind would blow her offstride. Still, she held her own physically and intellectually.

Our hostess, Ella Smith, was a heavy-set woman with a big smile, who exuded warmth and joy. She called us to dinner and put Cecile on my left at the table and the children opposite us. Our hosts sat at each end of the table. George said grace.

I had two helpings of turkey with dressing, cranberry sauce, mashed potatoes, corn, and gravy. While we ate, Ella explained that she had known Cecile's mother, who was dead, and her grandparents, who had moved to Washington D.C. Her two older brothers lived there now, as well. George told little anecdotes about Cecile's family to tease her.

The big surprise came after dinner. Ella brought out a cake with little candles and we all sang "Happy Birthday" to Cecile. She made a wish and blew out the nineteen candles with one breath. Everyone applauded.

Cecile served the cake. It was an exciting occasion for me. I not only felt that my relationship with Cecile had been strengthened, but that the Smiths were encouraging it. When it was time for me to leave, they told me to drop by any time. I came away with a feeling of satisfaction and happiness.

After that, I called frequently. Cecile would often say, "Why don't you come over and we'll study here? The Smiths are out and the kids will be in bed soon."

This became an enjoyable habit, and an almost weekly occurrence. Those were some of the happiest occasions of my life. Although Cecile was still going out with other fellows, I was pretty certain that we belonged together. As time went on, the study sessions became romantic episodes, too. Whenever we became overly stimulated, she would say, "You had better go home now."

I seldom argued.

When Christmas came, I spent the holidays in Philadelphia and she went to visit her grandmother and two older brothers in Washington D.C.

As spring came on, our interest toward each other intensified. We began to play tennis and to take walks along the banks of the Huron River. Also, we joined the other students wandering the Arboretum.

The Arboretum was a large, open park with many old trees and flowering bushes. The foliage of the trees provided dark shade and shelter. Winding roads and green, hilly terrain provided a romantic backdrop for walks, picnics, sunbathing, and studying. At dusk, especially, many couples would recline under the trees for their semi-privacy. The atmosphere was contagious, and Cecile and I enjoyed our weekend evenings in this outdoor theater of youthful romance.

By the end of the spring semester, we had fallen in love. I thought of her all the time, and when I was with her I was satisfied, even if we weren't talking. Unfortunately, she had to return to Washington D.C. for the summer to be with her grandmother and to work during summer vacation.

For myself, I returned to Philadelphia. I tried being a waiter in a fancy Chinese restaurant where the manager was a friend of Uncle Howard. Perhaps I had a subconscious rebellion at that kind of work; anyway, for some reason, I dropped a large tray of dishes every day for a week. After a week of smashed dishes, the manager tried me as a host, instead. I worked as a host for two weeks and then quit. The work was easy, but I was getting minimum wage and no tips.

The Helms suggested that I take a vacation. After a week or so of doing nothing in particular, I asked if I might return to Ann Arbor for summer school. Taking a course or two now could make the regular school year easier. They thought it was a good idea and I arrived back in Michigan just in time to register. A few frat brothers had stayed around for the summer session, as well. However, I was lonesome for Cecile.

I took the first clinical course for med students, in obstetrics and gynecology. We were on call for deliveries any time of day or night. It was a good course to get out of the way, to avoid being on call during the regular school year.

In this course, we learned how to interview a pregnant woman and to do a rectal and vaginal examination and to determine the degree of dilation of the cervix in a woman in labor. On deliveries, we usually only observed, but we did assist in a few cases where patients were confined in a correctional institution outside Ann Arbor. We also saw patients during our instructions of pre- and postpartum care.

In this course, we had constant contact with patients. The instructors were members of the junior staff who had recently finished their residencies in this field. As a result, they were young and enthusiastic.

I thought of Cecile frequently and we corresponded fairly often. She expressed delight when I quoted Yeats in my first letter. I could apparently write more eloquently than I could speak. Our relationship flourished in our correspondence.

During this summer, the news from China turned worse. Letters from my parents indicated that the Japanese were threatening to invade China proper from Manchukuo, their puppet state created out of three Chinese provinces in Manchuria that they had occupied six years earlier. Then headlines in the <u>Detroit Free Press</u> reported that the Japanese had skirmished with Chinese troops at Lukouqiao, or Marco Polo Bridge, near Beijing on July 7, 1937. The war had begun.

Already, the years of internal conflict among the warlords and the campaigns of Jiang Jieshi (Chiang Kaishek) against the Communists had caused much suffering. In Alpha Lambda, we were hoping now that, for a change, Jiang would unite with the Communists and other Chinese factions to repulse the Japanese.

The Chinese did resist. Though several cities fell to the invaders, China did not give up. By mid-August, we read frequent reports of heavy fighting.

Three months later, Nanjing fell to the Japanese. The Nationalist government fled westward, first to Hangzhou and then to Chongqing, a small city in the mountains, on the northern bank of the upper reaches of the Yangzi (Yangtze) River. Shortly after Nanjing fell, the Japanese sank the "U.S.S. Panay," a U.S. gunboat, and several British ships in the Yangzi.

All the overseas Chinese, including those of us at Michigan, thought that China would finally get help from the United States and Britain. However, the main interest of the western world lay in Europe where another storm was brewing. Also, any aid to China had to filter through a Japanese blockade. Nevertheless, China survived, continuing to fight on gradually receding lines.

These events played a large part in the lives of Chinese students living abroad. All of us intended to serve China someday with our educations and to assist in her modernization. We worried about our families and were terribly concerned about Japanese atrocities occurring in China, but we could do nothing.

The summer passed and once again the full number of students returned to Ann Arbor for the fall. I longed for Cecile to come back and I finally called the Smiths. They told me that she was due at the train depot soon.

By this time, I was brave enough to go and meet her at the station, where the Smiths were also waiting. Cecile hugged everyone, including me. The Smiths drove us all back to their house, but I excused myself and left, since I was not sure if I was in the way or not.

Cecile and I resumed our social life as before, despite the rigors of school. We played some tennis, went to movies, and took walks. At least once a week, we "studied" at the Smiths.

This year, the Double Ten celebration was attended by more Chinese students and more of their American friends than usual. The latest events in Asia had concerned everyone who followed the news. The Japanese invasion of China still progressed with alarming steadiness.

Cecile and I went to the dinner to celebrate our "anniversary," but the mood was gloomy. The Chinese students did express their patriotism, and many of the American students present showed a willingness to arouse America's awareness of the problem. During October, the situation in China had only worsened. Besides Hangzhou, the cities of Hanyang, Wuzhang, and Guangzhou had fallen to the Japanese by October 25, 1937.

Chapter Fifteen

When Thanksgiving approached, I sent Cecile a birthday card. I only found out later that her birthday would not always coincide with Thanksgiving. The Smiths invited me to join them again for Thanksgiving. I was too embarrassed to accept their hospitality again, though I wanted to do so.

Instead, I went to Detroit with two frat brothers, where we visited another family named Smith. We had a pleasant day and a fine dinner before returning to Ann Arbor. That evening, I went to see Cecile and spent the rest of the holiday with her and the Smiths.

I had many case reports to write, and Christmas seemed to approach quickly. In fact, I just barely finished in time for the new holiday break. Cecile surprised me with an invitation to spend part of the holidays with her family in Washington. I explained that I would be visiting the Helms and my Uncle Howard, and would have to see if I could make further arrangements once I got back to Philadelphia.

When the break began, I took the train back to Philadelphia and enjoyed a nice family gathering for Christmas at the Helms'. Their family had grown by two grandchildren, and all three generations were present. Since the elder Mr. Helm kept his apothecary open even on Christmas Day, he had to run in and out all the time to attend to his customers. His son carved the turkey with my help. Dinner was excellent, but I felt sorry for Mr. Helm. Even during the meal, customers interrupted him frequently.

The Christmas tree remained lit while we ate, casting a festive glow. The most exciting moments came when the radio broadcast a speech by the great Mohandas Gandhi, appealing for world peace. He spoke in a resounding British accent.

After dinner, I helped Christina and Helen, Gus Jr.'s wife, with the dishes. Later, the children opened their gifts. The adults had exchanged theirs the evening before. I had given Christina a white silk scarf from China which she seemed to like.

Christina and I talked about school, hers and mine, until quite late in the evening. She was pleased with what I was doing and reassured me that their family would see me through financially. I was still impressed that they would take on a total stranger from another country, especially an Asian. It took not only generosity, but courage. I would always remain indebted to them.

When I brought up the question of leaving early to see my uncle in New York, the elder Helms agreed, but showed some displeasure at the idea of my visiting Cecile in Washington. I had not told them much about her, so they were a little shocked.

Christina came to my rescue. She felt that it was fine for me to have a girlfriend. Later, thinking back, she expressed the opinion that her parents had been too strict with her, and that was the reason she herself never married.

I soon paid a brief visit to my uncle in New York and then took a train to Washington. Cecile met me at Union Station and introduced me to Fred and Florence Mattingley. Fred had dark hair that was already thinning; Florence was an attractive blonde with a narrow face. They drove Cecile and me to her family's home.

Their house had been built with distinct upstairs and downstairs apartments. I had never seen that design before. Cecile's grandmother, Gram, stood at the top of the stairs as we approached.

Gram was a lovely, stately woman with a disarming voice and smile. First she gave Cecile a hug and a kiss, then she shook hands with the rest of us. She addressed Cecile as "Twiddle."

Then Gram invited us to come in and sit. She sat down in her rocking chair and asked me about the train ride and the scenery. As the conversation progressed, I gathered that Florence and Fred were good friends of the family. Cecile brought everyone tea and soft drinks.

"I am going to start dinner," Gram announced. "I want all of you to stay. Do you like rice, Bill?"

"Yes," I said enthusiastically.

Gram rose and went to the kitchen. Florence and Cecile followed her to help, but she shooed them out again.

When dinner was ready, we sat down at the kitchen table. Cecile's eldest brother, Nelson, joined us. He was the breadwinner of the family and was just getting home from work. After washing up quickly, he came to the table and Cecile introduced us.

"Nel," said Gram, "why don't you start with the chicken and Cecile will begin with the potatoes."

We also had broccoli, corn, and homemade rolls. Best of all, Gram had cooked a small pot of rice just to my liking. The grains barely stuck to each other and a brownish crust had formed around the sides and bottom of the pot. I could see that Gram had experience in cooking rice this way. Still, I could hardly get over it, for this was the way my mother cooked it and I had not had it this way for a long time.

Nel was the tallest and heaviest person present. With a slightly round face and piercing eyes, at first he seemed stern. His features were Caucasian, except for the tan of his skin. He had a fine pair of hands with slender, tapering fingers, and worked as an excellent tool maker for the Navy.

As we ate, Nel was quiet at first, but he broke the ice by asking how my train trip had been. Fred and Florence joined in, and we talked about the Washington Redskins and the Michigan Wolverines, who had not done well that year. In the meantime, Gram urged everyone to fill their plates again. I did, without hesitation. For dessert, we had apple pie and tea.

After dinner, Gram occasionally mentioned Mae and Tiam Franking, the parents of Nelson, Cecile, and their brother Alason, who came between them in age. The Mattingleys left around nine o'clock and Gram and Cecile cleaned the kitchen. Nel and I talked then, and I found him friendly and well-read.

Cecile had planned sightseeing for the next day. We took the trolley cars to the Library of Congress, the Lincoln Memorial, and the Washington Monument. When we returned in the evening, Gram had prepared dinner for us.

After dinner, Nel went out for the evening. Cecile and Gram showed me pictures of Cecile's parents and of her brothers when they were children. I also saw My Chinese Marriage, the book Cecile's mother had written about her courtship and marriage. It had been published in 1921.

The next day, Alason and his fiancée, Phyllis, arrived to celebrate New Year's Eve. Alason appeared much younger than Nel, though the age difference was not great. More outgoing, he brought in an atmosphere of gaiety. Phyllis was reserved but pleasant. Fred and Florence arrived soon afterward. I learned during the evening that Alason was a musician, and also could sing, though he was partially deaf in one ear. This was due to complications from a mastoid operation he had had at an early age.

Gram had to cook a big dinner, but Phyllis and Florence assisted her. Cecile was relieved of that duty to help entertain the guests. However, everyone except Gram, Cecile, and I planned to go elsewhere late that night for the actual arrival of the New Year. By ten P.M., only the three of us remained. Gram wished us a happy new year and said good night. Cecile and I stayed up, talking and looking out the window whenever we heard unusual, festive noises outside.

Waiting for midnight became monotonous. We lay down on the couch to be close as we waited, but we were afraid that Gram might come in. Restraining ourselves, we were in each other's arms when the New Year arrived. Welcoming 1938 with quiet intimacy meant more to us than sharing all the noise outside would have. It was the most enjoyable New Year I had ever had.

On New Year's morning, everyone slept late except Gram, who spent the morning in the kitchen. When Cecile and I stirred around ten-thirty, Gram made us breakfast.

While we ate, Gram asked me about my plans to return to China, considering the war now taking place there. I could only respond that I would have to wait and see. Gram also began telling me anecdotes about the "naughty" things Cecile used to do as a child. Cecile was obviously special to her.

Gram exuded warmth. I liked listening to her talk. She used many youthful expressions and ideas; she kept in step with her grandchildren. Her manner was calm and sincere.

Nel rose about noon. All of us listened to the radio that afternoon to hear about the Tournament of Roses Parade and then to listen to the Rose Bowl. California defeated Alabama, 13-0.

Since I was leaving the next day, I suggested to Cecile that we all go out to a Chinese restaurant and have dinner on me. She consulted Gram, who though it was a fine idea for Nel, Cecile, and me. Gram declined for herself, saying that she seldom went out in the evenings.

Nel drove us to H Street in the heart of Washington's Chinatown. China Gardens was an excellent restaurant without grotesque decorations. It was very good, but the rice was not as good as Gram's.

At home that night, I said goodbye to Nel, since he would be leaving for work before I got up. I thanked him for his hospitality, and he told me to come back. Since Cecile and I had had such a beautiful and memorable evening the night before, we indulged in just one meaningful embrace and said good night. As I went to sleep, I felt full of joy and love.

Since Cecile had arranged a ride back to Ann Arbor, and I had a train ticket, we would separate temporarily. On the morning of January 2, I thanked Gram profusely for the hospitality that had made me feel so much at home. I also told her that the way she cooked rice was reminiscent of my mother's. Gram invited me back, too.

I wanted to give her a hug, but did not. She did not seem to want physical contact with people outside her immediate family. However, she did give me a warm handshake and squeezed my hand between both of hers.

Cecile gave Gram a kiss and a hug as we descended the stairs.

"Take good care of Bill," Gram said to Cecile.

Cecile rode with me to the train station. We held hands in the back seat of the taxi, but said very little. At the station, we waited about fifteen minutes. I wanted to kiss her and give her a big hug, but I was still reluctant to display affection in public. We shook hands and I thanked her, too, before I boarded.

As the train pulled out, I waved to Cecile from the window.

Chapter Sixteen

I could not afford to daydream about Cecile. Final exams were coming up. I had books and notes with me, and spent the train ride back to Ann Arbor studying.

Snow fell hard when I arrived. I could not get a ride from a friend to campus, so I took a taxi to the frat house. Three inches of snow had accumulated on the steps. Everyone else was already there, studying. My roommate, Raymond, was in our room. I greeted him and started unpacking.

Cecile arrived in town again the next day. I called her and we agreed that during finals we would only get together on weekends. However, I called her daily for a short chat.

Exams ended in a couple of weeks. A period of anxiety followed, as everyone waited for grades to come out. Cecile and I were both relieved to find that we had done satisfactorily.

During the semester break, Cecile offered to teach me to ski. A nice slope stretched between the University Hospital and the Simpson Memorial Institute for Research in Pernicious Anemia, just opposite the astronomical observatory. At first I was reluctant to jump, but it was fun once we started. We did this for several days without getting hurt, despite the many falls I had.

We also walked along the snowy paths through the woods by the Huron River. The first day, we saw that the river had frozen and that people were skating on it. The next day, Cecile and I went out with another couple to skate. I fell too many times and finally quit, but I enjoyed watching Cecile and the others glide gracefully on the river in the winter setting.

Raymond and Ruby were married in the Michigan Union on the Saturday before the second semester began. It was a simple ceremony, attended by our fraternity brothers and some friends, as well as a larger number of Chinese students. The couple left for Detroit, but they had only two days for their honeymoon before returning to Ann Arbor for the new semester.

On Monday, Raymond confided that they had gotten married without a license. He had gone to Detroit early on Saturday, and found the appropriate office closed. In any case, they moved into an apartment near the frat house and frequently came to visit.

In this semester, having chosen the surgical services, I had more chances to view operations. Also, I was taking an elective course in Junior Anatomy. The number of students in this class was limited, allowing us greater individual instruction for dissecting the more intricate structures, such as the muscles that move the eyeballs and the cranial and peripheral nerves and the sympathetic nervous systems. Coincidentally, my instructor was Bob Bartlett, the good friend of Paul Kwan, and I learned much from him.

As the semester progressed, letters from China arrived from various friends and relatives in the fraternity. All the news depressed us. The Japanese advance had reached central China and still continued. Since all of us dreamed of returning someday to help our native country, we followed these events closely.

A mass migration of the Chinese had been underway, as they transported schools, universities, hospitals, and factories by any means possible, but mostly by human effort. Everyone moved inland if they could, away from the invaders. People literally walked thousands of miles to escape the Japanese.

The only encouraging news was that China had not given up. The Chinese Communists were conducting guerilla warfare that kept the Japanese line thinly extended and prevented them from effectively advancing westward, at least for the time. Jiang Jieshi (Chiang Kaishek) had not fought much, but he had withdrawn with many divisions intact.

In the meantime, construction had begun on the Burma Road. When finished, it would allow the transport of supplies to the Chinese holding out in western China, including Chongqing, from Burma around the Japanese coastal blockade. Plans were also underway to build a road from that same area of China through the Himalayas in

Tibet. I later learned that the chief engineer for these projects was my friend and fraternity brother, Chen Fu Hua. He was a capable young man, but the task was stupendous. He told me that he was in charge of five hundred engineers and fifteen thousand laborers who constructed the Burma Road across six hundred miles in two years.

American support in this period remained minimal and the Japanese blockade remained effective. The Chinese attitude toward the American response was, "There was a lot of noise upstairs, but no one ever came down."

My senior year turned out to be relatively easy. We had more freedom in our clinical courses, which were divided into small groups for discussions after we saw patients. We would then interpret the lab results, including X-rays, blood counts, urinalysis, and blood cell appearance. Our discussion groups would center on our findings, offering a valuable mix of opinions.

We also observed more detailed methods of examination during rounds. One palpates for an enlarged liver or spleen in a certain way; a kidney required a different approach. Differentiating between an ordinary stomach ache and appendicitis was the most difficult, even for our teaching staff.

I was due to graduate in June, but I extended my education for a semester by taking fewer courses this spring and by doing dog surgery. I had two reasons for this. One was to watch developments in China a little longer. The second, related to this, was to decide if I was going to marry Cecile and take her back to China. I knew that Gram wouldn't like our going there, and I doubted Cecile was enthusiastic, either. She was due to graduate the following June.

During the Christmas holidays this year, I visited Cecile in Washington again. This time, we had serious discussions about our future together. Gram and Cecile's brothers felt it was unwise for us to return to China within the next few months. However, I had obtained an appointment as a house officer at PUMC, due to start in April of 1939.

In addition, I saw no future in pursuing my medical training in the U.S. I had written forty applications for internships around the country, but I was turned down in every case because the positions required U.S. citizenship. At the time, U.S. law prevented Asian immigrants from becoming naturalized citizens, so I could do nothing along this line.

Cecile and I were quite unhappy about my career problems, but we saw no solution. The Helms wanted to help, but could not see any way out, either. I finally decided that I should return to China myself to see how matters developed.

During the 1930s, China's political and military situation never quite stabilized, despite the ascendancy of Jiang Jieshi (Chiang Kaishek) at the head of the Guomindang, or Nationalist Party, starting in 1928. The Japanese, deciding to act before Jiang could consolidate the country, invaded Manchuria in 1931 and continued to threaten the rest of China. Meanwhile, Jiang's first priority had been to chase the elusive Chinese Communists.

In 1936, Jiang had driven the Communists into hiding in Yenan, with their military power apparently destroyed. Jiang persisted in pursuing them, however, while the Japanese gathered their forces in Manchuria. In December of that year, Jiang flew to Xian, to the headquarters of the Young Marshal, Zhang Xueliang. Jiang wished to persuade the Young Marshal, one of the few remaining independent warlords, to spearhead a campaign against the Japanese.

However, the Young Marshal surprised the Generalissimo by arresting his staff and confining him to a guest house. Zhang Xueliang pleaded with him to abandon his anti-Communist crusade. He wanted Jiang join a truce with the Communists to resist the Japanese. Jiang refused and many of the Young Marshal's officers wanted to execute him.

At this time, an unexpected visitor arrived from the mountain headquarters of the Communists in Yenan. It was Zhou Enlai, who argued persuasively for the unity of the Chinese against the foreign enemy. Jiang finally agreed to the truce and to participate in preparations against the Japanese. Zhang Xueliang released him.

The following July, the Japanese invaded China proper. From that time on, the East China Front of what would become World War II was at war. As we had observed, the Japanese advanced inexorably.

This was the backdrop against which I was about to return to

China, possibly to start my medical career. I had watched the new developments carefully throughout my senior year in med school, but the war had seemed to reach a point of stasis by early 1939. Meanwhile, I still had more work before I would receive my M.D.

First I finished my senior thesis, which was entitled, "Congenital Anomalies of the Genital Urinary System." The last and biggest stumbling block was the final oral examination. When the time for my final oral arrived, I was sitting anxiously in the chair next in line, waiting for my turn. The student ahead of me came out of the examination room pale and sweaty, with a disappointed look. My heart began palpitating at twice its normal rate.

When my name was called, I stood up and walked in on quivering knees. Fortunately, the candidate's chair was close to the door, so I did not have far to walk. I shut the door gently.

The Chairman of the Examining Committee was Dr. Fred Hodges, who smiled pleasantly and gestured to the empty chair. His colleagues on the board were professors of surgery, internal medicine, pathology, and neurology. I sat down to field their questions.

All of them presented fair and reasonable questions. Since I was extremely nervous, though, all the questions seemed difficult at the time. The final question came from Dr. Arthur Curtis, the internist who had suggested I take a leave of absence to go home after Bijin died.

"What would you do when a patient suddenly develops angina pectoris?"

"Give him a shot of a quarter grain of morphine."

Dr. Hodges smiled again. "That's all. Good luck to you in China."

He knew of my appointment at PUMC, though it had been contingent upon my graduation. Since his comment indicated that I had passed, I thanked the professors and left the room elated. I had earned my M.D.

Though I was very happy about this development, the following weekend became difficult. My next move was to return to China, and Cecile and I had to face our upcoming separation. We were ready to get married, at least psychologically, but knew that we would have to wait until I could be financially independent. Reluctantly, we agreed that one of two courses would be best. I would work at PUMC for a year and, after that, either she would join me in China or I would return to the United States to marry her and then we would go to Beijing together.

I informed my parents of these possibilities, but did not know what to expect. Being an Imperial Scholar, my father was very much of the old school of Chinese culture, yet he kept up with the times intellectually. My mother hardly ever traveled any distance from home because she got motion sickness in vehicles. Despite her limited view of the world geographically, she was broad-minded enough to say that she did not mind Cecile's national or racial origin as long as she was a good choice. My father surprised me by saying that a girl with parentage from two hemispheres might add much to our family tree. With these reassurances through the mail, I finally set sail once again for China on May 5, 1939.

This news was quite a contrast to the experience of Cecile's parents. Her father, Tiam H. Franking, had been a student from China attending the University of Michigan Law School. However, after he married Mae Watkins, an American of English and Scottish descent, his wealthy father withdrew all financial support. Tiam finished his education at the University of Detroit, which later became Wayne State University, while supporting himself.

Cecile's eldest brother, Nel, was born in Michigan, but Tiam took his family to China in 1912 and later became Dean of the Law School at Dongwu University in Suzhou. He served in that capacity for about four years and was eventually reconciled with his parents. Alason and Cecile were born in China and she was thirteen months old when Tiam was appointed to the Chinese Consulate in San Francisco. The family moved to the U.S., but unfortunately the young diplomat died in the worldwide flu epidemic in March of 1919.

Mae returned with the children to Ann Arbor, where news of their marriage had originally been received very badly. In 1924, Mae died of pulmonary tuberculosis, leaving her parents to raise the children. Contact with Tiam's family in China had gradually been lost.

❖

By this time, the Pacific crossing had become quite familiar to me. Since I had originally entered the country through Seattle, the

U.S. Immigration Service required that I travel through that city whenever I left or returned. So, once more, I took a train to Seattle, a ferry to Vancouver, and boarded a ship of the Empress line, this time the Empress of Asia. We made stops in Yokohama, Shanghai, and Hong Kong. I met a number of Asian students on shipboard, including Koreans, Japanese, Filipinos, and Chinese. We all had one quality in common, that we were returning to our home countries to work. Even the Japanese travelers were friendly, despite the war.

When we arrived in Yokohama, I wanted to get off and stretch my legs, though I was somewhat fearful of doing so. However, the Japanese immigration officer politely informed us that Chinese nationals should remain on board ship. So we played shuffleboard, deck tennis, cards, or checkers while the other passengers went ashore. At dinner, we discussed the situation in China, and how it might affect our individual futures.

We steamed out of Yokohama for Shanghai. In Michigan, I had obtained the addresses of fraternity brothers now living in Shanghai. Once there, I was able to locate one who contacted a few more. They gave me a quick trip through the city and took me to a fine restaurant for dinner. By the time I returned to the Empress of Asia, I was pleasantly exhausted and went right to bed. When I awoke the next morning, the ship was already underway southward. I joined everyone else out on deck to watch Shanghai disappear slowly in the distance. All the way to Hong Kong, we could see the China coast and, occasionally, portions of the Japanese Navy. We expected no difficulties because Canada was not at war with Japan. Still, knowing the unpredictability of war, we were uneasy.

Approximately twenty-four hours after leaving Shanghai, we arrived safely in Hong Kong. I was met by friends, mostly schoolmates from Michigan. After the greetings, I went home with the Poons.

The Poons had a large house in the Kowloon Tong area of the colony, occupied by the well-to-do. I had scheduled my arrival here in the south for late May so that I could visit my family in Toisan before returning to PUMC on July 1, 1939. However, between the time I made my plans and the time of my arrival, the Japanese had blockaded ports north of Shanghai and cut off Guangzhou as well.

Guangzhou lay only ninety miles north of Hong Kong, but the radio announced that no one was presently allowed through the Japanese lines separating the two cities. The Poons were very kind and invited me to stay as long as I wished.

Unfortunately, the war picture did not improve. I figured that getting to the other side of the Japanese lines was the major problem, and that if I could get beyond them to Toisan, I could probably make my way north to Beijing. While I waited for an opportunity, my father wrote and suggested that if I could not reach PUMC, I should return to the U.S. for further training. Two weeks after that, I received a letter from Dr. Houghton, the Director of PUMC.

Dr. Houghton explained that with the Japanese blockade on north China, I could not reach Beijing. Therefore, he had arranged for me to go to West China Associated University in the city of Chengdu. This lay in the west, still out of the reach of the Japanese advance. Dr. Houghton included a letter of recommendation that I could use when I arrived.

I was disappointed, but under the circumstances I realized the administration of PUMC had been quite helpful. Soon afterward, I said goodbye to my friends and left Hong Kong by boat for Haiphong. I hoped to enter China through the city of Kunming, in the southwest of the country, via Hanoi in French Indochina.

In mid-June, the tropical weather was hot and steamy, with much rainfall. From Haiphong, the train ran on a single-gauge track and the ride was very rocky. On board, the French colonists were very arrogant and inhospitable.

Since I had received no information that one had to order meals in advance, no lunch was waiting for me at the appropriate station. The train had no dining car, and I avoided the vendors in the station because of the possibility of disease. I ate bananas the entire trip.

The long journey to Kunming was unpleasant, with only one notable point. I happened to see a black French family who had a white French governess for the children. The man seemed to be some sort of government official. Since I did not speak French or Vietnamese, I spent the entire trip of several days in virtual solitude. When I finally reached Kunming, I was more glad than ever to be back in

China; at least I could communicate with people around me.

Kunming, being the "back door" to China, had become crowded and chaotic. Many other people like myself, desiring to get around Japanese lines, had also come to Kunming. The city was full of strangers, some desperate, all trying to protect their own interests without regard to anyone else.

I walked several miles from the railroad station, carrying my luggage, looking for a hotel or an inn. Around nightfall, I got a room in a partly-finished hotel. It was so poorly constructed that I could hear everything going on in the adjacent rooms. Nevertheless, I was relieved to have it.

By now, I was very hungry and sick of bananas. The hotel restaurant was crowded and disorderly and everyone had to yell and shove to order any food. Eventually, I got a bowl of hot noodle soup and settled down for the night. Despite all the noise, I slept soundly from sheer fatigue.

The following morning, I located the office of China Travel on Jinbi Road, one of the main thoroughfares in Kunming. I explained that I wanted to get to Chengdu by any means possible, and why. The clerks politely informed me that because it was wartime, government and military personnel had priority, and even they had a long backlog. The estimated time for an ordinary Chinese to reach Chengdu was two months.

At that moment, I wished that I had taken my father's suggestion of returning to the U.S. from Hong Kong.

By now, I was physically worn out and psychologically beaten down. I had no hope of reaching Chengdu in time to start my position, and was alone in a chaotic city during wartime. Then, the next morning, I woke up with nausea, vomiting, and diarrhea.

I got up, took some aspirin I had with me, and lay down again. While resting, I suddenly realized something. During my six years in Ann Arbor, I had met many Chinese students in various fields, many of whom were of course fraternity brothers. Most of them had planned to return to China; quite possibly, at least one or two people I knew were also caught in Kunming, waiting in this bottleneck as I was.

Chapter Seventeen

At midday, I felt better and decided to walk down Jinbi Road.

I walked slowly and stopped occasionally at corners, looking in all directions for a familiar face. In no more than an hour, I saw an officer in a Chinese Air Force uniform walking toward me. I crossed the street toward him quickly.

"Bill! What are you doing here?" He asked in surprise.

His name was K.C. Wang. He had studied aeronautics at Michigan before coming back here and joining the Air Force. He could not help me right away because he was on duty, but he gave me the names and addresses of more mutual friends who were now in Kunming.

I located the first one, Richard Woo. He welcomed me and invited me to stay in his apartment. I was relieved, but I also told him I was still having stomach trouble. Richard called a Dr. Kiang for me.

Dr. Kiang had been trained in Canada and had practiced in Hong Kong until the threat of war had caused him to move to Kunming. He examined me and found no serious problem. My intestinal flora had simply not acclimated to the new environment. Dr. Kiang gave me two prescriptions. In the course of our conversation, he mentioned his sister Victoria, who was studying nursing in Ann Arbor. I knew her, and on that basis we became friends. He visited several more times, and as a fellow physician and friend, I was not charged. I appreciated this, especially in my current circumstances.

Richard Woo became very helpful. He lived in Kunming, where he ran his father's branch office and processing plant for monosodium glutamate. "In about ten days, I am planning to go to Hong Kong for more raw materials. If you want, we can go together."

I was thrilled. Once this plan was set, I was able to enjoy Kunming a little. I spent one day visiting Richard's plant, which was in full operation and very impressive. The rest of the time, I walked around the streets of Kunming looking up other old friends.

One of them was Florence Wong, a medical graduate from Michigan who had been five years ahead of me. She had met a student from Shandong and they had been married for several years. However, she did not seem happy in this environment. She was a Chinese American, born in the U.S., but like so many in that period, she wanted to contribute what she could to a struggling China. I asked about her sister, Jennie, whom I knew. She had later married a chemist and was living in Chicago. Then I asked Florence if she would not be happier back in the U.S.

Florence shook her head. "I've learned to deal with the hardships here. I also feel that I'm contributing something, however small. They need more doctors here. Besides, I would not leave my husband."

I respected her devotion.

The next day, I was walking down the street when an air raid alarm sounded. People began running everywhere. I could do nothing but follow the crowd. With them, I ran to the outskirts of the city and hid in a cemetery. When everyone else returned, I followed them back.

The Japanese bombing had damaged the airport, according to the morning paper the following day, but no planes were destroyed and no one was killed. I had to run from these raids twice more while I was in Kunming, but the populace seemed to accept them as a matter of routine. I remained careful, but ceased to be afraid.

Richard explained that on the way to Hong Kong, he would have to spend a week or ten days in Hanoi on business. I told him that I was in no hurry anymore and would welcome a chance to relax in Hanoi, away from the crowd and confusion in Kunming. Yet when we actually boarded the train, I felt depressed. My trip to China had been a complete failure. I had not even been able to see my family.

At least returning to Hong Kong with Richard made the trip easier. He had taken this route many times and got us good accommodations on the train. We relaxed, talked, and watched the luxuriant tropical vegetation pass. At one point, the rain came down in sheets, leaving the jungle even more steamy than before. The railroad wound back through all the hills and mountains to Hanoi, where we arrived after the greater part of the day.

Richard knew the city, and we each took a pedicab right to a hotel. It was fairly modern, but open in the style of the tropics. The room provided mosquito bars for sleeping at night. That first afternoon, we got cleaned up and then rested, as the entire city did, in its tropical siesta.

I thought this a beautiful custom. The city closed from two to four P.M., then remained open for business until eight or even later. Late in the afternoon, Richard and I went to eat in Hanoi's Chinatown.

The Chinatown was large, and mostly Cantonese. Within this sector, people acted as though they were in Guangzhou (Canton) or Hong Kong. After a good dinner, we split up. Richard had to make some business contacts for the distribution of his product, so I decided to take a leisurely walk through town as I returned to the hotel.

On my way, I happened across a large lake in the middle of the city. Many people were sitting on or near benches by its shore, resting or reading by dim light or squatting together in conversation. Cool breezes from across the lake soothed everyone at that hour of the tropical evening. I returned to the hotel at about ten; Richard was still out doing business when I went to bed.

The next morning we had an American-style breakfast at the hotel — ham and eggs with toast. It was delicious, and for the first time this trip, I felt homesick for America, just from ham and eggs.

After that, we walked downtown to a department store to browse. Richard wanted to buy perfume for his wife. I wanted to find some for Cecile. The store had many varieties of fragrances, all reasonably priced compared to prices in the U.S. We bought several bottles, making our selections with the help of an attractive young local woman in the store. Richard bought some other items, but I had to watch my money.

We toured the downtown area and were both surprised to see an American movie dubbed in Vietnamese. It was a western, and featured Gary Cooper speaking that language. Since we did not understand the dubbing, and felt silly reading English subtitles, we left.

That evening, Richard had more business appointments. After dinner, I walked back to the lake alone and tried to strike up conversations with some of the local people. They could tell by my clothes that I was from elsewhere, but they were friendly. I avoided a few beggars, but I found a Vietnamese student who spoke some English.

This student explained that the French were exploiting his country. He told me that the French would not allow the Vietnamese to hold positions in the local government, no matter how educated or capable they were. Very bitter, he hoped that the French would soon be driven out. I agreed with him, and in fact he aroused my feelings against the French here considerably. In later years, the kind of psychological suffering and abuse that the French inflicted upon the younger, educated generation of Vietnamese eventually brought on the war in which the Vietnamese finally defeated the French colonials at Dienbienphu. It was also the French, as representatives of the white man in Asia, who mistreated them so badly that they would fight anyone white, regardless of nationality.

During the successive days Richard and I spent in Hanoi, I became fond of the lake area. I spent much of my time underneath the shady trees watching the children playing along the shore and the old men smoking and chatting or even playing chess or checkers. Since most of them did not speak any English, I usually just watched them quietly. Some responded graciously with gestures and an attempt to communicate; others simply looked up and then returned to their activities.

Occasionally, I would see a couple of young women in their distinctive local styles. They wore long gowns of white or colored silk or cotton, slit high up each side. However, they also wore loose, long trousers underneath the gowns. Their dresses were very similar to the Chinese qibau, except that Chinese women didn't wear trousers beneath their dresses. No matter how attractive a Vietnamese woman was, however, her teeth were always stained black. I could never get used to the sight. The stain came from the juice of the betel nut, which they chewed to protect their teeth and for the slight "high" it gave them.

I customarily went to Chinatown for lunch when Richard was on business at that hour. Most of the small restaurants were run by families who were either Cantonese, Hakka, or Fujianese. I was usually able to strike up conversations with them.

All of them had tales of woe. Some had left China long ago because of the civil wars, at first among the warlords and later between the Guomindang and the Communists. New arrivals were fleeing the Japanese. Many had lost their earnings, houses, and land when they fled. In addition to those here, many others had gone to Saigon, Indonesia, Thailand, Malaysia, the Philippines, and Burma.

Though displaced, their lives were bearable. They looked toward the future, not the past, with lives of hard work. Their devotion to the care of their families, and their self-reliance, in fact supported the Bank of China in Hanoi, which at that time was the largest bank in French Indochina.

For the first time, I began to realize that the Chinese were everywhere in Southeast Asia. A smaller percentage were just adventurous merchants. They had left China for business reasons and had succeeded throughout the area.

Richard concluded his business in Hanoi after a few days. We packed up and boarded the train for Haiphong. The weather, of course, remained hot, humid, and rainy, but the train did have electric fans to provide a little ventilation.

I found Haiphong rather small and dull after Hanoi, but it was a busy seaport. We got off the train on a Sunday morning and found no one to get our luggage. Since we were pressed for time, we entered the luggage area ourselves and simply took it out in a cart to our ship. We were lucky enough to get passage out on the same day. If we had wished, we could have taken all the luggage from the train with us.

Once we had settled into our staterooms on board ship, we ordered some cold drinks for relief from the heat. Then we went out on deck to bid goodbye to Haiphong. Having felt the oppressive atmosphere under the French colonials, I had no regrets about leaving the place.

Time passed quickly on the way back to Hong Kong. We arrived very early in the morning. Since we had not known ahead of time when we would arrive in Hong Kong, no one met us at the pier, though Richard's wife of several years was waiting for him in Hong Kong. I thanked him profusely for his hospitality, especially when I had been ill in Kunming, and for accompanying me back to Hong Kong. After I wished him well in his business enterprises, we parted.

When I arrived again at the Poon residence, only the servants were awake. I had written to the Poons about my ill-fated trip, so they were expecting me. The servants gave me a nice breakfast while we waited for the family to awaken.

The Poons received me courteously, but not with the same enthusiasm as when I had first arrived from the U.S. I didn't understand this change of attitude, and was uneasy remaining in their house. However, my hostess, Ching, suddenly developed abdominal symptoms, including severe pains. After careful thought, I concluded that she had a peptic ulcer. Subsequent examination proved my diagnosis correct, and the Poons asked me to stay with them until she improved. I agreed.

In the meantime, I wrote to my family and explained that I had simply come back to China at the wrong time. I could not reach them, even though they were only a short distance away. By the time I was ready to leave, Ching's condition had improved, though I told her to remain on the regime of antacids and restricted diet. At the time, the antacids were in powder form and had to be wrapped in small packages.

I learned later that the Poons thought I had returned from China because I had become spoiled in the U.S. and could no longer take the physical hardships like those in wartime China. That was the reason for their cool reception when I first arrived from Indochina. However, all worked out well. By the time I was ready to leave Hong Kong again, Ching's illness was under control and she was very appreciative.

Before I left, one night I had a nightmare and kicked the wall in my sleep, causing me to walk with a limp. This allowed Ching to take care of me, giving me daily soaks. The others teased me for being a patient, and the mood in the house returned to normal.

I met some other Americans in Hong Kong who had worked at PUMC. They gave me some career advice, suggesting that I write to Dr. Max Zuninger, who had previously taught surgery at PUMC. I wrote to him out of desperation.

Finally, I left Hong Kong again for the U.S. in mid-September of 1939. The Poons and other friends came to the dock to see me off. Once more, I boarded the Empress of Canada and stayed in one of the special third-class cabins. As before, most of my fellow passengers in that class were Chinese, and after dinner we would sit together and discuss the wartime situation and China's future. We criticized the Guomindang for not resisting the Japanese more effectively, but on the other hand, none of us was going back to help, either.

Everyone on board followed the progress of the war closely. So far, the Nationalist Chinese army had done little but fight rear-guard actions and retreat. One exception had been the vigorous defense of Nanjing, which had still resulted in a Japanese victory. Some passengers brought up the suggestion that the Japanese might blow us up in mid-Pacific, but we did not actually worry about it since Japan still was not at war with Canada.

The periodic safety drills became more exciting under these wartime conditions, but fortunately they were not necessary. We arrived safely in Shanghai. A short time later, we steamed away again.

As I watched the China coast disappear in the distance, I wondered if the Japanese navy would allow us to reach the high seas without any trouble. Enemy ships patrolled everywhere, but we passed unmolested. Then, as we left Asia behind, sadness overcame me. I had spent the greater part of my life in getting an education, and now that I was ready to contribute to China's health problems, I was leaving China once again instead. Existing conditions there were bad, and the future very unpredictable.

On the other hand, perhaps China would simply swallow up these conquerors, as it had other conquerors over the centuries. In 1939, America's attention remained focused on Europe. Help from the U.S. seemed unlikely.

We arrived in Yokohama about four days after leaving Shanghai. Those of us of Chinese origin were again told not to go ashore. The Japanese officers still seemed polite, but they referred to a "little misunderstanding between our two countries," in explaining the situation.

For the first time, all the Chinese on board began to get acquainted, totalling about fifty Chinese passengers and perhaps a hundred Chinese service staff members and sailors. Most were Cantonese, so I could communicate with them comfortably. As on my earlier trips, many of the workers looked up to some of us as the intelligentsia of the new generation of Chinese, and were reserved toward us at first. However, once they found that we bore no prejudice on the basis of class, they became more friendly. They showed us around their quarters, the engine room, and other areas usually off limits to passengers.

That evening, we were treated to a special Chinese banquet prepared by the ship's Chinese crew. It was a sort of patriotic celebration. Not all of the Chinese passengers were professionals, and more of us became acquainted at dinner. Most of the passengers ran small businesses, such as restaurants, grocery stores, and laundries. A few were government officials. The mood was pleasant, and the dinner was excellent.

One day shortly after lunch, I was napping on deck when the sound of cheering woke me up. I joined a small gathering on deck that was reading a news bulletin. It reported that the Nationalist Chinese army had defeated the Japanese soundly at Taierzhuang. Not only Chinese passengers, but everyone else, joined the celebration. It was only one battle, but it was the first actual victory by the Chinese we had heard about.

As before, I disembarked at Vancouver. The rest of the return trip remained the same; I took the ferry to Seattle and the train to Philadelphia. After visiting the Helms in Philadelphia, I was reunited with Cecile in Washington. Then I received a letter from Dr. Max Zuninger in response to my query from Hong Kong. He had obtained an internship for me at Bethesda Hospital in Cincinnati.

Chapter Eighteen

The week before I left for Cincinnati, the administrator of Bethesda Hospital wrote to me. He explained that the hospital had a resident who was of Japanese descent. The administrator expressed hope that he and I would have no friction because Japan and China were at war. I wrote back, saying that I had no personal feelings against Japanese people, and that medicine should have no battle lines drawn anywhere.

When I reported to duty, I received a warm welcome from the house staff, including Dr. Tashiro, a Japanese American who had more dislike for the Japanese than I did. We got along well. Professionally, he acted as a big brother to me, showing me many practical tricks of the trade regarding intravenous injections, emergency room care of accident cases, and suturing small lacerations. He also gave me information regarding the idiosyncrasies of certain surgeons we would assist during operations.

The chief surgical resident was Tom Edwards, a tall and robust fellow. Friendly and talkative, he always seemed more like a politician to me than a physician. He pursued the ear, nose, and throat specialty and later got a residency in that area at the University of Cincinnati.

The chief medical resident was Jack Sharp, a friendly and genuinely warm friend. On one occasion, he invited me out to a burlesque show. The next morning in the hospital, he jokingly told all the nurses where I had been the night before. I just laughed and told them that he had taken me to a better show than I expected.

All the interns and residents looked forward to at least two years of training before going out to practice. Gordon Strand pursued general surgery and during this time, he developed appendicitis and had his appendectomy done under local anesthetic, just to see how it felt. James Brown, who was going into obstetrics and gynecology, fre-

133

quently played tennis or ping pong with me on our days off. Eleanor Waskow prepared for internal medicine, and had a good rapport with everyone.

A tall, handsome fellow named Don Barker did research on white rabbits, pertaining to plastic surgery. One day he asked me if I would mind having a piece of my darker skin grafted onto his arm. Two days after the transplantation, his arm developed pain, swelling, and a temperature reaction. His body rejected my skin, but we were thereafter known as "brothers under the skin" anyway.

Pat Fulton, my roommate in the interns' quarters, liked women and was known as a "cocksman." He took life as he found it and, where his duties were concerned, he did the minimum. At least two or three times a week, on the spur of the moment, he would ask me to cover for him because he had to go out for a while. I always obliged, since I was staying in most of the time, anyway. His personal activities wore him out, though; on one occasion, when the phone awakened him, he grabbed his gooseneck lamp and spoke into it repeatedly, too sleepy to understand what he was doing.

On weekends, we all played bridge and poker. We had to work as a team, and in order to get along, we had to develop a group identity. Habits and patterns formed, and as a result, I learned these card games as consistently as I learned my professional endeavors. When an emergency occurred, we would work as a team to take care of it as efficiently and expeditiously as possible. Then we would return to our games.

The mood became close and jovial. One Sunday afternoon, I was off and left alone while the others went to assist on an appendectomy. I decided to take a shower and began singing a Chinese song that I still remembered. As soon as I turned off the water, I received applause and loud laughter from my companions, who had returned.

The most memorable experience I had in this period was not lighthearted, however. I was on rotation in the maternity hospital while Ernie Colglazier remained busy most of the night. I was on second call, but I was not needed in the evening, so I went to bed. He woke me abruptly at about 2:00 A.M.

"I need help, and quickly," he said.

On the obstetrics service, we slept in our scrub suits, so I was ready. I hurried out with him and he explained the situation. A pregnant woman had died of a heart attack, but the unborn fetus was still alive. He wanted to do a Caesarean section to save the baby.

As we were preparing to begin, a woman's voice behind us said firmly and menacingly, "Don't you dare."

It was the mother of the dead pregnant woman. Without permission, we could only stand by helplessly as the fetus died. I later learned that the family was Christian Scientist.

At the time, I knew nothing about Christian Science, but was appalled at the event. Since then, I have learned something of the principles of Christian Science. However, this particular experience has remained with me.

Another unexpected episode occurred when I was still in the OB service. One day, just before lunch, a car horn began honking loudly and incessantly at the emergency entrance of the maternity hospital. Our staff hurried down immediately. It was a taxi, and the driver was standing by nervously.

"A lady's having a baby in my cab! Please —"

The first nurse to get there made way for me. Others brought sheets, blankets, and instruments. Nurses and other auxiliary staff stood in a circle around the car while two nurses assisted me with the woman in the back seat. The baby's head was already halfway out and the mother was moaning in pain.

One nurse held the mother's head and told her to breathe deeply as I guided the rest of the head out of the birth canal. The slippery body and limbs followed. I placed the baby on the sheet and blanket already laid on the floor of the back seat.

A nurse gave me hernia tape to tie off the umbilical cord in two places. I did, and severed the cord between the two knots. While waiting for the placenta to separate, I handed the baby to one of the nurses. Gentle Creole massage on the mother's abdomen helped induce the placenta to detach itself, and I removed it.

I covered her properly and accompanied her up to the delivery room. Later, when she was resting satisfactorily in a postpartum room, she asked if her baby was a boy or a girl. Because of the unusual situation during delivery, I hadn't noticed the sex of the baby. When someone found out, and we told her, she was ecstatic. It was a boy, and she had two girls already.

We gave the mother and child antibiotics for several days because the birth had occurred in non-sterile conditions, but no complications arose. They went home healthy within a week. It was the most exciting delivery I was involved in, especially because I did it as an intern alone, without a staff doctor to rely on. It gave me a great deal of confidence.

Most of the staff members at Bethesda were very good physicians and surgeons, but a few were characters. Pop Schuman, a moderately obese man in his late fifties, knew his way around the abdomen and his experience made his surgical work seem easier than that of other surgeons. He was an informal man, calling me "Willie" and always telling Confucius jokes. I didn't understand half of them. However, he was kind and pleasant and I felt at ease around him.

I gained some respect for my medical opinions with a patient assigned to me for "workup." He complained of pain in the upper right quadrant of his abdomen. The staff man did the preliminary studies, including a gastro-intestinal series and gall bladder visualization. Nothing was found to explain the patient's pain. I examined this patient daily and was certain that I felt a mass near his right kidney. The staff man did not agree, and requested a consultation with a professor of urology from a nearby medical school. The professor came and said the patient had no kidney problems, so they decided to explore for gall bladder disease. In doing so, they found a tumor, a hypernephroma of the right kidney. I felt pretty cocky after that, but I kept it to myself.

On another occasion, a Chinese patient was admitted to the hospital with abdominal pain and distension. He was assigned to me because he spoke very little English and I could communicate with him in Chinese. The usual studies were done and his gastro-intestinal series demonstrated a questionable mass in his small intestine near the ligament of Treitz.

I assisted Dr. Dan Early in surgery. He was highly thought of by the house staff. During surgery, we had an older visiting doctor whom

I didn't know. When we visualized the tumor the stranger said, "Just do an externalization and close him up. It's a malignancy and you can't do much about it." Then he left.

When he was gone, I pleaded with Dr. Early. I said that the mass seemed well circumscribed and asked that he resect it and do an anastomosis if at all possible, malignant or not. Culturally, colostomy and exterialization of bowels was simply not acceptable to Chinese at that time. Dr. Early acquiesced. He dissected out the lesion, resected it, and did an end-to-end anastomosis. That allowed the patient to continue normal bowel activity.

Later, to our gratification, the mass turned out to be a benign granuloma, not a malignancy. The patient was cured. Dr. Early thanked me for convincing him not to listen to the visitor.

The other man turned out to be a professor who was observing Dr.Early's technique and judgment. This was part of qualifying process for the American Board of Surgery. Dr. Early's decision made his judgment look very good.

In July of 1941, I was appointed co-resident with George Brown. Both of us were interested in surgery, but the hospital only appointed one resident in medicine and one in surgery. George kindly agreed to alternate with me, six months in medicine and six in surgery. He was a good man to work with. In August, he invited Cecile and me to spend a week with him and his wife at his parent's summer home in Wisconsin. His parents were gracious. His father was an avid fisherman, and we learned to cast from him.

Don Barker, my "brother under the skin," put his car up for sale at this time. It was practically new, with only six thousand miles on it, painted light blue on a streamlined body. His wife was about to have their first child, and he needed money desperately. He offered to sell it to the first person who came up with five hundred dollars. None of us had that much on hand.

Somewhat hesitantly, I called Christina Helm up for a loan. She agreed that the car was a good buy and loaned me the money. I promised to pay it back in monthly installments of fifty dollars.

All my colleagues were envious. I learned how to drive, and began to enjoy my new car. The first time I drove alone, I took out half the flower garden by the exit from Bethesda Hospital. I improved, however, and in particular drove to movies and to play tennis with some of the nurses.

One evening, I was driving a student nurse back to the hospital quickly, since she was almost late. I was too close to the car on my left and knocked off its door handles. Both cars stopped, and the nurse hurried on foot to the hospital, which was now nearby.

I got out to deal with the middle-aged couple in the other car. They were angry, but mellowed when I told them I was an intern and had not been driving long.

"Where did you come from, young man?" the woman asked.

"I came from China originally, but I've been here for some time. I went to medical school at the University of Michigan."

Other cars began to honk, since ours were blocking traffic.

"My brother is a missionary in China," said the woman. "He likes the people there very much." She turned to her husband, who had been standing quietly. "Isn't he a nice young man? Just let him go back to the hospital and we'll have the insurance company take care of our doors."

The man made a gesture of despair. "Let's go."

His wife shook hands with me. "Be careful and good luck."

They left. I was grateful that they were compassionate people. I drove on to the hospital very carefully.

The year passed quickly. As a resident, I had more responsibilities both in caring for patients and in supervising the new interns. Dr. Tashiro had moved on to the University of Cincinnati for further training. Since surgical training required some time spent in pathology, I took three months with Dr. Edward A. Gall, a hard taskmaster and an excellent teacher. He cleaned out some of the dead wood in the hospital and was so inspiring that by the following spring, I had obtained a residency in pathology at the University of Cincinnati.

I never took it.

The reason began much earlier, only about halfway through that year of residency. December 6, 1941, fell on a Saturday and I was on call for the surgical service. We had several car accidents and two emergency appendectomies. I assisted in all those procedures throughout the night. By the time I got to bed, it was about six o'clock Sunday morning. I went to sleep in my scrub suit and slept until about noon. When I rose, I turned on the radio and showered. Shortly thereafter, a serious announcement came over the radio. Pearl Harbor had been destroyed in a sneak attack by Japanese planes.

I got dressed in a hurry and rushed to the hospital floors. There, I asked the nurses if it was true, and they said everyone had heard the same. In fact, everyone was walking around in a mixture of anger and disbelief. Hospital business continued, but no one had the same devotion as usual. Everyone was cursing the Japanese, and I was afraid to go out for fear that I would be mistaken for a Japanese. Later, I obtained a lapel pin in the form of a Chinese flag from the Chinese embassy as a means of identification.

Dr. Tashiro heard about this and asked if I could get a Chinese emblem for him too. I had no personal objection, but was uncomfortable with the deception involved. Anyway, it turned out to be impossible for me to get another.

In the following months, various interns and residents around town were drafted one by one. Although I was not an American citizen, I was subject to the draft, which would make me an enlisted man. It was a precarious, unpredictable situation.

One day a medical recruiting team came to the hospital asking doctors to sign up. I asked their commanding officer for advice. He suggested that I enter the armed services as an enlisted man. After serving for three months, I could apply for citizenship and then, being a doctor, I would be able to apply for a commission as an officer. Although he was right about the rules he quoted, I did not feel I could trust the proper execution of those rules. Once I was enlisted, I might get lost in the paperwork and remain an enlisted man for the duration. I did not take his advice.

The work at the hospital grew heavier as more physicians left. I continued working, and waiting to see what would happen. Time passed uncomfortably for all of us.

One evening early in the summer of 1942, Pat Fulton, my former roommate, came to say goodbye. He had been working in another hospital, but was now preparing to join the Navy. I was touched at his coming to visit. At the end of the year, I learned that he had been killed at Guadalcanal.

In June of 1942, I read a news item in the Journal of the American Medical Association: "Nationals of cobelligerent countries who have had similar training as Americans in medical education may apply for a commission in the United States Army." As a graduate of the University of Michigan Medical School, I applied right away.

About two weeks later, an answer came from Washington. If I could prove that I was Chinese, they would give me a commission in the U.S. Army Medical Corps. I searched for my old Chinese passport and sent it in with a short cover letter. Since my residency in pathology at the University of Cincinnati was about to start on July 1, I informed the university that I was going into the army. Giving up the job was something of a risk, since I had not actually received my commission, but the alternative was reporting for work knowing that the commission was probably coming.

Two weeks later, a telegram arrived from Washington addressed to "First Lt. William Q. Wu." The instruction read, "Report to Fort Lewis, Washington, by September 2, 1942."

Chapter Nineteen

Notification of my commission excited me, as it was extremely good news. If necessary, I would have gone into the U.S. Army willingly even as a private, but that would have wasted my ability and training in medicine. Now I felt I could truly contribute to the war effort, and at age thirty, I was mature enough to handle the vicissitudes of life — and war.

For many years, Japan had humiliated China and caused untold suffering among its people. Now, Japan had audaciously attacked my adopted country, which had offered me so many tremendous opportunities in life. I was elated at receiving my commission and promptly called both the Helms and Cecile to tell them about it.

The army had left me sufficient time to visit the Helms in Philadelphia and Cecile, too, in Washington, D.C. The senior Helms, whom I had recently been addressing as "Mom and Pop Helm," were getting older and I might not see them again. Christina and Cecile were young, of course, but then the war made my own return uncertain. It was another time of difficult farewells.

I spent two days in Philadelphia this time. While there, I visited several clansmen, including Cousin Feng Chiu. He was quite pleased to see me again.

"I knew you would grow up to be like your father," he said. He gave me ten dollars for luck, and as a parting gift. I never saw him again.

The evening before I left, the Helms had a fine farewell dinner for me.

"We know you'll be a good soldier," said Pop Helm. "We'll be waiting for you to come back, as always."

I struggled to hold back tears, for I feared that I would not see them again.

Christina was crying quietly. "William has gone through so

141

many hardships. He'll serve Uncle Sam with honor. I'm sure he will do well." She looked at me as she spoke.

Mom and Pop Helm shook hands with me and then hugged me.

Christina kissed me on both cheeks and then hugged me, too.

"I know you're a lieutenant now, and able to take care of yourself," she said. "I'll take you to the train station tomorrow, anyway."

I wore my officer's uniform for the first time on the way to the Baltimore and Ohio Railway Station. Christina and I didn't say much to each other on the trolley. After I bought my ticket to Washington in the station, I turned to say goodbye.

"I hope you'll have fun with Cecile," said Christina. "I am not ashamed to say that I am envious of her." She appeared pensive for a moment, then gave me another hug and a kiss on the cheek. Then she gripped my arms and held me at arm's length. "I am proud of you. Take care of yourself. I'll be here to greet you when you come back."

I fumbled for words, then merely said, "Thank you. I'll write." Then I climbed up the steps into the train.

Cecile and Fred and Florence Mattingley met me in Washington.
They were surprised to see me in uniform, and in fact I still felt a little strange in it. We greeted each other and returned to Cecile's. Gram was waiting for us at the top of the stairs, as before.

"Welcome back, Bill," said Gram. She shook my hand. "How distinguished you look."

When the initial greetings were over, we all sat down. I was stiff and uncomfortable in my uniform, sitting with my military cap in my lap. Cecile took it from me and set it aside. Gram, always observant, spoke up.

"Bill, why don t you take off your jacket and be comfortable?"

"Thank you. I'd be happy to." I took off my jacket and relaxed.

Everyone had a cocktail except Gram and me. We had tea. That evening, Gram prepared a good dinner for us all. The

Mattingleys left shortly after dinner.

Gram sat with Cecile and me until about nine P.M., speculating on what army life would be like and kidding Cecile about some of her antics as a child. I felt that Gram seemed to like me a little more each time I visited. Despite the large generation gap between us, she was always knowledgeable and up to date.

Cecile had to work, but she managed to get two days off, and of course we had evenings together. We visited the usual tourist spots in the city as before. This time, the only important part of the experience was holding her hand in mine.

At that time, I had not received any military instructions except to report to Fort Lewis at the proper time. I was surprised when, as Cecile and I walked around the city, enlisted men in uniform saluted me. I actually learned how to salute by imitating them as I returned their salutes. However, I was afraid of chancing across other military courtesies with which I was not familiar.

Cecile now worked as coordinator of the China Unit of the Army Map Service. Her brother Nelson remained a toolmaker for the Navy, and was gratified that his work was now more important than ever. Alason also worked as a civilian in the government. Al and Phyllis came over for dinner twice, specifically to see me before I left for the army.

On my last evening there, Gram spoke to me alone on one occasion. "I am pleased to see you both here," she said. "I wish you could stay longer, Bill. Twiddle will be with me, of course, but I don't want the poor child tied up waiting for you."

I agreed. Privately, I knew that Cecile had many activities and friends in Washington, and would not be "tied up." Gram was concerned, though, because she and Cecile were close friends as much as they were grandmother and granddaughter.

On the last evening before I had to leave for Fort Lewis, Cecile and I talked a great deal about our relationship up to that point, and about the uncertainty ahead. We were lying on the couch together, kissing and talking, but the atmosphere of war dispelled the feeling of romance. Even so, we felt close, and understood that after the war, we would get married.

The next morning arrived too soon. I had never really unpacked. Gram cooked a breakfast of ham, eggs sunny-side up, and toast. As usual, she and I had tea while Cecile drank coffee. Then the Mattingleys arrived to take Cecile and me to Union Station.

Gram shook hands with me before we left as always, but also patted my hand with her left. "Bill, good luck to you and take care of my Twiddle when you come back. Take good care of yourself." Her tone had a sadness and finality that worried me. However, she maintained her stateliness and dignity, only beginning to weep briefly as we descended the stairs from the apartment.

On the way to the station, Cecile and I sat in the back seat holding hands. The four of us made small talk. Fred did all the work, first driving us and then buying my ticket and checking my luggage. I shook hands with Florence and him, and turned to Cecile.

At this point, there was not much left to say. Cecile gave me a big hug and kissed me while starting to cry. Then it was time to go. I grabbed my hand luggage and, as I ascended the steps, I turned back to Cecile and the Mattingleys, and saluted them.

I had good accommodations on the train, but I felt tired and lonesome. Once more, I was off on a new adventure alone, leaving behind everything and everyone familiar. I thought of my parents and siblings in China and wondered if I would ever see them again.

The scenery across the country remained as beautiful as ever, and the Rockies were stunning, as always. This time, though, I could not keep my attention on the sights. The war atmosphere was not conducive to the finer things in life.

My anxiety increased as the train approached Seattle. When I arrived, though, I was surprised to find that the Commanding Officer had sent a car from Fort Lewis to meet me. I showed the driver my orders. We exchanged salutes and he opened the car door for me.

As we drove to Fort Lewis, about forty miles away, we made small talk. Then, at the Fort, he introduced me to the C.O.

I saluted him properly.

"Glad to have you on board, Lieutenant. The sergeant will take you to the officer's quarters."

At the officer's quarters, I first met Ralph Christensen and Jim McCabe. Ralph, Jim, and I became good friends immediately. It so happened that Ralph was about six feet, one inch tall and Jim was just a little shorter. In a photo of the three of us, I appear to be standing between two telephone poles. We started addressing each other as "Cousin," a habit we never dropped.

Our group was temporarily assigned to an evacuation hospital for our training. My first job was as mess officer. This consisted mainly of inspecting the kitchen and the food.

The sergeant usually offered me a cup of coffee, which I always refused. A dental officer, a lieutenant as I was, advised me not to get too familiar with enlisted men. Later on, I realized that he was too straight-laced and had become unpopular because of it.

Ralph came from Oregon and Jim from Montana, so they were both more familiar with the Northwest than I was. On one occasion, I found myself going to Seattle with them and their two dates, who were nurses. Since I had no date, I was clearly in the way.

After dinner, we returned to the car and they turned their attention to their dates avidly. I told them that I was going to visit someone in town and would return to camp by bus. They protested, but weakly, and I left.

I remembered that Calvin Chang lived in Seattle now. Calvin, a Michigan alumnus, was doing graduate work part-time at the University of Washington and working for the Navy in Puget Sound as a paymaster. I enjoyed a brief visit with him that night and continued to spend time with him for some time on my free weekends.

Meanwhile, our training continued. After two months in Fort Lewis, I received orders to report to Camp White, Oregon, where I was to join the 22nd Field Hospital. It was made up of both Chinese Americans and white Americans. I felt this meant I would eventually be sent to China.

When I arrived at Camp White, the entire unit was out on a hike. The only people left in camp were the Commanding Officer, who had no intention of hiking anywhere, and a sergeant on duty to handle matters such as my arrival. The sergeant helped me move in, and I waited anxiously to meet the officers of the group when they returned.

When the unit came back, I went out into the corridor. The first Chinese American officer to pass me wore a scowl. When I advanced a step to greet him, he muttered, "Hi," and walked on to his room.

I was disappointed by this reception, but the other officers followed him in. They all were more friendly. I introduced myself and we chatted briefly before they went into the quarters to relax.

Most of the Chinese Americans came from the West Coast, especially the San Francisco Bay area. Major Jake Yee was the oldest, at about forty. Lieutenant Eli Eng was a medical administrative officer, while Captain Bob Lee and Lieutenant Chet Fong were dental officers. Lieutenant Fred Jing and the unpleasant fellow I had met first were the others.

The remaining officers were Major Tom Oliver, Captain Nick Saliani, Captain Charlie Marsten, Captain Kirk Swan, and another dental officer named Lieutenant Steer. The Executive Officer, Lieutenant Colonel Bob Johnston, shortly afterward became Commanding Officer of the field hospital.

That evening in the mess hall, I began to get acquainted with everyone, including Captain James D. King, the sour-faced fellow I had met first. I happened to sit down across from him and he remained unsociable at first. However, when I heard his name, I asked if he was the James D. King who had written an article in the Journal of Experimental Surgery.

King lit up like a new man. He told me that he was a graduate of PUMC, and of course I replied that I had received a position there a few years before, though the war had prevented me from getting there. We talked about some of the staff members at PUMC and I learned that he knew my friend Paul Kwan. By this time, we had become friends.

Later, in private, he explained his aloof attitude. He had very little regard for the Chinese Americans he had met, especially

146

in that unit. He complained to me that they knew very little about China or America. In his opinion, they were not intellectually stimulating and cared only about money and women, though all of them were married.

King felt that he had nothing in common with them, and he associated with them no more than necessary, even in the Army. I did not share his opinions, but I respected his accomplishments. In addition to his article, he had been on the faculty at Ohio State University before joining the Army.

I established a good rapport with him, and also with the other officers in the unit. My ability to speak both Cantonese and Mandarin helped me to deal with them; of course, I had Ruby to thank for the Mandarin. My language ability would also be handy if we were sent to China.

Many of the U.S.-born Chinese Americans from the West Coast had attended Chinese schools as children to learn the language and cultural traditions. However, most of them were not well aware of the social, political, or economic changes taking place in China during that time. They were a transitional generation after their immigrant parents.

One of them, dental officer Chet Fong, brought his wife to visit. March Fong had a sharp, commanding presence. Many years later, as March Fong Eu, she became California's secretary of state, the first Asian American to hold that position.

We trained in Camp White for several weeks. During this time, the U.S. government passed a law allowing Chinese immigrants to become naturalized citizens under certain conditions. This new law made me eligible for the first time.

Medford, Oregon, was the nearest town to us, and we went there for leisure. It was a fruit canning center, and of course fresh fruit was available there. In March of 1943, I was granted U.S. citizenship in Medford.

When I took my oath, I was the only one present in uniform. The other new citizens were all older Europeans, many of whom spoke English with a marked accent. I celebrated with fresh fruit.

Becoming a citizen had a transforming effect on me psychologically. I had been living in the U.S. for a long time, but had never been able to apply for citizenship before. My habits and thinking were more American than Chinese, as my friends and family reminded me on my trip back to Toisan. Yet in all that time, I had never really felt that I belonged.

Without some assurance of belonging, the safest course had always been to return to China to work. I still wanted to do this in order to contribute, but I wished to do it as an American, since I felt myself to be one. As a citizen, I now had the option of living in the U.S. after all, if I could find work. I could vote and criticize the government without being an outsider. For the first time, my citizenship had become consistent with the daily facts of my life over the years.

I became closer to the Chinese Americans in my unit, and even preached to Jim King, who was already a citizen. I argued that as Americans, we could only pursue one course, which was to be loyal to Uncle Sam and to contribute our best to the United States. This would indirectly aid China, anyway. I also said that in the caring for the sick, no barriers should exist.

He agreed halfheartedly, and we let it go at that.

We finally received our orders to go overseas. First we were ordered to sail from the West Coast. By the time we left, though, we had been ordered to board a train for Camp Kilmer, New Jersey, instead.

So I took another long trip by rail across the country. We arrived at Camp Kilmer in the evening and struggled to get ourselves and our dufflebags organized, since the camp was under a blackout. The long journey had fatigued us, and we were glad to flop down onto our bunks. We did not know how long we would be there.

We remained in Camp Kilmer for four days. During that time, Cecile was able to visit from Washington. We had time for only one evening together, but it was a memorable one. Her former roommate, Peggy, came along as a "chaperon," but her attitude was so liberal that she was really just a companion.

Since our camp did not allow visitors after early evening hours, I had reserved a room for them at the Hotel Rogers in a small town nearby. I also obtained a pass to spend the evening off the post. Cecile, Peg, and I ate a good steak dinner at the hotel over a pleasant conversation. We talked about schooldays in Ann Arbor and about living under wartime conditions now. Also, we pretended that my going overseas now might actually be enjoyable in some ways.

When we went up to the hotel room, Peg withdrew into the bathroom and allowed Cecile and me some privacy. A few minutes later, she came out again.

"If you want to wash up before bedtime," she said, "you better do it now. I've made myself a bed in the bathtub."

This surprised me, but it was a strong hint, as well.

According to my pass, I was only supposed to spend the evening out of camp, and return before midnight. However, Cecile and I agreed to share the night together. With the dangers of war looming ahead, the pass seemed insignificant.

When morning arrived, I got up and found Peggy already reading in her makeshift bed. I absolutely had to be back in camp by seven A.M., so I hurried to get ready. Cecile and Peggy rode out with me in a taxi.

At the gate to Camp Kilmer, we all became weepy, since this was my real farewell before going to war. Cecile and I embraced tightly and kissed as she fought back tears. I also gave Peg a kiss and a hug, and she tried to smile through her tears.

I showed my pass to the solemn guard at the gate, who could see Cecile and Peg still watching from the taxi. He nodded and winked sternly.

"Thank you, soldier," I said quietly.

Chapter Twenty

The next day, my unit was ordered to board the <u>Mauritania</u>, a British passenger ship. We walked to the ship from the camp, carrying all our belongings for over a mile. Oddly, this turned out to be one of the single most difficult tasks of the entire war.
All of us carried too many unnecessary items at this stage, and we had had a relatively easy time of it so far.

As we walked, a number of enlisted men set down their duffel bags and claimed that they could not go on. The situation became so difficult that even the sergeant, who was usually very tough with them, expressed sympathy. He urged them to take it slow and easy, and herded everyone to the embarkation area.

By the time we got there, all of us were hot, sweaty, hungry, and exhausted. At that point, the Red Cross came to our rescue;Red Cross women brought out coffee and doughnuts, which we needed. After that one-mile march to the New Jersey shore, the rest of the war did not seem so scary.

As an officer, I shared a stateroom on board ship with seven other officers. The bunks were comfortable and we were told that the Prince of Wales had once stayed there. However, when we went to see the enlisted men's quarters, we found a terrible mess.

The ship was transporting many other units besides ours, and many of the units were much larger. The ship had been converted to a troop carrier, but the hold did not have enough bunks for all the men. Many of them just slept on top of their dufflebags on the floor. At night, the heat in the hold was so great that many of them came out on deck to sleep.

Even so, after two or three days, everyone settled into a routine and became acclimated to the environment. For entertainment, we had movies — but not ordinary Hollywood entertainment. Instead, we watched daily installments of the British Army in North Africa, chasing Rommel with tanks. Field Marshall Montgomery was the star, of course.

Our real entertainment turned out to be poker and blackjack, played among the officers in the dining room or in staterooms. It became a daily ritual in our room, but the stakes were high. In addition to those of us bunking there, we always had visitors. At one point, we learned that the air corps pilots had played for such high stakes that their commanding officers had set a ceiling on their bets to avoid serious problems.

Our first surgical case ocurred during an emergency alarm. We had become accustomed to them and had learned exactly where to go when they sounded, regardless of where we happened to be on the huge liner at any given time. During one of these emergency drills, a soldier fell and fractured his left cheekbone just under his eye. One of the surgeons performed the operation and we returned our attention to poker.

We were tossed on the high seas day in and day out, without knowing where we were or where we were headed. Unusually rough seas always caused a certain amount of anxiety, especially because we had no idea of our destination. Since we were sailing alone, without an escort or convoy, some soldiers argued that enemy subs were probably chasing us.

Then, after about three weeks, we docked outside of Rio de Janeiro, Brazil. Rio was a magnificent port with a huge statue of Christ overlooking the harbor. We were not allowed to go ashore, even though we were docked all day. The only exception was one soldier who had developed a high fever and abdominal pains; he was taken to American authorities in Rio and left behind.

Even from shipboard, we felt refreshed just to see land, with mountains and buildings. We were anchored too far away to see any women clearly, though the soldiers tried. Then we sailed again.

After we left Rio, we zigzagged all over the South Atlantic. At one point, we even sailed toward the South Pole. Our speed picked up for a while, and later we learned that enemy subs really were chasing us. Several days later, we sighted land again.

We had reached Table Mountain, part of Capetown at the tip of

Africa. This time we were all given liberty to go ashore. Adjusting our sea legs to land again was peculiar and we got a good laugh from watching each other.

The white Africans were conservative and hostile. I had expected a more cosmopolitan atmosphere in that crossroads of the world. Even in this time of war, when our nations were allies, the white South Africans on the street made nasty comments about us. They shouted "Chinks!" randomly at the half of our unit that was Chinese American.

We walked through town looking for a Chinese restaurant but did not find one. Then we ran across a Chinese man on the street, who directed us to the Chinese Seaman's Club. It was the only Chinese orqanization there, and had no more than forty people.

When we introduced ourselves there, they welcomed us enthusiastically. The Club members got together and cooked us a special banquet. We felt a marvelous feeling of brotherhood based on national origin and ancestry and returned to the ship in a happy mood.

The next morning, we set sail for Columbo, Ceylon. When we arrived, we found that it was hot there, and during our brief stop a number of us bought Khaki shorts in the hope of wearing them with our uniforms. Unfortunately, we were not allowed to, since they were not regulation. We set sail one last time and soon arrived in Bombay, which turned out to be the destination of our ocean voyage.

After debarkation at Bombay, we were transported to a permanent British Army camp nearby. Our quarters were satisfactory, but had no doors anywhere, apparently to allow the tropical breeze to blow freely. The camp commander assigned native attendants to all our officers.

The attendants, all of whom were barefoot at all times, were strange to us, but efficient. They served us tea in the early morning. After we were dressed, we went to the mess hall for breakfast. The evidence of British colonialism appeared there, too; the very fine breakfast was served by Indian waiters who were fancily dressed but also barefoot.

The British Army officers maintained an aloof and leisurely attitude toward us and the camp. They didn't seem concerned with any exigency, including the war. The lax atmosphere made us uneasy, and we were glad when our orders came through three days later.

Bombay was a large city and its architecture was mostly western. It was teeming with millions of people, but upon leaving, I remembered mainly filth in all but the largest thoroughfares and packs of beggars who chased us down every street as went from one place to another. It was a sad commentary on British colonialism. We were not sorry to leave.

Our entire field hospital unit now took a train across the country from Bombay to Assam, on the eastern border of India. Except for the Indian crew in the locomotive and one British officer in each car of the troop train, only our men rode the train. We had all of our hospital equipment as well as our own food supply, some of which we had just purchased in Bombay before leaving.

From this city in the southwest of India, the train took seven days to reach our destination. Each time the train stopped for water, fuel, or any other reason, we saw crowds of children showing the havoc of starvation, disease, and overpopulation. Our men threw money to them and sometimes C-rations, our canned food. Even worse, many children begged for cigarettes to smoke. Sometimes, feeling sorry for them, we threw those, too.

For most of the trip, the officers had comfortable facilities, meaning electric fans and regular sleeping cars. However, we had to change trains approximately twenty-four hours from our destination. We bivouacked in a YMCA facility near the banks of the Bramaputra River.

Some slept on the floor in the building and others in hammocks slung between trees. The YMCA had a refreshment area that was open. We were warned not to eat any fresh fruit or vegetables for health reasons, but they had canned peaches.

The first soldier to look at the can shouted, "This iscrazy! Peaches from Oregon in this hole!"

All the cans were stamped, "Medford, Oregon, U.S.A." We stuffed ourselves with peaches from home, while fighting off mosquitoes. Then we went to sleep, still fighting them.

153

The next morning, our master sergeant woke up everyone. We broke camp quickly and gathered our personal and hospital material. On our way to the train station, we could see Hindu women on the opposite bank of the river, beating and wringing their laundry as they washed it. The water flowed muddy and yellowish.

On the new train, all the cars were third-class and we were so crowded inside them that some of us had only floor space. Being of small stature, I found a comfortable spot by padding a baggage rack with a short overcoat and getting a boost up there from a couple of the men. They reinforced the rack with rope and I was able to sleep there.

This part of the journey was as dreary as the earlier portion. We saw the same pitiful scenes of hunger, revealed in people with prominent ribs and protruding abdomens, as well as swollen legs. People in threadbare clothing ate with their hands, squatting on the ground. Even the few cows we saw, holy as they were, showed signs of starvation. Everything in the tropical subcontinent seemed slow and dragging. War was on, but in the countryside here we saw no evidence or awareness of it.

We arrived in Assam after a miserable journey, and then had to walk a half-mile carrying our equipment to our campsite on the edge of the jungle. This camp was semi-permanent, made mainly of bamboo and thatch. The quarters, called bashas, barely allowed room for two cots each. They were hardly high enough for anyone to stand, and had floors of only packed mud.

Apparently another American unit had just moved out; we found Wrigley gum wrappers and match covers from New York, Cleveland, Detroit, and other American cities. Not a single cigarette butt had been left behind, however. The local scavengers had already come through for them.

The sounds from the jungle remained with us constantly, especially the monkeys squeaking and chittering as they swung from tree to tree. We were supposedly en route to another place, but no more orders came through. Each day, we merely performed calisthenics and hiked in small groups into nearby villages.

One day, some of our Chinese American enlisted men ran across some members of the 38th Division of the Nationalist Chinese Army in India, under the command of General Sun Liren. This division was known and respected in India because it had rescued a British garrison, helping them break out of a Japanese encirclement. Their division headquarters lay only a few miles away.

One Sunday I rode with some other Chinese American officers over to visit the 38th Division. We arrived first at their dispensary, and the Chinese soldiers there welcomed us. Two nurses there were quite pretty, and inquisitive about our unit. They showed us around and introduced us to some of their officers. Their headquarters building was huge compared to ours. When we asked about it, they explained that they had built it themselves.

The Chinese Army had also built roads leading into the camp and a recreation center large enough to show movies. The nurses invited us to a Beijing opera there the following week, which was put on by the soldiers. We accepted.

At the opera, the nurses pointed out General Sun. He was erect, handsome, soldierly, and proud. The show was quite professional, but watching a Chinese opera in the midst of the jungles of Assam felt odd.

After the show, we thanked our hostesses and drove home. Later, we learned why they had wanted to befriend us. They knew we would eventually be going into China, and they asked us to take some items to their families. When the time came, we agreed.

A few days later, our unit was assigned to the U.S. Army's 20th General Hospital on a temporary basis. It was made up of personnel from Pennsylvania and served American and Chinese forces in the area. For the first time since we had left home, we actually worked in medicine again and cared for patients on a regular basis.

Most of the patients came from the Chinese Army, suffering from malaria, relapsing fever, and typhus. The surgical cases involved gunshot or shrapnel wounds. After we had worked there a week, my respect for the personnel of this hospital rose a thousandfold, from the orderlies to the chiefs of the various services. Everyone worked diligently and efficiently.

The officers established this professional atmosphere. On one occasion, I happened to see Lieutenant Colonel I.S. Ravdin, Chief of

Surgery, making his rounds. When he entered, all the nurses and other medical officers came to attention, ready to accompany him.

"At ease," he said. "There is much work for all of us to do. I know you are all very busy. Go and do what you have to do. I'll do my own dressings." He pushed his dressing cart himself; obviously, he was no prima donna. Later, he became Commanding Officer of the 20th General Hospital. By the end of the war, he had become a brigadier general.

In our camp, only one basha was big enough for a group to play cards or for people to write letters or read. One night, it was invaded by the sacred cows of India, who were protected by Hindu religious beliefs. They wandered in, dropped manure all over the floor, and moved on. We were all annoyed.

The next day, another cow walked into camp. One of our officers shot it with a hand-made bow and arrow. It stuck into the animal's side but did no serious injury. The cow ran away.

The following morning, a large contingent of natives arrived from a nearby farming village. They demanded an apology and reparations. To avoid unnecessary disturbances, the Commanding Officer met their demands. The officer who had played Robin Hood claimed it was a wild cow, but that did not make it less sacred; he was severely reprimanded.

Altogether, we spent three months in India. Then one evening, our bridge game was interrupted by a messenger. He brought us an order by telegram from the headquarters of the China-Burma-India (CBI) Theatre. One of the three platoons in our field hospital was ordered to go to Kunming in the morning.

Lieutenant Colonel Johnston picked me, two other officers, and twenty-some enlisted men to go. I knew I had been chosen because I spoke two dialects of Chinese. We were all surprised and excited. We dropped the bridge game and hurried back to our bashas to pack.

Since we had been ordered to report to the airstrip at 0600, or six A.M., we spent all night getting ready.

Chapter Twenty-one

On our maps, the Himalaya Mountains in Tibet bewtween India and China contained blank areas. Called "the Hump," the forbidding altitude and harsh environment of those areas had not been mapped. If we went down there and survived, we would have to find our own way out.

Early in the morning before we left, our mess sergeant prepared a special breakfast of spam and eggs, for which the men had traded cigarettes. Our Commanding Officer had been in China as a medical missionary the year before, and he said a prayer before we left for the airstrip. Our platoon said goodbye and mounted the truck.

We arrived at the airstrip about fifteen minutes early. The area was silent, deserted, and shrouded in early morning fog. We climbed off the truck and lined our material along the side of the runway.

At 06:00, a sergeant drove up in his jeep out of the fog and climbed up to a wooden shack. I followed him.

"We're part of the 22nd Field Hospital," I explained. "We're scheduled to leave for China."

"I don't know anything about it, sir."

I showed him our orders.

"I guess you are," he said. "Well, just leave your stuff where it is and wait for the plane."

I returned to the unit and told them we would have to wait. After a half hour or so, two C-47s came down, one right after the other. The pilots jumped out and walked to the wooden shack. I chased after the first one and identified our unit.

"Well, just have your men throw the stuff in and get on board. We'll be leaving soon." The pilot went into the shack.

I got the unit into the planes, but was not very impressed with the haphazard manner of the pilots.

When we finally took off, I decided it was just as well that no one had told us what flying over the hump would be like. It was thrilling, but rough. We were flying into clouds and out again constantly, except when a snow-covered peak suddenly appeared in front of us. Then the plane would bank sharply or climb steeply. Some of us needed oxygen and most of us got sick from the stormy ride.

Perhaps two hours later, the weather improved. The sun came out and the ride became steadier. Two hours after that, Kunming appeared in the distance. As we approached, we saw a plane burning on the ground. We grew tense, but we landed safely.

A pleasant, smiling Chinese liaison officer met us at the airport. He took us to a newly-erected camp about twelve miles southeast of Kunming. We were relieved to find that our quarters here were made of wood, complete with wooden floors, and that the ceilings were high enough for us to stand comfortably. We also had both an officer's club and an enlisted men's club for recreation.

Kunming stood on a high plain, so the evenings were cool, even after a hot summer day. After moving into the camp, most of the officers went into town for dinner. We were welcomed at a Cantonese restaurant on Jinbi Road. It was one of the most satisfying meals any of us had eaten in a long time. Because of the wartime inflation under the Guomindang government, it cost ten thousand yuan, or Chinese dollars, for each of us. That came to five dollars in American money.

As we relaxed after dinner, Captain George Reeves commented that he was happy and relaxed instead of depressed for the first time in weeks. "During the time we were in India, I don't recall seeing a single smiling Hindu. Here, as soon as we landed, we met the smiling Chinese liaison officer. Everyone on the street here seems to be relaxed and pretty happy."

The rest of our outfit followed us over the hump during the next two weeks. Our field hospital became part of Yunnan Force, or Y-Force, a U.S. task force assigned to support the Nationalist Chinese Army. Brigadier General Frank Dorn commanded Y-Force.

Two of the Chinese American officers who could speak Mandarin were requested to help out in a sick ward of a Chinese artillery unit nearby. Fred Jing and I went. In the meantime, ten Chinese nurses were assigned to our unit to learn some English and some of our methods.

Fred and I worked every day and saw some of the worst illnesses of the war. Located in an old ancestral temple, patients suffered from malaria, relapsing fever, and dysentery. Lice and fleas covered the pale, poorly-nourished soldiers. Some men had swollen abdomens and legs; many had worms. The mortality rate was high, and continued to be, because we were not prepared for these problems and the Chinese lacked medicine.

We did manage to get some drugs to treat malaria and relapsing fever after a great deal of red tape, but we could do nothing about the typhus. Every day, Jing and I had to delouse ourselves at our own unit before going to our quarters. The rest of the field hospital had begun working side by side with a Chinese field hospital that had moved nearby, commanded by a Colonel Lo. The two groups were preparing for coordinated work when we were ordered to the front together.

During this time, I was promoted to captain.

One day Colonel Lo requested my services, and my C.O. sent me on loan to him. General Tsai Zhang, the commander of a division in the Chinese 53rd Army, was a V.I.P. in need of medical help. He had fought the Japanese in Manchuria, and had resisted them at invervals all the way to Yunnan Province here in the southwest. General Tsai had marched many miles with his troops, and they respected him highly. Colonel Lo escorted me to the general's headquarters.

I saluted General Tsai and he struggled to rise from his chair. He was obviously in great pain. A brief examination showed that he suffered from prolapsed hemorrhoids so bad that he only walked, if at all, bent over with his feet apart like an old man. I made arrangements for surgery the next day at our own field hospital.

During surgery, I used spinal anesthesia and removed three partially ulcerated hemorrhoids. He remained at our hospital for four days, as the pain subsided. When the time came for him to return to the Chinese, he still had some residual pain, but now walked erect, like a soldier. Just before he left, he reached into his pocket and handed me a piece of coarse jade.

"I've suffered from this for a long time," he said. "I don't know how to thank you for your skill in relieving me of my misery. I'm also proud to have been operated on by a Chinese American surgeon. This little piece of stone is all I have to express my gratitude." He shook hands with me and gave me a salute.

I returned his salute and thanked him. He took a jeep back to Colonel Lo's outfit.

Shortly afterward, our unit received orders to go to Baoshan, at that time the northern terminus of the Burma Road.

General Dorn gave us a briefing on our upcoming trip. We would go on foot with a mule train carrying our supplies. Since we would be vulnerable to Japanese planes on the main road, we would have to march overland. He said we would have a story to tell our grandchildren, but we had no idea how right he was.

Soon after the briefing, our unit was hiking up mountain slopes and down through the valleys. That first day on the march, we walked until it was so dark that we couldn't see. Finally, when we came across some water holes in an open field, we stopped.

We boiled the water to make instant coffee and ate our C-rations. After that, we strung up our hammocks with mosquito bars and went to sleep. In the open field, we couldn't sleep any later than sunrise, so we rose early. For breakfast, we ate more C-rations and we brushed our teeth with coffee.

On the second day of marching, we came across an old road that some of the local people claimed had once been traveled by Marco Polo. It seemed old enough; the footing was terrible. The granite steps on the slopes had been worn down to the point where they were sloped and slick, and our mules picked their way up these steps only with difficulty.

After three days of climbing, we descended a slope to the banks of the Salween River.

Just as we marched down to the river, we suddenly found ourselves in the middle of action for the first time. Mortar shells were falling in front of us from over the mountains beyond the river. As unaccustomed to war as we were, some of us stood still, looking around to see which hill the shells were coming over.

"Take cover, stupid!" Someone yelled.

We all jumped for cover. Fortunately, the shells all fell short, so no one was hurt. Darkness arrived about an hour later, and the shelling stopped.

Our unit found a relatively protected area in which to bivouac for the night. Some of us used hammocks, but others slept in sleeping bags under small tents. During the night, the river rose and carried away some of our equipment.

When we got up in the morning, we were still blithely unaware of the realities of war. While we prepared breakfast in a casual manner, members of the American Advisory Command appeared from over a hill. They told us that a fierce battle was raging not far away. The Chinese were so far holding their own against the Japanese, but casualties would be coming soon. The Advisory Command led us quickly to a bridge about a mile downstream from where we had spent the night. At this point, our field hospital split up into our three platoons, as it was originally designed.

U.S. Army Rangers had thrown up a narrow, swinging rope bridge over the river here that swayed precariously as we crossed it. We moved in small groups, at intervals, and reached the other side safely. Then each platoon situated itself in a naturally protected area among the bases of the surrounding hills, within easy access of the roads.

Once our platoon was settled, we sent an officer and an enlisted man forward to scout for incoming wounded. The gunfire had been growing progressively louder as time passed. Within an hour or so, the first wounded was carried to us by stretcher.

This Chinese soldier had his left foot blown off and his right leg broken. We could not handle severe injuries, and could only give him morphine for his pain before sending him back to an evacuation hospital. It was frustrating. However, we were able to care for the other wounded. They required preliminary cleansing and debridement of the wounds and then dressings. After that, we sent them back to the rear echelon. We kept the walking wounded with us overnight and then sent them on to Colonel Lo's Chinese hospital to the rear of us.

This went on for two days. Then the gunfire stopped and the latest wounded told us that the Japanese had retreated. This was our

first experience in rendering care to the wounded, and the ugly results of war had become clear to us for the first time. Yet we also felt
confident now that we could do the job a field hospital was assigned
to do.

The next morning, we received orders to move forward. Ahead
of us, Chinese forces with U.S. military advisors were advancing,
and we had to remain a short distance behind them. As soon as we
hiked over the nearest hills, we looked out over a beautiful valley,
spread out below us.

Our hospital unit spent all morning in a careful, gradual descent.
By the time we reached the valley floor, the U.S. command headquarters had already been set up in large tents. We were instructed to
set up our hospital there and for the first time all three platoons of the
hospital worked together. No gunfire sounded for two days. This
was good for the men in combat, but we became uneasy because we
did not know what was happening up ahead.

The following day was Sunday, pleasantly cool and sunny. Most
of us went to church, where the chaplain mainly prayed for us. Then,
after lunch, I had a visitor.

Colonel Lo's hospital had set up just a few miles behind ours.
Today, remembering me from the time Fred Jing and I worked under
him outside Kunming, he came to pay a social call. He arrived on
horseback, with a pony behind him.

Colonel Lo knew more about the military situation than our
American advisors. He told me that the Japanese were now retreat-
ing quickly behind Snow Mountain to regroup on the other side. Since
it would be several days before we could advance, he had come to
take me to one of Yunnan Province's natural hot springs. He had
brought the pony for me to ride.

I was happy to accept his invitation, but I had never ridden on
horseback before. Since I did not want to appear scared, I said nothing. Remembering how cowboys mounted their horses in the movies, I put my left foot in the stirrup, grabbed the pommel of the saddle,
and hoisted myself up energetically.

I promptly fell off the other side.

The Colonel looked down kindly. "You are accustomed to riding regular horses, not ponies," he said. "I apologize for bringing you the little pony. Please take my horse."

I declined vehemently. On my second try at mounting the pony, I had better luck, and mounted with some dignity. I followed Colonel Lo for over an hour on the most memorable ride I ever had. As we constantly either climbed or descended slopes, I nearly fell off many times and hung on hard all the way. I enjoyed bathing in the hot springs very much, but I was never sure if it was worth the ride. On the way back, I was much more comfortable, and had no trouble.

Colonel Johnston was somewhat put out that he had not been invited. Before I left, I had explained that Colonel Lo wanted to speak Mandarin with me. When I returned, I thanked both colonels, one for taking me and one for allowing me to go. Colonel Johnston was a kind man in a missionary sort of way, but he found it hard to play soldier. All of us respected him as a fine person, but not really as a C.O.

We relaxed somewhat during the lull in this pleasant valley. Each day, we pursued the daily practice of setting up facilities for emergency care and definitive treatment. No wounded came in for four days, and then we were ordered to advance again. Colonel Lo had been right; we were headed for the base of Snow Mountain.

The mules we had received from the Chinese Army had tired and nearly starved during our march, but they revived during our stay in the valley. We packed them again and began to march. The advisory headquarters remained behind.

As we marched, we began to throw away unnecessary equipment. Soon each of us carried only a minimum of clothing and other personal items. With the mule train carrying the supplies, the march was not too bad. Then, at the base of Snow Mountain, American Headquarters informed us that we would have to return the mules to the Chinese. From that point, we acted as our own beasts of burden.

In addition to our personal belongings, each of us had to carry some hospital equipment. We started up the slope of Snow Mountain. Since the monsoon season here had begun, gullies of water ran down the mountainside. Some of them became leaping cataracts. Planning our advance on this mountain was as difficult and dangerous, as planning the assault against the enemy just beyond it.

Colonel Johnston decided to send us up one platoon at a time. The first two platoons would leave men posted at intervals to tell the following platoon what to expect ahead. Unfortunately, my platoon was the last one to climb.

We started late in the day, six hours after the first platoon left. By now, we were climbing with heavy gear in knee-deep mud under the constant rain. In the treacherous footing, we took four hours just to reach our first post.

The soldiers at the post had set up a tent on the slope and built a fire. We put up hammocks between trees, but the rain was our real adversary. For a short time, we rested, heated C-rations by the fire, and ate. Then we moved on.

By the time we reached the second post, night had fallen. Our orders instructed us to reach the top, but we had to stop here on the timber line for lack of visibility. The rain continued to beat on our helmets, and we were worn and tired. We put up one tent and slung our hammocks to spend the night. Despite the rain, we were able to make coffee and heat more C-rations.

The cold jungle around us remained quiet, but we were scared. We had not heard from the unit of the Chinese Army that was supposed to be advancing ahead of us. No sounds of gunfire had reached us, either, and we had no idea how close the Japanese Army might be.

The atmosphere on the mountain that night was eerie. However, the exertion had worn us out. Though we were cold, wet, and dirty, we slept without trouble.

Chapter Twenty-two

In the morning, our mood improved. The sun peeped through the close, hanging clouds briefly. We used water from the mountain streams to wash and make coffee. By this time, we were all accustomed to using our helmets to heat C-rations and our canteens to boil water. Those of us who knew how to use chopsticks cut them from branches of bamboo, which still grew at that altitude. We stuck them into our leggings for safekeeping and set out again for the peak.

Four hours later, we reached an open area short of the peak. It was barren, and we were shivering with the dampness and the cold. For the first time, we heard voices from people outside of our unit. They were Chinese soldiers, coming back down this route.

I approached one of their officers, who said he was the company commander of an ordnance unit supplying the troops on the front lines. However, he said the advance had stalled because the Japanese had been prepared to defend this route. The Chinese soldiers were just now returning from the peak to attempt a flanking maneuver farther down.

Captain Kirk Swan commanded our platoon. He decided we should wait here. Within an hour after we had set up a temporary tent, the Chinese soldiers came streaming down the mountain. Every so often, some would get out of line to warm their hands over our fire before going on. A few of the walking wounded suffered from pain. We gave them a shot of morphine, the only type of service we could offer under the circumstances.

Despite our orders, we were stranded and becoming frustrated, cold, and scared. We had no communication with our own hospital unit or the American liaison staff. Our rations were growing short, and we were hungry now that we had to ration our supplies carefully. We were supposed to stay just behind the Chinese front lines to handle the wounded, but we had not received specific orders to move with the Chinese line.

At one time, we had been told that supplies would be air-dropped to us, but they never arrived. Later, we learned that the pilots had not been able to locate us because we were out of sight above the cloud line. Our rations were dropped by mistake behind the Japanese.

We spent a miserable day and night in that barren area. More Chinese soldiers poured down the muddy road. I tried to talk to the Chinese again, but they were under orders to march on the double, and they ignored me as they hurried past. We were getting nervous; once the Chinese had pulled back completely, we would be exposed to any advance by the Japanese.

Finally, Captain Swan decided that Sergeant Haas and I should follow the Chinese down until we reached someone who could explain the situation and give us instructions. This decision lifted everyone's spirits, and the two of us started back down the mountain.

Sergeant Haas and I spent all day sliding down the muddy trail, falling into the mud and tripping over rocks and fallen branches. We, like the rest of our unit, now had only D-rations left — thick bars of chocolate. On the way, we passed the other two platoons of our field hospital, but they knew no more than we did. However, they were closer to the headquarters down in the valley and had sent people there for more supplies. At both stops, they gave us rations and coffee before we continued.

We finally reached our liaison headquarters down in the valley around 18:30 hours, or six-thirty P.M. When we reached Colonel Stoddard, the Commanding Officer of all American personnel attached to the Chinese 53rd Army, we actually collapsed to the ground in exhaustion. He didn't mind our informality, since he had already heard from others about conditions up on the mountain.

Colonel Stoddard asked for a report. We described conditions in general on the mountain. Then he asked us to explain our presence. We told him that our platoon was isolated, low on rations, and without directions or communications.

In the meantime, the mess detail had prepared ham and eggs and rice for Sergeant Haas and me. It was a feast for us and Colonel Stoddard allowed us to gulp it down while we continued to speak.

166

He told us that the movements of the Chinese fighting units were not yet certain, but that their flanking maneuver had been successful. The Chinese units still up on the mountain above our platoon would be advancing down the other side now, since the Japanese were beginning to withdraw. He told us to spend the night there in the valley and then to return to our station the next morning.

Sergeant Haas and I begged for another day of recuperation. We also pointed out that we should take supplies back with us.

Colonel Stoddard nodded thoughtfully. "We didn't plan it this way, but we just bought a cow from local Chinese farmers. Since you need food so bad, why don't you just take the cow up the mountain? Divide it among the American personnel as you see fit."

We agreed, and he granted us another day in the valley. The Headquarters personnel had been enjoying cool, sunny weather and good food, for which they had bartered with local farmers. The personnel sympathetized with the plight of our platoon, and they fed us well. We enjoyed this respite, but it was over quickly.

The following morning, we had another fine breakfast and then got underway. After days of rain and thousands of soldiers' footsteps, the route had become even rougher and muddier than before. In addition, the cow did not want to go up the mountain.

The higher we got, the more barren the mountain became, and the cow resisted even more. As we ascended, grass for the cow disappeared entirely and the weather grew colder and damper. We had to force the cow to keep going, which made the climb extremely difficult.

Altogether, we spent over two days fighting the terrain, the elements, and the cow as we climbed. On the way, we spent two nights with the other two platoons of our field hospital. By the time we reached them, the cow had become so scrawny that no one else wanted anything to do with it. When we arrived back at our own platoon, no one there wanted to slaughter it, either. With the limited equipment we had on Snow Mountain, it would have been quite a job.

Captain Swan suggested that Sergeant Haas and I take the cow on up to the peak, where the Division Liaison Headquarters was now located, in search of help. After climbing another two hundred feet, the cow collapsed from hunger and exhaustion, and simply expired. Sergeant Haas and I sat down to consider the situation.

I knew that if we left the cow, the Chinese soldiers would make a feast of it; by their standards, it was still worth the effort. Some of them passed by, and through them I managed to locate the ordnance officer we had met earlier. In exchange for a quarter of the beef, he agreed to put a guard on the cow while we pushed on to the headquarters on the peak.

Sergeant Haas and I continued our ascent and came across the Chinese field hospital under the command of Colonel Lo. One of his men led us to him, and he was kind and courteous, as always. He offered us hot rice soup and other food from his depleted rations. We ate while we explained our dilemma.

Colonel Lo sent several of his men to slaughter the cow for us, and I gave them a quarter of the meat, too. Colonel Lo refused it at first, but I insisted. He finally accepted, and sent two of his soldiers to transport the remaining beef with Sergeant Haas and me to the peak.

When we arrived, we presented ourselves to Colonel Ringler, who was in a foul mood — his usual mien, I learned later.

"Where have you been?" he demanded. "We received an order from HQ that Captain Wu is to be assigned here as a division medical officer to replace Major Young. He was wounded and sent to the rear."

I saluted. "I never received orders to that effect, sir. We just came up to bring the beef."

"I heard about that, too. Where's the cow?"

I explained the situation, and he dismissed the Chinese soldiers who had helped us. Before they left, I thanked them and asked them to convey our gratitude to Colonel Lo. I was ordered to remain under Colonel Ringler, who ordered Sergeant Haas to bring up all my belongings from the other station.

In the meantime, the Colonel also sent out a call to the regimental advisors for them to come and get their share of the beef. After it was all divided, each regiment received only three-quarters of a helmet of meat. Even so, everyone was glad to have it.

The peak, of course, was even more engulfed in clouds than the lower stations. Anyone more than a short distance away turned into a shadow, then vanished from sight. We were deliberating the best way to build a fire in the rain in the middle of the cloud when one of the regimental commanders called on the telephone. He recommended that we eat the meat as soon as we could cook it, because the meat his group had received had just been snatched by a hand out of the clouds. The thief escaped easily in the dense fog.

We took a long time getting a fire built. Once it was going, we were able to boil the meat and give everyone a taste. It was not very appetizing. This was a poor return on the effort Sergeant Haas and I had made, but of course the cow had sacrificed the most.

When Sergeant Haas returned, he helped me set up my hammock and sleeping bag. When I climbed in, water squirted out of my bedding on all sides. I slept in it with all my clothing on, including my trench coat. All of us, to keep our feet warm, heated our canteens and used them as hot water bottles. Since I had a private supply of nembutal, I took one to knock myself out. It was the best way to sleep in cold, water-soaked bedding.

This period on the mountain was one of the worst experiences of the entire war. The most eerie moment occurred once when I walked carefully through the clouds to the edge of the peak in order to urinate. I looked down and found myself standing on the half-buried body of a Japanese soldier, who seemed to be staring at me with one open eye.

After two more days on Snow Mountain, word arrived that the Japanese had withdrawn, leaving the far side of the mountain and the next valley clear. We broke camp immediately and started down out of the clouds. It took an entire day to reach the valley. In the evening, we set up camp on relatively dry ground at the base of the mountain and spent a pleasant night in a warm breeze.

The morning dawned sunny and clear. At last, we dried out ourselves and our belongings. We could see the clouds still ringing the mountain peak, but they were behind us now. In the afternoon, we began to march, moving from one jungle village to another.

At each village, the local populace feared us. The Japanese had treated them very badly. When we met them, we tried to show that we were friends, not enemies.

During this time, my old outfit caught up with the advisory group. Captain Swan requested that I rejoin the 22nd Field hospital, and he had Colonel Stoddard's approval. Colonel Ringler didn't like the idea, since I had been acting as his interpreter with Chinese officers. However, he consented, and I was glad to return to medical duty and old friends.

The three platoons of the hospital reunited for the first time in many weeks and we were jubilant at being together. When we reached a broad, grassy field bordered by a forest and a small village, we pitched our tents and set up the field hospital again. Ahead of us, the Chinese troops had once again caught up to the Japanese, who had taken up another defensive position.

We prepared for several days to handle the wounded Chinese as they came back from the front. However, Colonel Lo's field hospital had set up only a mile away, and the Chinese soldiers kept bypassing us to go there. After we notified Colonel Lo, however, he arranged to send us the most serious surgical problems, since we had better equipment and more medical supplies. We worked at this site successfully for about four weeks.

Since our unit was about forty percent Chinese American, many of us went into the local village on our free time. At first, we had to convince them that we had good intentions. We played a little with some of the children and gave them candy from our C-rations. This broke the ice and after a while we were able to purchase or barter for eggs, chickens, and pork.

One day, a Chinese American enlisted man saw that we appeared to have a new member in the outfit. The newcomer seemed to be a very laconic Chinese American who was noticeable only in front of the chow line for every meal. The soldier who noticed him at first said nothing, since the entire outfit had been separated for so long at Snow Mountain. He also did not want to embarrass the man. Finally, however, he mentioned his observation to his sergeant. The sergeant approached the stranger and discovered that he was Japanese.

This Japanese soldier had been cut off from his unit when the Japanese had withdrawn from area. He had been hiding in the woods, trapped by the Chinese lines ahead of us. When we arrived, he had seen the Chinese Americans and realized he might pass as one of us. He stole a G.I. uniform, probably from a dead soldier, and simply walked casually into camp at mealtimes to get in the mess line. Since he could speak neither English nor Chinese, he had had to bluff his way through the line without ever attempting to speak. He had done this three times a day, every day, for a couple of weeks before he was caught. At that point, he was turned over to the Chinese Army. Though he was an enemy, I was glad he was caught by us rather than killed by the villagers or left to starve in the woods.

Soon we were ordered to advance again; the Japanese ahead of us had withdrawn once more. We packed up and began to follow the advancing Chinese line again. Then, as we approached the walled town of Tengchung, we heard gunfire. The Japanese now held out there. American P-40s were already periodically bombing the town. It was time for us to set up again.

With several others in our unit, I began to scout for a suitable location. Just on the outskirts of the next village, I noticed a Buddhist nunnery inside a walled compound. We entered the compound slowly and found no one.

"Is anyone here?" I called out in Chinese.

A moment later, two nuns came out in their habits, showing their shaved heads. I told them that we were an American hospital unit and asked if we could use part of their compound. They agreed without hesitation, said "Welcome," and then fled back to their quarters.

Obviously, the Japanese had mistreated them, too. Before we moved into the compound, we instructed our men to treat them with as much courtesy as possible. Then we prepared for the wounded.

To this point on the campaign, we had not been able to set up all of our equipment in full preparation for surgery. All our locations had forced limitations on us. Now, for the first time since Fred Jing and I had worked in two Chinese artillery wards near Kunming, we were prepared to do all the work for which we had been trained.

We placed three operating tables in front of the Buddhist altar and arranged our equipment and supplies in the outer courtyard. As the wounded came in on stretchers, they would be examined and given priorities. Two corners of the courtyard were designated for postoperative patients. The walking wounded would be sent on to Colonel Lo's Chinese field hospital, which subsequently found us and set up nearby.

Fortunately, the nuns' quarters were isolated from the mainstream of activity. From time to time, we could see them shyly peeking out at us. None of us disturbed them.

Our staff slung hammocks between the many trees in the courtyard. The Chinese Army assaulted Tengchung at nightfall, and the casualties began coming in a short time later. The gunfire continued all through the first night.

Captain Swan did his first amputation, on a soldier who had already lost his left foot. Then Captain Reeves tended a gunshot wound in a soldier's abdomen and one of my classmates from Michigan, Captain Marsden, also operated on abdominal injuries. Then two patients came in with gunshot wounds in the head. I treated them.

Since all three operating tables were busy, I had to wait until Captain Swan finished his current work. Then I debrided the patient's wound, removing all the bony fragments I could see, and cleansed the area, including some of the contused brain. Since part of the dura matter was torn off, and we had nothing with which to cover that area, I just closed the scalp over it tightly. The wound was in the right frontal region and the patient suffered no apparent neurological deficit from it. We gave him some sulfa drugs and later sent him on to Colonel Lo for disposition.

My next patient had a penetrating gunshot wound of the head. He was aphasic and had weakness in his right extremities. I took a moment to remember my medical school neurology and some of the automobile accident patients I had seen in Cincinnati. From this experience. I knew that my patient had an injury on the left side involving the speech area. However, we had no X-ray facilities with which to locate the bullet. I decided only to give him some sulfa drugs and to debride the entry wound. We kept him for several days, and the scalp wound healed. He improved to the point where he could walk, but he still could not talk. At that stage, we sent him on to Colonel Lo.

We stayed at this location for a number of weeks. Since none of the other medical officers were interested in caring for the craniocerebral injuries, they began pushing them all to me. I found these injuries interesting. Also, I did a few abdominal operations, some thoracostomies and amputations, in addition to numerous minor wounds. Not having done any serious medical work for a time, we found our hands a little rusty at first. Within a few days, though, we had regained our dexterity.

None of us were expert surgeons, since we were all only two or three years out of medical school and at the level of residency. However, the volume of work we did each day near the front developed our abilities quickly. We had to make decisions instantly and muster our own resources as we could to meet the needs of each case. Without professors or department heads to consult, we could only turn to each other for advice. We did a creditable job for the Chinese fighting men, and became expert surgeons before long.

Even the nuns admired our diligence. Though afraid of us in the beginning, they later told me that they prayed for us every day, with incense and Buddhist chanting. After a while, they would come out and chat with us when we weren't too busy. Their smiles and gestures told us that they were glad to have us there. They even laughed at some of the antics that the enlisted men put on just for them.

Chapter Twenty-three

We spent several weeks in the Tengchung area, and gradually established a regular routine. During the days, we checked our patients, changed their dressings, and dispensed medicine. We usually worked late into the night, and kept separate shifts. Though the patients and doctors could not communicate verbally in most cases, a good relationship developed through gestures, smiles, and translators like me. To those of us who could speak Chinese, the patients expressed sincere thanks to the hospital as a whole.

War injuries required very little diagnostic acumen. Whenever we heard the distant sounds of gunfire, we prepared for new patients. The gunfire usually began in the evenings and lasted long into the early morning hours. We persevered, despite insufficient lighting, inadequate operating facilities, and unskilled help.

Captain Swan frequently complained, saying sarcastically that "Massachusetts General was never like this." Yet he and everyone else met the challenge as professionals. We matured as we worked, and became more somber as we saw the destruction of war, day after day.

Tengchung was an old border town in southern Yunnan. Little fighting occurred during the day, and we could see it in the distance. Outside the city wall, ponds of water lilies shone in the sun, and the wind swept across a carpet of green rice plants. In the daytime, the only sign of war was an occasional bombing raid by American P-40s and P-38s to knock out the city wall for the Chinese attackers.

Toward the end of our stay in that location, we ran out of intravenous fluids. We contrived a substitute by boiling water from a nearby spring, filtering it through fine gauze, and adding the proper amount of salt to make a normal saline solution. This worked without apparent complications. At one point, we requested supplies, but they were dropped near the Japanese, who got them just as they had received our food supplies up on Snow Mountain.

The villagers in this area also feared us at first. While we stayed in the area, however, we gradually won them over. As they grew to trust us, they began to sell us items that they had hidden from the Japanese. When we had truly befriended them, they even gave us a banquet put on by the entire village, in appreciation of our contribution to the Chinese Army. We enjoyed it very much, but noticed that the young women in the village were hanging back very shyly. Some of our men became bold enough to ask them to eat dinner with us, and a few reluctantly accepted.

Our Chinese American enlisted personnel were the first to make these overtures. Later, I pointed out to Captain Swan that these young men all craved female companionship and that the villagers and their daughters were friendly. As a result, he gave our enlisted men later hours to be out during our last two weeks in the area.

One evening, when casualties were light, they invited me to join them. I was surprised to find that the parents of the village girls were very liberal toward our men's friendship with their daughters. Some of the families invited the men to stay overnight.

On one occasion, I spoke to the father of an eighteen-year-old girl. He explained that before the Japanese had been driven back from this area, they had required the villagers to send twenty teenage girls into Tengchung every two weeks for sex. Since the alternative was a massacre of the entire village, the villagers had complied. This had continued for four months prior to our arrival.

"All our daughters in this village, from the age of sixteen and up, have submitted to Japanese sexual cruelty. However, we don't love them any less. You Americans have rid us of our hated enemy, and most of our girls are willing to give themselves to make the Americans happy."

This was, in fact, an open invitation to the entire field hospital, but I told the Chinese American enlisted men just to invite a few more close friends to the village. I wanted to prevent the situation from getting out of hand. Shortly after this, we received our orders to leave anyway.

Another field hospital had arrived to relieve us. Tengchung still held out, but we were ordered to pack up and start the long journey back to Baoshan. Fortunately, we were not required to climb back over Snow Mountain. That would have destroyed our morale; climbing it once had been enough for a lifetime, and Sergeant Haas and I had already climbed it twice.

The return march took us about a week. We stopped periodically to trade with the villagers. In exchange for sulfa drugs, aspirin, and cash, we obtained eggs, chickens, pork, taro, and sweet potatoes. Our only drink remained the water we boiled. Finally, at markets and vending stalls along the road, we were able to buy tea. Also, we purchased bananas, one of the few uncooked foods in the area safe enough to eat.

At one point, we came across a division command post of the Chinese Army. We stopped to pay our respects, hoping to be offered some food and a place to spend the night. The Chinese soldiers asked us to wait, and went to consult their superiors. One of them came back shortly and said, "Our C.O. welcomes you. Please stay and rest."

We entered the area, and General Tsai Zhang came out to welcome us. He invited us to have dinner and to bivouac there for the night. Then, when I stood to greet him, he forgot all his military protocol and rushed over to grab me in a tight bear hug. He invited me to his private tent, and we chatted over tea and Chinese cookies.

General Tsai was eager to tell me that he was well. In fact, since he had recovered from his hemorrhoid surgery, his division had successfully fought the Japanese and driven them back, though his 28th Regiment under a Colonel Mao had sustained heavy losses. Suddenly the General pulled out a folded Japanese flag with blood stains on it.

"I would like to present this to you as a memento," he said. "You made me a soldier again and I have regained the respect of my colleagues and soldiers. I even led my men into battle again. I'm eternally grateful to you. We may or may not meet again, but I'll never forget you."

I thanked him and accepted the flag. The next day, our unit continued toward Baoshan. As he suggested, we did not meet again, but I appreciated his gift.

On succeeding nights, we looked for any convenient shelter. One night, Sergeant Hobbs and I shared an abandoned building that had apparently once been used to store grain for animals. We placed two large boards across shaky benches and tried to sleep on them. Almost immediately, we were attacked by hordes of huge ants and peculiar bugs that we had never seen before. Though we were dead tired, we had to retreat. Outside, we slept on the boards restlessly, exposed to mosquitoes and other more familiar pests.

In the morning, Captain Swan ordered us to move out early, before we pursued our attempts at hygiene with our limited water. He had learned that only about a hundred yards down the road, we could get a semblance of breakfast and hot water for our Nescafé. We refreshed ourselves there, then marched on.

Since we were not retracing our march forward, we did not see the same villages on the way back, nor did we see many of the same landmarks. Two landmarks, however, told us that we were successfully returning through the same general area. We re-crossed one of the smaller branches of the Salween River on a bridge, and a short time later passed the old road of worn granite steps that Marco Polo had reportedly traveled. After two more days, we reached Baoshan again and were transported by truck to the area now designated for our hospital.

All of us were glad to be back. We felt that we had returned to civilization. When we piled out of the trucks, we got to work setting up our "permanent" tents. The sun came out, and a small stream nearby provided water. We washed our threadbare uniforms, set them out to dry, and bathed in the stream. Since we were camped in an open field, we had to dig security holes by each tent in case of air raids. After that, we were free to sleep peacefully for the first time in weeks.

Since we were too far from the front to have casualties of any kind here, we relaxed during the day, as well. Colonel Johnston began making plans for us to go on R & R in small groups. We would be going to a resort area.

I pleaded with Colonel Johnston not to send me to the R & R camp. Instead, I requested a pass to Chongqing, where I had many friends. He acquiesced.

To get there, I would have to make the trip from Kunming. I went to Kunming by truck and located the office of the transportation officer.

He was a Lieutenant Menjou, a jolly fellow with a big moustache. "What can I do for you, Captain?"

"I'm going to Chungking." That was the English name for Chongqing then.

"Well, I can get you there next Tuesday, but not this week. We only go once a week."

"That's fine. Thank you."

I returned to the officer's quarters in Kunming, and learned that Lieutenant Menjou was considered a decent fellow who could be trusted. His brother happened to be the movie actor, Adolph Menjou. The following Tuesday I returned to his office, and he put me on the plane to Chongqing as he had said.

From the airstrip, I hitched a ride with some other American officers into town and billeted at the officers' quarters there. The following day, I began looking up my former schoolmates. As usual, if I found one, I would learn where to find the others.

I located Raymond and Ruby Huang first. Raymond now worked for the American Information Service, Ruby for the Chinese National Airline Corporation. They put me in touch with Huang Soong and Bob Suez.

An electrical engineer working for the Chinese Air Raid Detection System, Huang Soong told me that their system was so effective that they not only knew when the Japanese planes took off, but also where they were going, how many there were — and in some cases, the names of the pilots. With this level of advance warning, most of the Chinese and American personnel in the area fled to safety during air raids, though the bombs destroyed buildings and other facilities. During my ten days there, I ran successfully from three air raids.

My friends in Chongqing invited me out to dinner. However, I knew that the wartime inflation had made their Chinese money virtually worthless. I insisted on treating them instead, and in turn they showed me the best eating places in the city.

Actually, after a week of relaxation in Chongqing, I began to feel restless. Compared to my experiences on Snow Mountain, life in Chongqing seemed criminally luxurious. I left Chongqing early and arrived back at my unit a few days before my orders had expired.

When I reported back to Colonel Johnston, he was surprised. "Didn't you like Chungking?" he asked.

"Well ...." I couldn't really answer.

"Anyhow, welcome back."

During the Salween Campaign, I had lost track of time. It was now the spring of 1945 and progress against the Japanese had continued on all fronts. The 22nd Field Hospital was reorganized as new personnel were brought in. The army reassigned most of the officers.

My new orders assigned me to the Station Hospital in Chongqing, next to the China-Burma-India Theater Headquarters. When I remembered that Colonel Johnston thought I didn't like Chongqing, I was suspicious of his motives in assigning me there, but I had no serious objections. I bade him farewell with a handshake and a salute.

Colonel Johnston saluted back and winked. "Good luck, Willie."

In Chongqing, a new kind of army life started for me. The Station Hospital had only about thirty-five beds. They were used mainly for high ranking officers; just a few enlisted men were treated here. Also, as part of American courtesy to allies, we extended our medical services to the diplomats of the different countries represented in Chongqing.

In fact, we in the hospital staff attended more embassy parties in Chongqing than most other officers, partly because of our medical care. I gave rabies shots to the son of a Russian embassy official and penicillin to the Danish Ambassador, who had pneumonia. Also, I operated on a Chinese admiral with a thrombosed hemorrhoid and gave vitamin B-12 shots to George Atcheson, the chargé d'affaires of the American Embassy.

Atcheson, a hard-working diplomat who had the understanding necessary to deal effectively with the Chinese and the American personnel in China, possessed a boundless command of facts about Asia. While his manner was unassuming, he could drive a hard bargain in negotiations. All of us liked and respected him, and enjoyed treating him. In turn, he looked after us. He later became General MacArthur's political advisor. Then, while flying home to consult with the State Department, he vanished over the Pacific.

Our unit also became acquainted with diplomats Richard and Jack Service. Jack later became a controversial personality because of his leftist leaning. We saw Lieutenant General Joseph W. Stilwell only once, near the end of his command of the China-Burma-India Theater, but we met his successor, Major General Albert C. Wedemeyer, several times.

I received a call from General Wedemeyer's office once. A Japanese prisoner who had been borrowed from the Chinese for interrogation had become ill. I went to make a diagnosis.

The prisoner had a fever and bad chills, but he had to be returned to the Chinese Army within twenty-four hours, so our interrogators couldn't wait long. The case fell to me because I was Officer of the Day. I had him brought to the hospital under escort by field-rank officers from both allied armies.

At the hospital, I ordered the lab technician to do a blood smear for malarià and relapsing fever, and a urinalysis. In the meantime, I checked his throat, but found no local infection or respiratory problem. Then the blood smears were ready.

Sergeant Berry had identified malaria in blood smears easily on other occasions, so I accepted his judgment that none was present here. When I took over the microscope, I was gratified to see the spirochetes of relapsing fever. I gave the patient an ampule of marphasan and some aspirin. The next morning, he had become well enough to be interrogated. After the officers left, Sergeant Berry and I congratulated ourselves.

The next day, Theater Headquarters called and thanked the hospital unit for its good work. However, no one on duty that day knew what they were talking about.

One day, General Claire Chennault's room attendant came to the hospital for a tooth extraction. He was a young man of Chinese

180

descent, who now had a swollen jaw. Since he saw me first, he explained the problem to me in Chinese.

Major Stuart, the dental officer, exploded. "We are not allowed to render service to Chinese personnel — even if they are employed by the American army. We are strictly responsible for the American armed service people, American civilians, and the diplomatic corps!"

The young man shrugged, and responded in English with a distinct New York accent. "Oh, I was born in Brooklyn. I graduated from high school there."

Major Stuart motioned him into the dental chair. "I don't think Brooklyn is part of the United States, but I'll take care of you, anyway."

When the job was finished, General Chennault's man thanked Major Stuart profusely in a Chinese manner and bowed repeatedly as he backed out the door.

Our unit also had three older medical officers, two corpsmen, and two nurses. The older officers were colorless individuals with no genuine interest either in the war effort or their medical pursuits. They performed minimal duties but always enjoyed themselves at parties. Of the others, nurse Nancy Wong was the best. She had been born and raised in Canada and had come to China a few years before.

Before working in Chongqing, Nancy had actually been at the front with the Chinese Army. She had sustained several leg wounds. Now she walked fairly normally, but was slightly bowlegged. Since she spoke English, the patients enjoyed joking with her.

Colonel Clark was in charge of the G.I. section of the China-Burma-India Theater. He epitomized the phrase "an officer and a gentleman." At one point, he developed an upper respiratory infection that progressed to pneumonia. I had to go to his quarters to give him penicillin. When he improved some, he came to the hospital to finish his course of treatment. As a result, we established a close doctor-patient relationship.

A month after he had returned to duty, he telephoned me. "All the hospital personnel are up for promotion. However, since you're a recent transfer, you're not eligible. Well, based on time of service you are, but the table of organization won't fit you in. So if you want to be promoted, you'll have to be reassigned and leave Chungking. Or, you can stay here and remain a captain."

"Well, may I think it over? I'll report to you tomorrow, if it's all right with you."

"Come over to my office at ten in the morning."

I agreed. Actually, the next morning, I arrived at his office a little early.

"What's your decision?" he asked.

I felt sheepish, but also a little bold. "I really want to be promoted and remain in Chungking as well."

Colonel Clark shook his head a little and then swung around to his teletype. He wrote out a message and then let me read it: "Promote Captain Wu to Major and keep him here in Station Hospital in any way possible."

Two days later, he called me again. "Congratulations, Major Wu. You are to remain with the hospital."

Our officers' quarters in Chongqing were very comfortable. For breakfast, we had bacon, eggs any style, pancakes, cereals and juices, just like at home; obviously, it was quite a contrast to the field hospital on campaign. I realized, though, that caring for the wounded in battle had been much more satisfying than treating civilians and top brass.

Colonel Cox was known as the "rudest man in Chungking" among American personnel. At mealtime, everyone tried to avoid him. He always sat at the middle of a long table in the center of the dining room. One day I was a little late for lunch, and found all the peripheral tables full. I sat down across from Colonel Cox.

Colonel Cox began to question me as soon as I sat down. "Are you a native of China, originally?"

"Yes, sir. I was born in southern China and grew up there until I was about eleven, then I went to the States."

"Then you don't speak Chinese. You must have forgotten most of it, if not all of it."

"On the contrary, sir. My father was an Imperial Scholar and he made me keep up my Chinese for years by requiring me to write book reports for him. When I was at the University of Michigan, I lived in a Chinese fraternity and my fraternity brothers taught me Mandarin. Also, I came back to China several times while I was in school and traveled to Peking, Kunming, Chungking, and other cities."

"Well then, tell me what 'hong' means."

"I couldn't quite catch the tone, sir."

"Anyone who's studied Chinese knows what 'hong' means!" he growled angrily. He turned to Captain Mueller, a veterinarian sitting nearby who apparently had taken some Chinese lessons. "Mueller, tell Wu what 'hong' means! He doesn't even know his own language."

Captain Mueller was surprised and embarrassed. "Sorry, sir. I've forgotten."

"'Hong' means 'red'!" the Colonel bellowed. "Anyone who knows Chinese knows that!"

"Well," I said, "there are four tones in speaking Mandarin. 'Hong' as you pronounced it meant nothing, but in the second tone it means 'red.'"

By the time I got away, the dining room was nearly empty. Still, word of the episode spread to other officers' quarters around Chongqing. Some of the other officers who had been subjected to the Colonel's abusive treatment decided to get back at "the old man."

Two days later, I entered the dining room at lunch time and felt a tense, expectant air. Colonel Cox was already seated in his usual place, and I was glad to see that all the seats at his table were taken. When I looked around for an empty seat, Captain Mueller waved to me.

"I want you to meet my guests — Major Harold Stevens and Lieutenant-Colonel Kermit Roosevelt."

I shook hands with them and sat down. Actually, I had already met Lieutenant-Colonel Roosevelt. He had come to me as a patient, with an open wound near his right kidney that needed a change of dressing; he had sustained it while fighting in North Africa shortly before he was transferred here. I found him a congenial and dashing sort of person.

Suddenly Major Stevens demanded loudly, "Wu, what does 'hong' mean in Chinese? I presume you know your own native language."

I was amazed. Before I could reply, Lieutenant-Colonel Roosevelt interrupted.

"Leave the man alone. It's we who are ruining their language."

I was so embarrassed and uncomfortable that I simply left. Even if I had responded, Colonel Cox might have used anything I said against me. The other officers at the table were now in the OSS, the forerunner of the CIA, and safely out of his command. I later learned that Colonel Cox had kicked them out of their officers' quarters the year before without good reason, when he had the authority. They had been waiting for a chance to get back at him, and they did so at my expense.

All the medical officers at the Station Hospital took turns on sick call. After a period of time, we realized that one soldier in particular came in almost daily. His complaint remained the same, that his feces contained blood. All of us examined him and checked his stools by culture and microscopic examination. We found nothing to account for the problem. Still, he kept coming back, day after day.

Finally, one day when I had run out of suggestions, I said, "I suppose you're eating out at all kinds of Chinese restaurants, and your intestinal flora may be upset by the food."

"Oh, no, sir," he said. "I always eat in the Army mess."

"Oh. Well, maybe you should go out to eat more often. As you probably know, most Chinese foods are well cooked." Gradually, we began to see this soldier less and less. Finally we assumed he had been transferred.

Despite my duties, I also arranged to see my friends in Chongqing occasionally. Some of them even came to visit me at the hospital, expressing their gratitude and pride in the fact that I had come back to China for the purpose of serving both the U.S. and China. One day, when I was visiting Raymond and Ruby, she mentioned that the Chinese would like to have a dinner dance.

"American officers are often entertained by various organizations," Ruby said. "We can't just have a dance, because the Chinese government prohibits us from holding any social functions, except to entertain American service people."

"You're an American officer," said Raymond. "If you will come as our guest, that will meet the requirement."

I agreed, and we had a successful party. Many old schoolmates from Michigan attended, and all the Chinese seemed happy to have a chance to dance and socialize. I took several of my colleagues to make it more legitimate. Afterward, several similar parties were held, and later Cecile observed that one benefit of my going off to war was that I improved my dancing.

Apparently through my Chinese friends, some of the medical students and residents at Central University Medical School and Hospital in Chongqing heard that I was working in an American hospital. They were anxious to update their information, and asked me for help. I gave them all the medical journals that I had, which I received from home, and also my medical books. They explained that the U.S. State Department had sent specialists to work with them in several surgical areas, but none in neurosurgery. Many of their patients were dying from brain tumors and intracranial infections. In fact, they asked if I would come and operate on their patients. I explained that I was not a specialist, but simply had some limited experience with war injuries outside Tengchung. Even so, I was tempted to try helping, but Army regulations forbade it.

This consideration, however, prompted my decision to become a neurosurgeon if the opportunity developed.

Rumors of all kinds circulated in Chongqing. One incident created much dissatisfaction among the Chinese high command; General Stilwell called Jiang Jieshi (Chiang Kaishek) a "peanut," and expressed his lack of respect in other ways, as well. Other Americans were frustrated by the undercurrent of feuding between the two allies. Disrespect for the Guomindang was spreading widely, fueled especially by the luxury in which Madame Jiang was living. She had demanded that American pilots flying over the Hump transport personal items for her, such as silk sheets, taking space away from critical supplies. Meanwhile, other air corps pilots went on leave at times to areas controlled by the Chinese Communists. They returned with glowing reports of the order, honesty, and courtesy of people in those areas. As American military personnel continued to exchange comparisons of this sort, their dissatisfaction increased.

When President Roosevelt died in the spring of 1945, the Generalissimo gave a reception for the American field rank officers and invited them to a memorial service which he personally conducted. I had just been promoted to major a short time before, so I was able to go.

Coincidentally, Zhou Enlai had come to town to negotiate with the Guomindang at that time. He attended the reception. I saw him at some distance, a distinguished man wearing a khaki Zhongsan uniform, and holding a pith helmet. Very few people spoke to him. He was the most conservative of the Communist leaders and the only one whom Jiang would accept for negotiations.

I started to approach him, but a fellow officer stopped me.

"Observe military protocol," he reminded me.

I did not approach Zhou after all. Years later I wished that I had taken the opportunity to meet him. He remained a major figure in China, and later stressed moderation during periods of extremism such as the Cultural Revolution of the 1960s.

Personally, I felt that the United States should stop trying to mediate between the two Chinese factions. If the U.S. would simply choose one and back it fully, then pressure could be applied to govern more democratically. As it was, neither Chinese faction was democratic.

The U.S. continued to try reconciling the two Chinese groups without understanding the blood feud between them — each side felt the other had betrayed it, and they had fought a bloody civil war from 1928 to 1936. In addition, grassroots sentiment among the Chinese people had consistently turned against the Guomindang during the war years, as corruption, nepotism, and uncontrolled inflation ran wild. By the late 1940s, the Chinese people felt that Jiang had had his chance, and failed.

Chapter Twenty-four

One Sunday, in the last week of July, 1945, I was working at the hospital. Sergeant Ward came up to me and said, "Major, you're going home."

"There are quite a few sick patients here. I'll go as soon as I'm through."

"No, you don't understand. An official order just came through for you to go Stateside. It's a forty-five-day leave."

I was so unprepared that the idea took a while to sink in. When I finally realized I had orders to go home, I was ecstatic. I finished what I was doing and the next day I briefed my replacement on all my patients. Then I began to make plans for my trip.

By now, I had spent twenty-seven months overseas. I immediately sent a cablegram to Cecile, with whom I had been corresponding regularly. She had recently gone on loan from the Army Map Service to the State Department as a Chinese analyst.

When I cabled her, she was working with the Chinese delegation in San Francisco, where the United Nations was first being organized. When my cablegram arrived from CBI headquarters, it flashed on the U.N. teletype screen. As a result, my proposal for marriage was visible to every delegation in the U.N.

I managed to leave Chongqing soon after my orders arrived. Colonel Clark, whose office had issued the orders, was leaving for Washington, D.C. the following week. Since he knew my fiancée lived there, he told me where to get in touch with him and arranged for my trip home with other returning servicemen.

The trip would take a week, because of the route, flight changes, and military priorities. Before we left Chongqing, we were briefed on the dangers of flying over the Hump. Then in Kunming, we were issued jungle knives, emergency rations, and oxygen supplies in case we went down in the Himalayas. The irony struck me; I could not help remembering my first flight over the Hump, which had been so casual. Now the briefings made us all nervous, but the flight was uneventful.

We refueled at Abadan, Iran, and then stopped in Cairo, Bengasi, Oran, and Casablanca. We stopped in Cairo and Casablanca for two days each and were able to stretch our legs and loosen up. From Casablanca, we flew to Newfoundland — a strange route, I thought. From there, we went to Montreal in a heavy rain, and then flew south to Washington, D.C.

Four of us had been entrusted with important medical information, which we had to take to the Army Surgeon General's office in person. We landed August 8, 1945. We got into a cab, and the driver spoke enthusiastically.

"How about that bomb, eh? The one that destroyed Hiroshima? And it was only the size of a baseball!"

We had no idea what he was talking about and shrugged him off as a kook. Since we had been in the air for most of the past few days, the news of the atomic bombs had never reached us. Of course, we caught up with events as soon as we could.

Once we had delivered our material, we shook hands and parted. I called Cecile from the nearest drug store and then took a cab to her apartment. She and the Mattingleys were waiting for me when I arrived.

Cecile and I greeted each other with hugs and kisses, but I could still hardly believe I had come back. The full emotional impact did not develop until the next day. We discussed our wedding plans, and decided on August 19 for the wedding date, about a week later.

Two friends from Ann Arbor, Jim and Peggy Hunt, came to Washington for our wedding. They now lived in Kalamazoo, Michigan. Peggy was Cecile's matron of honor. Since Colonel Clark was in town, I invited him, and we were delighted when he came. Cecile and I were married and prepared for a honeymoon before my leave was up.

In fact, I asked Colonel Clark at the wedding what I should do. The war seemed to be winding down now, after the bombings of Hiroshima and Nagasaki. Yet it had not actually ended.

"Your present orders are to return to Chungking when your leave is up. However, if you want to stay home, write me requesting a change of station before you go on your honeymoon. I'll see what can be done."

After the wedding, Cecile and I sneaked out of our wedding reception before it ended. Fred and Florence Mattingly, who had helped arrange our wedding plans, took us to the Wardman Park Hotel on the northwestern edge of Washington. We checked in with a bottle of champagne that Cecile's brother Alason had slipped me at the reception. In our room, we enjoyed a wonderful wedding night. Our feeling of closeness was enhanced by our long separation.

Just before midnight, we both felt hungry. All we had eaten that day had been some hors d'oeuvres at the reception. I called room service and tried to order.

"Where have you been?" The room service operator demanded. "There's a war on!"

So we starved through the rest of the night. In the morning, bacon and eggs had never tasted so good. Then we packed up and reached the airport by noon, where we left for Cincinnati.

We visited Nikki Sharp, the wife of my former fellow resident Jack Sharp at Bethesda Hospital. Cecile and I had gone out with them when Cecile had visited me in Cincinnati before the war. They now had a three-year-old daughter, but Jack had not returned yet from his Navy tour.

My old friends from Bethesda greeted me enthusiastically and admired the major's gold leaf on my army uniform. I had left Cincinnati as a new first lieutenant three years and a couple of months before. However, though I enjoyed the reunion, the atmosphere of camaraderie in my time as a resident there had passed. We had all experienced three long years of wartime, either at home or overseas.

After a couple of days, Cecile and I went on to see some of her relatives in Columbus, Ohio. Cecile's Great-Uncle John Gilmore Monroe was Gram's brother and his daughter had married a man named Hobart Munsell, whose son John was therefore Cecile's second cousin. We had visited the Munsells once from Ann Arbor, when we had gone to Columbus for the Michigan-Ohio State football game.

The Munsells welcomed us and made us feel at home, as part of the family. In particular, they asked about my wartime experiences,

189

which I was glad to share. Their favorite anecdote was the story of how Sergeant Hass and I had forced the cow up Snow Mountain.

Next, Cecile and I went back to Ann Arbor. Our trip was casual and light-hearted, and my beautiful and loving bride was effervescent and carefree. We traveled with all the joy and hope associated with starting a new life together.

On our return to Ann Arbor, we visited places that we had frequented as students. They included the Arboretum, the arcade just off State Street, and the University Hospital. One block down from the hospital on Ann Street, we passed the house where Cecile had lived with her grandparents during most of her childhood.

We also paid respects at the grave of her mother in the cemetary at Geddes Avenue and Observatory Street. Near the entrance, my old Alpha Lambda Fraternity house stood on Geddes, where we had enjoyed many parties a short distance from Camden Court, where she had lived when I had first met her.

Most of our friends from our student days were gone. We made no special effort to look anyone up. Instead, we simply enjoyed reiminiscing.

After a couple of days, Jim and Peggy Hunt drove to Ann Arbor from Kalamazoo and picked us up at the Michigan Union. We relaxed in Kalamazoo for few days and then all four us went to Chicago. In Chicago, we checked into a motel near Lake Michigan.

One afternoon, we went to a sandy beach on the lakefront for a cookout. The sun was bright and the water was clear, with gentle waves. We swam and sunbathed leisurely. Lying in the sand and gazing at the clouds, we felt our future was as open as the blue sky.

While sitting in the sand and running my hands through it, I noticed that my new wedding ring had slipped off. I panicked momentarily and all four of us began looking for it in all the different places around the beach where I had been.

I really did not see how we could find a wedding ring lost in the sand. However, Cecile suddenly called out excitedly that she had found it. I was greatly relieved and have taken great care with it ever since.

At the end of our visit in Chicago, Jim and Peggy drove us to

Midway Airport on their way back to Kalamazoo. Our idyllic honeymoon was coming to a close. On the plane home, we began to feel the real uncertainties lying ahead. My orders to return to Chongqing when my leave was over still stood.

When the Mattinglys drove us from the airport in Washington to our apartment on D Street, we found our furniture in disarray. All the drawers had been yanked out. In the bedroom, we found gift boxes scattered all over and most of our wedding gifts missing. However, they had missed a pearl necklace I had given my bride. It lay in a small box on the floor, among the larger boxes strewn around.

We were disappointed, of course, but the damage was done. First we reported the theft, then we cleaned up the mess. To our surprise, the police were able to return a camera and a few other stolen items to us a few weeks later.

In the meantime, new orders had arrived for me: "Report to Fort Meade, Maryland, after your leave is up." I called the fort a few days early to confirm this, and I was told that I didn't even have to show up in person. Since the war clearly would end soon, reporting in by phone would be sufficient. Moreover, my discharge was already being processed. Finally, they informed me that I had been awarded the Bronze Star for my services in the Salween Campaign. I was on terminal leave, and able to turn my full attention once again to civilian life.

Now I looked for a place to continue my medical training. First I signed up for a postgraduate course in general surgery at George Washington University Hospital. Later, I took another course there in neurosurgery. At that time, I met Dr. Walter Freeman and Dr. James Watts, whose combined work pioneered the prefrontal lobotomy procedure that first was popular and later discredited in treating major psychosis.

Cecile was still working as chief of the China Unit in the Army Map Service. At home, Cecile and I settled down and kept house. She also did creative writing, especially poetry.

One evening, she and Florence Mattingly held a poetry reading. Later that night, Cecile told me that she had had trouble reading her poem aloud because her throat felt tired. As she was talking to me, her voice sounded oddly nasal. However, the next morning, her voice had become normal again.

A problem persisted, however, when I came home in the evenings. Cecile began to complain of being unusually tired, after only routine work. She tried taking a drink of water, but choked on it, unable to swallow. Yet, as before, she felt fine the next morning.

Cecile's family doctor found nothing wrong. I took her to an Army ear, nose, and throat specialist. After he examined her, while she was dressing, he told me nothing was wrong with her physically. However, he gave me the name of a good psychiatrist.

This upset her considerably. At home, she wept and fell asleep. When she awoke, she looked much better. Suddenly I exclaimed, "I know what it is — myasthenia gravis."

In the days that followed, she also mentioned that the frying pan seemed heavier than usual. Another day, she dropped a jar of cold cream without knowing why. Yet she did not have the classic symptom of myasthenia gravis, a drooping eyelid.

Then one afternoon, when she was taking a nap, I noticed that her eyelids did not close completely. As time passed, her voice became worse and swallowing required great effort. She choked on liquids frequently.

Now her symptoms completely fit a disease called myasthenia gravis, but I had never seen a case of it. From what I remembered, it was a disease in which unusual fatigue would occur, but the patient would respond to rest. However, I was frightened. In medical school, I had learned that it had no cure.

I researched the subject in the Library of Congress and at the medical school at George Washington University. Dr. Henry Viets had developed a diagnostic test for myasthenia gravis. If the disease was confirmed, a drug called neostigmine was an effective treatment, though no cure existed.

In addition, Dr. Alfred Blalock, a professor at the Johns Hopkins Medical School, had achieved good results in some myasthenia cases with thymectomies, but the mortality rate was twenty percent. He had stopped the operations because of the high mortality rate.

I had already taken Cecile to several physicians, some of whom had given less depressing diagnoses. However, their suggestions were not helping her any. Reluctantly, I took her to see Dr. Walter Freeman. I was afraid he would confirm my diagnosis.

Dr. Freeman, an excellent neurologist, was known as the dean of psychosurgery in America. He did confirm the diagnosis, and sent us to Boston, to see Dr. Henry Viets, who was the nation's expert on myasthenia gravis. It was December, 1945.

Dr. Viets was a lecturer at Harvard and the Director of the Myasthenia Gravis Clinic at Massachusetts General Hospital. A large, well-proportioned man, he met us with a cordial manner and a beaming smile. We felt comfortable with him at once. After we chatted briefly, he examined Cecile and gave her another prostigmine test. Prostigmine was the major drug treatment for the disease, supplemented at times with ephedrine and guanadine. Cecile tested as a myasthenic.

At this point, Dr. Viets felt she should be put on a medical regimen, but that she did not need hospitalization, especially since I was a physician. If an emergency developed, I could give her injections of prostigmine myself. We took the train back to Washington and stayed with friends in case we needed more help.

In a week or so, Cecile became much worse. I had to carry her piggyback up the stairs, and she descended the stairs by sitting on a pillow and sliding down, one step at a time. One night, she had difficulty breathing. In a short time, her lips were blue.

I wasn't sure what to do. From her symptoms, however, I judged that I did not have much time to deliberate before she would die from lack of oxygen. I felt that a normal injection of prostigmine into her muscle would not take effect fast enough. Instead, I gave her an ampule of prostigmine intravenously.

Fortunately, this revived her enough to continue breathing. I called Fred Mattingly immediately. He drove over, carried her down to the car, and rushed us to Gallinger Hospital.

Chapter Twenty-five

By chance, the hospital maintenance staff had just cleaned the steps, and the water had frozen. Fred slipped on the sheet of ice and they both fell to the pavement. Fortunately, the fall did no serious damage, and we soon had Cecile in a respirator — an iron lung.

The nurses who put her in the respirator were novices. They put her inside it in the usual recumbent position, on her back. She resisted, because she could not expectorate the huge collection of mucus in her throat and trachea while she was on her back, and she was unable to speak. When the nurses put her in this way, she was in danger of suffocation.

Cecile pulled her head all the way into the machine, forcing the nurses to turn it off. I tried to explain, but they considered me just a husband, even though I told them I was a doctor, and in uniform, signifying my rank as a major in the medical corps.

They ignored me anyway.

Finally, Cecile managed to turn herself over. In a prone position, she was able to expel the mucous and breathe. By the time the resident finally arrived, the struggle was over.

Cecile remained in the respirator for several days, and then gradually was weaned away from it. She had to be tube-fed for many weeks, however, because she was too weak to swallow. After about three months, she was strong enough to be transferred.

We returned to Boston, where Dr. Viets put her into the Baker Memorial section of Massachusetts General. He adjusted her medication and several weeks later she improved enough to be discharged. However, her speech was still unintelligible, and she could not swallow if she was in a sitting position.

One evening in the hospital, she was talking with another young woman who had myasthenia, and the two of them spoke in such a slurred manner that a third patient asked them if they were speaking

Chinese.

Dr. Viets expressed surprise when I told him that I had kept Cecile alive by giving her the prostigmine injection into her vein instead of into her muscle. He had never heard of that being done before. Apparently, it had been riskier than I had realized.

Cecile's cousin, Marilyn Sager, lived with her husband Bill in Cambridge, a Ph.D. student at Harvard. They invited us to stay with them, and offered to help care for her.

We were eternally grateful for this. It allowed us to remain in the area, near Dr. Viets, and it released me to pursue a residency in neurosurgery. Dr. Viets kindly wrote several letters of introduction for me to the directors of some neurosurgery training programs in Boston.

First I went to see Dr. Jason Mixter, who had come out of retirement to run the neurosurgical service at Massachusetts General when other doctors had left for the armed services. However, Dr. Mixter explained that the program in neurosurgery was up in the air, and that no new appointments would be made soon. Next, I visited Peter Bent Brigham Hospital. Dr. Elliot Cutler, Surgeon-in-Chief at that hospital, was a brigadier general. I was still in uniform, since my discharge had not come through yet, and so was he. Dr. Cutler asked if he could be of help.

I explained my purpose. He was sorry, but post-war plans for residency were not established there either. I was discouraged, but moved on.

At Boston City Hospital, I met Dr. Donald D. Munro, Surgeon-in-Chief of the Neurosurgical Department. He received me cordially in his office and gave me the first good news I had received in a long time — he had an opening for a neurosurgical fellow, as the position was called. I told him briefly about my medical background, and then felt I should explain my wife's illness.

Dr. Munro nodded. "I know that your first responsibility is to look after your wife, but if I give you this appointment, I expect you to fulfill its responsibilities to the utmost. I won't tolerate any excuses. Do you think you can handle it?"

"Yes, sir." I would have to.

When Cecile's condition had been first diagnosed, I was terribly disturbed and depressed. Our life together was just beginning. For my own enlightenment, I read everything I could find on the subject and asked neurologists about it when I could.

Myasthenia gravis is an auto-immune disease in which acetylcholine anti-bodies affect acetylcholine receptors at the neuromuscular junction, causing an abnormal transmission of nerve impulses. Myasthenics also frequently have enlarged thymus glands, and thymectomy often benefits the patients, though no one knows the reason.

Patients with myasthenia gravis often have ptosis, or drooping eyelids. In more systemic cases, the muscles involved in swallowing, speaking, and chewing weaken. Next, muscles used to breathe may be affected. Obviously, without treatment, such patients will not survive.

Now Cecile had become so severely ill that I could not understand her speech. We began to write notes to each other, but she became so fatigued that I couldn't read her writing. Then she would cry in frustration. She still had trouble swallowing, breathing, and walking, as well.

I was finally discharged from the army in March of 1946. On April 1, I started the residency program at Boston City Hospital, or BCH. Adjusting to the new environment there was tougher than usual, with Cecile's condition on my mind. Fortunately, Leon Becker, the chief resident, was very pleasant, as were the others on the service.

Dick Strain, who had been on the teaching staff at Vanderbilt University as a general surgeon, had arrived just ahead of me. Three of us were resident fellows — Irving Perlmutter, who had been a commander in the Naval Medical Corps, John Paget, president of his graduating class at Tufts Medical School and also recently out of the service, and me.

Dr. Munro's associates were Dr. Walter Wegner and Dr. Price Heusner. Before long, we had all heard about and witnessed the idiosyncracies of each staff man. In a way, it was part of our training.

Dr. Munro terrorized everyone, including the patients. He hated to see any of us sitting down, even to read a medical journal. According to him, the wards were full of patients and if we were doing our jobs properly, we would not have time to read.

Even though we always made our rounds of each patient every day, he always found something wrong when he made his rounds later. He forbade patients to smoke, many years before the link between smoking and cancer was suggested. Not only did he consider it unhealthy, but he hated the smell and the fire hazard. Therefore, all smoking materials were taken from any patient admitted to our service, and locked away. If Dr. Munro caught a patient smoking, perhaps if a friend or relative had smuggled cigarettes in, the patient was dismissed from the hospital.

In the operating room, Dr. Munro was a prima donna of the old school. Nothing we did was right, but he seldom gave us any proper instruction. After the operation, or at least when the main work was done, he would allow the first assistant to finish. With Dr. Munro, we learned mainly by observing. His surgical technique was not the most meticulous, but he usually accomplished the job satisfactorily. He was scrupulously honest; his operative notes always included difficulties he had experienced and minor errors he could have avoided.

Dr. Wegner, on the other hand, put everyone at ease. He took the time to teach at bedside as well as during operations. A soft-spoken man, he was tidy in his work and stable in his personality. Not colorful but steady, he possessed a genuine concern for both patients and residents.

The youngest of the three, Dr. Heusner, was a Rhodes Scholar and a showman, but he was also truly a good surgeon. He could be very sarcastic at times, but he was always willing to teach at any time of the day or night. In fact, he would just as readily give us a discourse at three in the morning as three in the afternoon.

We frequently called him at night for advice, and he told us what to do. If we were really in doubt, he would come over at any time. He believed in the pyramid system of residency training, though, which required that the chief resident be informed of all the situations and handle them if at all possible.

Dr. Heusner had developed one bad habit when he had been ill with pleurisy, however: he had become addicted to codeine. Since he knew where it was kept in our ward, he would take one or two tablets every day during rounds.

In the meantime Cecile's illness, which had been termed "fulminating myasthenia gravis," had stabilized but not improved. I had to take the subway to check on her, whether or not it was my night off. The other residents always covered for me when I had to leave. This way, I felt that I was not neglecting either her or my work, although the urgency of both her condition and the training program took a toll. I was grateful to my colleagues, who helped me avoid inciting Dr. Munro's wrath.

We shared our wards with the neurological service; each group had seventeen beds. The female patients were on the sixth floor, male patients on the seventh. The staff offices lay on the eighth. Dr. Derek Denny-Brown, a world-renowned neurologist, and Dr. Jackson Putnam, Professor of Neurology at Harvard, had their animal laboratory on the ninth floor.

Shortly after I arrived at BCH, I was given a room in the house officer's building. This building had a swimming pool, handball courts, a reception parlor, and an elegant dining room with a lofty ceiling. It had some of the best and worst food of any hospital there, but it was usually good, especially at lunch. On Sunday evenings, I was introduced there to baked-bean sandwiches.

At lunch hour, our group usually sat together with one or two staff members. We discussed patients, possible diagnoses, and methods of treatment; these were extensions of the discussions begun on our rounds. Elderly women served us lunch. They had worked there for many years, and sometimes even had trouble carrying fully loaded trays. However, they were all tender-hearted, and liked to pamper us. In particular, when we had steak for lunch, they would slip a second one onto our plates with a wink. All two hundred residents at the hospital had a special affection for them.

One day at lunch, I heard a familiar voice coming from a nearby table. I looked over and saw Kirk Swan — Captain Swan, who led my platoon up Snow Mountain. Of course, we were both civilians now. I rose, and we greeted each other enthusiastically.

Kirk explained that he had started his residency at BCH shortly after he graduated from Harvard Medical School, but the war had interrupted it. Now he was continuing his surgical training there. I told him briefly of what I had done since leaving the field hospital, including Cecile's illness and the immense amount of medication she needed every day — two ampules injected every two hours. We parted after lunch.

After that day, interns and residents began stopping me in the hospital corridors. Many of them were total strangers, but they could read my name on my white uniform. Each one of them handed me some prostigmine, courtesy of Kirk Swan. At BCH, each service sent in a daily requisition for drugs, and Kirk was requisitioning some for me through his own service. He helped me a great deal this way. The G.I. Bill paid for my neurosurgical training, but I earned only $25.00 a month as a resident.

Kirk had always been a happy-go-lucky sort of person. He would capitalize on opportunities, but became depressed easily when matters did not go right. During the Salween River Campaign, he and Captain Marsden had frequently mixed the hospital's supply of ethyl alcohol with candy from their C-rations for flavoring, and drank the mixture as a beverage. Since I have no tolerance for alcohol, I didn't join them, but I often sat nearby and listened to them talk. They were usually depressed, and dwelled on the dark outlook we had ahead of us in those days.

On a happier occasion, before our unit had left for the front, Kirk had been involved with one of the pretty Chinese nurses, Shiao Li. While we were on the Salween Campaign, Shiao Li wrote to Kirk in Chinese. He would hand the letters to me, saying, "Willie, I'm at your mercy." I translated all of them for him.

Unfortunately, after I had been transferred to Chongqing, I had learned that she was in a nearby hospital with tuberculosis. Another nurse from the campaign, who was now in Chongqing, took me to visit her. She asked me about Kirk and the hardships of our campaign, but I had lost track of Kirk at the time; he had been transferred to another unit, too. She said goodbye to me in English, and died about a month later.

I didn't get a chance to tell Kirk until I saw him at BCH.

"What a pity," he said sadly. "She was such a cute kid, and we did have fun together."

Even before the war, though, he had been married with a young son. Now that he was home, his family life was re-established. The second time we ran into each other at BCH, he said, "I want to invite you to come over to have dinner with us, but I want you to cook the rice. I miss the stuff."

I laughed. In China, he had often proclaimed that he would never look at rice again. That weekend, I met his wife and his handsome four-year-old son.

After several days had passed, I realized that I had not seen Kirk in the residents' dining room for some time. I asked the assistant resident where he was.

"Oh, you know Kirk. Last Tuesday, he was late for a scheduled operation at 8:00 A.M. and couldn t find a place to park. So he parked in the superintendent's spot."

"That sounds like Kirk, all right."

"So he was suspended for two weeks."

When Kirk returned, I told him I was sorry to hear about his suspension.

"Don't be concerned, Willie. I enjoyed the extra vacation."

After three months at BCH, I was promoted from fellow to assistant resident. My predecessor had just been drafted. On this occasion, I was surprised at Dr. Heusner's new attitude toward me.

"You were promoted because you've done the scut work with diligence and dedication. Now you are to tell other people to do it, instead of doing it yourself. If anyone gives you any trouble, just let me know. Also, if you need help, call me directly. You are going to have more opportunities to operate on service cases, with one of us looking on, but you'll have to make more of your own decisions as well."

This situation developed even sooner than I expected. Leon Becker, the chief resident, really was an auto mechanic at heart. He was always working on cars when off duty, and later he built and raced cars. Also, he made some of his own surgical instruments. However, the hospital could not always locate him when he was needed for emergencies. On one such occasion, Dr. Munro became enraged at Leon and ordered me to take over his responsibilities for about ten days. During this period, I had more opportunities to assist Dr. Munro with his private patients, as well as to handle more service cases. In the meantime, Leon was happy, since he spent his suspension making more instruments for himself.

As assistant resident, I alternated with Leon on night calls. When I was on night call, I began learning to take decisive actions alone in emergencies. We wore scrub suits for pajamas on this duty and I gained valuable experience in making diagnoses.

One day during our rounds, we met a Chinese patient. He was a recent immigrant from Guangzhou, who had sustained a back injury when he was hit by a car. Dr. Heusner asked him a few questions, and found that he spoke very little English.

"We'll have to get a Chinese student in here to interpret for him," said Dr. Heusner.

"What's wrong with Willie here?" Irving Perlmutter asked.

Dr. Heusner turned and looked at me. "Well, I never thought of him as Chinese, just as one of us."

I thanked him for the compliment and interpreted for the patient. He had been in Hong Kong just before coming here, and had been used to seeing traffic on the left side of the street in the British fashion. When he had crossed a street here, he had looked the wrong way and was hit from behind. However, he was not seriously injured.

I had mixed feeling about being "just one of the boys" in the resident group. Though gratified to be considered a friend and colleague, I wondered if I was losing my identity as a Chinese. I was glad to be an American, and one of Uncle Sam's adopted nephews, but I was physically and to some extent culturally Chinese.

Really, though, there was no danger of my forgetting that. People always reminded me that I was different, even when their intentions were good. Patients who had served in the China-Burma-India Theater would ask where I was from out of curiosity. Colleagues would ask, in casual conversation, if I would be returning to China when I finished my residency.

Leon, being very generous as a chief resident, let me do some of the cases that fell to him. He also taught me how to do a myelogram, an important diagnostic test for ruptured intervertebral discs and spinal cord tumors. The procedure is simple, but doing it with little or no pain to the patient is a challenge.

One evening, an emergency operation had to be done on a compound, comminuted depressed skull fracture. It was at night, and Dr. Heusner told me to take care of it. The surgery proceeded all right, but before we began, we had to do a diagnostic spinal tap, according to Dr. Munro's standing instructions. I asked Dick Strain to do the tap, while I helped hold the patient. Someone else was clipping the patient's hair at the same time. Dick struggled with the tap, as the patient moved periodically despite being semicomatose. Finally, he told me that he had the spinal needle in the right place, but that there was no fluid.

Still holding the patient, I said briefly, "No fluid, not in." It came out sounding like pidgin English.

We argued, and he challenged me to do the tap instead. We exchanged places and I began. Luckily, my first attempt was successful and pinkish cerebro-spinal fluid dripped out of the needle.

"Well, I have to hand it to you," said Dick. He repeated, "No fluid, not in," every time he saw me during meetings after that.

My residency progressed well, overall. However, Cecile's condition was not improving.

Chapter Twenty-Six

While I was becoming acclimated to the field of neurological surgery, I also got used to the illness that plagued my wife. The Sagers did more than yeoman duty in looking after her. When I was not present, Bill Sager gave her the shots she needed. She was still so ill that she had to have injections every two hours, day and night. Since she had to be awakened at these intervals, I did not get much rest even on my nights off, but I was glad to be with her.

Suddenly one day, the Sagers called me at the hospital. They were frantic. Cecile had trouble breathing and could hardly swallow. Without hesitation, Leon Becker drove me home in his jalopy as fast as he could — with his interest in racing, that was fast. We carried Cecile out to his car and rushed her back to one of our neurosurgical beds.

We reported this to Dr. Munro, who was kind and sympathetic in this crisis. He examined her and then called Dr. Denny-Brown, who responded quickly and examined Cecile himself. After his examination, he adjusted her medication and ordered his chief resident to have the respirator available. Her condition remained critical, so Dr. Munro and Leon Becker told me to forget about my hospital duties for the time being and stay with her.

Under the care and supervision of Dr. Denny-Brown and his staff, she gradually improved, but only slightly. She could only get out of bed with help, and could only swallow food that did not require chewing. To eat, she had to lie down and aid her swallowing by a jerky movement of her head. Her voice was unusually nasal and could hardly be understood.

I stayed with her on my nights off, and whenever the night had no calls. When she became too fatigued to hold a pencil, we simply held hands. After she fell asleep, I would kiss her good-night and leave. This routine continued for about three months.

Dr. Denny-Brown, being an excellent physician, always took time out from his teaching and research duties to visit Cecile. Though she and I realized that he could not do very much, we found his afternoon visits comforting and reassuring. Cecile looked forward to it each day. As a doctor, I realized then that seeing each patient daily was a very important element in the art of medicine.

At that time, Dr. Denny-Brown had plans in mind that we were not aware of. About a month after her hospitalization, he drew me aside and discussed the possibility of radiating her thymus gland, since she was too weak to take any surgical procedure. He told me that some people in England had experienced success with this technique. Cecile and I of course agreed, and she received a series of radiation treatments.

Her improvement from this therapy was discernible, but not dramatic. Even after a few weeks, I still could not understand any more of her speech. She could swallow more easily, but still had to jerk her neck in order to force the food down. Though life had become more bearable, Cecile was getting discouraged.

When the end of 1946 approached, Dr. Munro secured a new position for me at the Cushing V.A. Hospital in Framingham, Massachusetts. He thought my year with him had given me a strong background in dealing with trauma to the head, neck, and back, but we had seen very few brain tumors and cervical and lumbar spine problems. Residents were not allowed to do those operations at BCH, anyway. At Cushing, I would have the opportunity for a wider variety of cases.

Cushing V.A. Hospital had been converted from an Army Hospital during World War II. Newer than BCH, it was staffed by the neurosurgical department of Massachusetts General Hospital. Drs. J.C. White, William H. Sweet, Thomas Ballantine, and Sam Louis carried out most of the teaching. Since there were two full wards of paraplegics, Dr. Munro was a consultant here.

We worked harmoniously, in a more relaxed atmosphere than I had during my previous year at BCH. An additional year of maturity and experience made the most difference, and Dr. Munro had ruled partly through fear at BCH, though he could also be kind and helpful.

The staff at Cushing established a different kind of rapport.

In the fall of 1947, I received a letter from Dr. Viets inviting me to attend the First International Meeting of Myasthenia Gravis, which would be held at Massachusetts General Hospital. At the meeting, I listened to Geoffrey Keynes talk about the one hundred thymectomies he had performed on myasthenics in England. His statistics indicated that young female patients who had suffered from the disease less than three years improved markedly. Some needed no further medication and others required only minimal doses. Many regained their health to a normal or near-normal degree. This was so encouraging that I was unable to pay attention to the rest of the meeting.

That evening, I told Cecile about it, and we discussed it with Dr. Denny-Brown. He talked to Dr. Viets about the possibilities, especially in relation to Cecile's depression. Her slow progress was eroding her will to live. Dr. Viets reluctantly approved our decision to have a thymectomy done on Cecile. He arranged to have Cecile moved to MGH and made special preparations for her.

Then, the day before the surgery was planned, the arrogant and unsympathetic resident informed me that he would not schedule the operation unless I produced two units of the correct blood by the next day. This looked impossible on short notice. Bill Sager and Harold Kwart, another Ph.D. candidate at Harvard with Bill, donated blood. So did our friend Frank Judge, a Canadian graduate student at the Harvard School of Business. We offered our heart-felt gratitude, but we needed more. Finally, I called Kirk Swan for advice that night.

"Don't worry, Willie," he said. "I'll have two units of blood for you tonight."

He took two units from his surgical service and sent them over to MGH for Cecile's operation. I thanked him profusely, and told him that I was indebted to him forever.

Dr. Oliver Cope performed the thymectomy. I watched from the gallery as he did a sternum-splitting incision and then removed the thymus gland. The operation was completed successfully.

Dr. Benjamin Castleman, Chairman of the Department of Pathology, reported no malignancy. This good news was followed by

205

an immediate improvement in Cecile's overall condition. However, her prescribed level of prostigmine now caused an adverse reaction. An overdose of the drug could be as dangerous as lack of medication would have been before the thymectomy. Instead of taking the medication at the same level, Cecile secretly began to stockpile the extra amount. When she was about to be released from the hospital, she showed her cache to Dr. Viets. This surprised him, but when he realized that she was much improved, he was pleased. If she had not saved the extra medicine, the overdose would have killed her. He could hardly believe she had improved so fast.

After she had been discharged, we returned to the Sager's home.

My position at Cushing was due to end in December of 1947. I had accepted a fellowship to follow it at the Lahey Clinic. However, while Cecile was recovering favorably from her thymectomy, I received a call from the Lahey Clinic, saying that their position would open early, at the first of November. The Cushing administration was kind enough to let me go, as I wished.

I had begun to feel at home at Cushing, and I had enjoyed the guidance of some of the field's outstanding doctors. However, the arrangement at the Lahey Clinic would allow me to spend much more time with Cecile. Their fellows were given a stipend, but no room and board. We would take our calls at home when on duty and we were rotated between the New England Baptist Hospital and the Deaconess.

Cecile's daily rebound from the operation continued. She took only a few prostigmine tablets a day now, instead of thirty or more ampules every twenty-four hours. We had a new life, with a future.

As a result, the ambience of the whole Sager household began to change. Everything seemed lighter. I had to get up earlier now, to drive our old Ford to the Clinic or one of the hospitals. One morning, Corky Sager, the Sagers' first daughter who was three years old, got up early also and asked me to fix her a bowl of corn flakes. I did, and hurried on my way.

This became a daily pattern. She was a cute, talkative child, but when I was in a hurry, I would often think of Clifton Webb in a movie in which he overturned a bowl of cereal on a child's head while babysitting. However, Corky and I became good friends.

In January of 1948, Cecile and I moved into our own apartment. We felt that we had burdened the Sagers long enough and Cecile was well enough for the move. However, we took an apartment in the same building, and Marilyn Sager would still be able to check on Cecile occasionally.

My work at the Clinic differed from my previous experience. Here, we were assigned to see patients at the Clinic just as doctors in private practice would see them in their offices. We treated some as outpatients, and had others admitted to one of the hospitals. After seeing patients in the mornings, we would assist during surgery in the afternoons. Among the many other fellows were Irving Perlmutter and Dick Strain, who had been with me at BCH.

Three staff surgeons worked here, headed by Dr. Gilbert Horrax, who had been trained by Dr. Harvey Cushing and who had worked with him for eighteen years. A stern and stately gentleman, Dr. Horrax was precise in his movements and proper in his manners. He was kind and reassuring when I first met him in his office, but he was also reserved, and without warmth. Dr. James Poppen was considered to have one of the finest surgical techniques in the country and Dr. Kenneth Livingston, a gifted surgeon, had been a fellow at the Clinic himself just a few years before.

Now that Cecile had improved enough for us to socialize, our friends began to invite us out. The first time, we were the guests of Wesley Watson and his wife; Wes was a resident under Dr. Denny-Brown and he had helped care for Cecile when she was last hospitalized. His wife was a charming young woman of Russian origin. Her parents were also there, and they all made us feel at home. Wesley was particularly attentive to Cecile, and set up a reclining chair for her at the dinner table out on the lawn.

The Antonellis invited us over, and Pat entertained us at his piano. His wife cooked a marvelous lasagna dinner. He had already given up neurosurgery, and entered a general practice because he had a family to feed.

When Cecile improved enough for us to entertain, we prepared a Chinese dinner and invited all the neurosurgical fellows and their wives, as well as Ken Livingston and his wife. Afterward, we found ourselves pleased, very tired, and somewhat astonished to be back in social activities. Our friends reciprocated, and we gradually established a closer bond with many of them. We also got to know some of the surgical nurses, who helped the fellows immensely, especially at first.

The first time Cecile and I ever watched television, we saw the Harvard-Yale football game of 1948 at Dick Strain's. It interested all of us, but we were quiet most of the time. I felt that watching television was a social hindrance.

The senior fellow at the Clinic was usually Dr. Horrax's first assistant in surgery. The rest of us, in order of seniority, would assist Dr. Poppen, and then Dr. Livingston. Each of us looked forward to our infrequent opportunities to be the first assistant to Dr. Horrax, but the night before that chance would arrive, we were usually ridden with anxiety.

Dr. Horrax was meticulous, always exact and neat, but he also complained constantly, with mild cliches. The first time I assisted him, I was so nervous that I was actually trembling.

"You smoke too much, Dr. Wu," he said. "Help me, just gently. No jerky movements; my goodness gracious."

The scrub nurse came to my rescue. Every time I was not sure what to do, Miss Weggie put an instrument into my hand. Dr. Horrax was so intent on his work that he gave very little actual instruction. Occasionally, when an anatomic structure such as the optic nerve or the chiasm was exposed, he would point it out. "Just take a peep. My goodness gracious, don't get so close. Hold this retractor, gently now, that's it. Come on, help me, suction and coagulate quickly!"

Dr. Horrax always gave orders as though his assistants had no idea what to do, but late in the operation he would turn the patient over to his first assistant, saying, "Thank you. Close it neatly and make sure that all bleeding points have stopped." He trusted us more than his words indicated.

In addition to the more glamorous surgical exercises, we also attended weekly conferences in radiology and pathology. On Saturday mornings, the senior fellow was in charge of a review of all our X-rays, pneumoencephalograms, ventriculograms, and arteriograms. We would give a brief history of each case and exchange opinions. The staff men also sat in, and we were gratified to have a fairly high percentage of correct diagnoses.

On Wednesday evenings, Dr. William Meisner held sessions on microscopic pathology. First he would show us slides of cells taken from certain kinds of benign and malignant brain tumors. Then unidentified slides would be distributed, and we would have to identify them.

These sessions, as well as our daily activities with patients, took us along the road to becoming neurosurgeons. I was prompted to remember, however, a comment by Dr. Munro back at BCH: "Specialists are a dime a dozen, but a good doctor is hard to find." Pure medical knowledge was only a part of the art of medicine.

Life was improving quickly now. Cecile was now definitely on the road to recovery, and we had much time together.

Chapter Twenty-Seven

In the spring of 1948, Cecile phoned me at work to say that a Chinese student at Harvard had called. He knew us, and thought we might like to meet two visitors from China. We invited all three of them to dinner that weekend.

His guests were a Dr. Chang and a Dr. Lau, members of a recruiting team from a medical center called Shangya. Known in English as Yale-in-China, this center lay in the city of Changsha, south of Lake Dongting. They were seeking medical specialists to come work at their center.

I had been hoping for this kind of opportunity since before World War II. We discussed their hospital, their equipment, and their staffs, both in the hospital and in their medical school. They offered me a position, with generous benefits. I would be allowed to organize a new department of neurosurgery, with a fund adequate to purchase neurosurgical equipment and an EEG laboratory. An animal lab would also be available. Cecile was willing to go. I told them I was interested.

Dr. Chang asked if I knew of a good hematologist who might also be interested in their center. I suggested Dr. Shuchu Shen, who was working in Harvard's Thorndike Laboratory at BCH. At the time, he was further advanced in his field than I, so I knew he would be sufficiently qualified. They later contacted him and found that he was also interested.

About a month later, I received an urgent letter from the wife of Paul Kwan, my old fraternity roommate who had worked at PUMC. I had never met his wife Anna, but she was writing to me for help. She explained that since I had last seen Paul in Beijing, he had first opened a surgical practice with a colleague in Shanghai, and then had spent the war years in Hong Kong. Now, however, he was ill with cancer of the colon. Her letter was self-sacrificing and heart-rending;

she wanted him to come to the U.S. for further treatment, regardless of what might happen to her.

I could not help her directly, but I contacted Dr. Frederick Coller in Ann Arbor, who remembered Paul well. As Professor and Chairman of the Department of Surgery at the University Hospital at Michigan, Dr. Coller wrote back, compassionately offering Paul a job in his own department of surgery at Michigan. This would allow Paul, a U.S. citizen, to return to the U.S. and earn a living while he received more treatment.

Paul arrived in Michigan a month after that, and wrote to me. Dr. Coller had examined him and told him that he needed another operation. Unfortunately, his cancer had spread, and only palliative relief could be accomplished. Dr. Coller gave Paul a position as an anesthetist. This allowed him to work sitting down. All of us knew his days were limited.

At home, Cecile and I continued to enjoy a greater social life. Harold Kwart, one of the donors who had given blood for Cecile's thymectomy, and his wife Helen invited us to the Toll House outside of Boston. There we ate boiled lobster dinners for the first time. Cecile required only one injection of prostigmine to attack the lobster. On the way home, she complained of fatigue in her hands and jaw, but she had been able to eat a real meal out, sitting up normally without choking.

On another evening in 1948, we attended a special convocation at M.I.T., as the guests of our friends George and Sally Cherniak. The speaker was Sir Winston Churchill.

The restless and anxious crowd in the packed auditorium waited for Churchill to appear. World War II had only been over for three years, and he was a genuine hero. Finally, President Killian of M.I.T. escorted him to center stage, to a standing ovation.

President Killian approached the podium to introduce Sir Winston, but as soon as Sir Winston sat down on the stage, he recognized some dignitaries seated in the front row. He casually got up, waved, and walked to the edge of the stage to chat. His leonine face wore a smile and he walked about the stage greeting friends while President Killian stood awkwardly at the podium. Finally, the President introduced him, and he spoke.

Churchill's booming voice was familiar from all the wartime radio broadcasts and movie newsreels. His voice permeated every corner of the auditorium. He spoke in a relaxed manner, looking straight ahead through his horned-rim glasses. Although I listened as though spellbound, I later remembered his presence, not his words. When he had finished, he gave us the V-sign with his fingers.

The audience applauded and gave him another standing ovation.

Not long afterward, another reminder of the war reached me. Cecile and I were walking through Harvard Square at lunch time when I heard someone shouting my name.

"Major Wu!" The voice was familiar, but I could not identify it.

I looked around and saw a young man walking forward quickly, with a big smile. He extended his hand and we shook. I introduced Cecile to him, still trying to remember who he was.

"I'm no longer Major Wu," I said. "You're not a G.I. any more, either." Then I recognized him. He was the persistent soldier from Chongqing who had kept complaining about a digestive problem. We embraced spontaneously.

"I've quoted you many times," he said. "You remember how I kept pestering you doctors every day about my bloody stools? You told me to eat more Chinese food and eat less in the mess hall. I followed your advice and never had any more trouble. In fact, I've told many people about your advice. I still eat at Yee Hong Guey once a week here in Boston's Chinatown."

"I'm glad I could help," I said, laughing. Apparently that army food had been even worse than all the jokes implied. "It's good to see you again." Cecile and I both wished him luck.

As he walked away, across Massachusetts Avenue, he slung a gray book bag over his shoulder with "Harvard" printed on the side. I was glad he was doing well, and flattered that he recognized me, based on a casual remark I had completely forgotten.

During that fall of 1948, I came under greater pressure in my training program. As a senior fellow at the Clinic, I carried more responsibility than before. With the help of Miss Samsel, the chief neurosurgical nurse, I assigned assistants to scrub with the staff

212

neurosurgeons and I also organized the weekly meetings. I was generally the first assistant to Dr. Horrax, though it was not always possible. By this time, I had become acclimated to his idiosyncracies and was able to concentrate on mastering his surgical technique.

Contracts arrived from Yale-in-China for Dr. Shen and myself. However, the news from China had been bad for some time, and a Communist victory seemed imminent. Dr. Shen and I met several times to discuss the situation. Our positions were due to start in the coming summer of 1949, but we decided to wait and see what would happen.

My training at the Clinic would end in June of 1949. As that time approached, I began to hear the future plans of my colleagues. Irving Perlmutter and Dick Strain decided to go into private practice together in Florida. Ernie Sachs joined the staff of the Hitchcock Clinic at Dartmouth. Others went off to different parts of the country.

My own dream of returning to China was shattered by the turmoil there. The political situation became more unstable and unpredictable. Even if I had been willing to risk the environment myself, I would not consider taking Cecile, whose health was still fragile. Despite her improvement, she might still need sophisticated medical care in the future.

While I was reaching this conclusion, Dr. Jost J. Michelson offered me a position as an assistant in his practice. The salary was minimal, but it was just barely adequate. I accepted the position.

At the end of June, I left the Clinic with blessings and kind words from Dr. Horrax and Dr. Poppen. Their tolerance and guidance had been crucial to me. They had also helped me write my first scientific papers. The first, written with Dr. Horrax, was on oligodendrogliomas; the second, written with Preston Weadon and Dr. Poppen, was on benign tumors of the spinal cord. The article on oligodendrogliomas appeared in the Journal of Neurosurgery, and the one of benign tumors of the spinal cord was published in Surgical Clinics of North America. Now, having finished my training at the Lahey Clinic, I was ready for private practice.

I found private practice to be a radical change from training. Though I consulted with my senior partner frequently, most judgments and decisions were mine to make. At the same time, when I was treating patients I thought were my responsibility, Dr. Michelsen would sometimes take over, and utilize my services merely as an assistant. Though I now had opportunities to work at prestigious institutions, such as MGH, through Dr. Michelsen's influence, I felt that I had the burdens of private practice without the benefits. In many ways, my position with Dr. Michelsen was much like a residency.

Even so, I did continue to learn from Dr. Michelsen, not only in surgical technique, but in handling referring physicians, patients, and their families. Also, I became something of an itinerant neurosurgeon. We operated frequently at the Malden Hospital in a suburb of Boston, and once a week at Phillipsburg. We even took occasional trips to Cape Cod. Since Dr. Michelsen had a Buick Roadmaster, a chauffeur, and a private surgical nurse, these trips could be quite pleasant diversions from the routine. However, I was known only as Dr. Michelsen's assistant, and had no professional identity of my own.

I discussed this with Cecile and with some of my former colleagues still at the Clinic. Finally, I told Dr. Michelsen that I was not happy with the arrangement. He promised to alter the situation, but nothing changed. Several months later, in the winter of 1949-50, Cecile and I began to consider leaving the area so I could try establishing private practice on my own.

Before we reached a conclusion, I had one of my more unusual patients of this time. He was a lobster fisherman who had been in partnership with his grown son. His son had been drafted into the armed services and the father came in shortly afterward complaining of stomach trouble and various other aches and pains. Neurosurgical tests showed nothing. Consultations with internists revealed no organic disease. One day I took the time to talk with him at length about his illness. His real desire was to get his son back on a hardship basis, because at his age he could not run his fishing business alone. I explained this to the Red Cross and asked them to pursue his hardship claim.

In the spring, Cecile and I had decided to leave Boston. When I told Dr. Michelsen, he was surprised.

"You will find it hard to get along on your own, as an American of Chinese origin," he said. "If it doesn't work out, you may always come back here."

I thanked him. We parted as friends, but he had also issued me a challenge. I believe that most Americans are fair-minded and if one is conscientious in his profession, they will recognize it. I had this impression when I was in the armed service.

One day when Cecile was home alone, a very large woman of Italian descent came to the door. She asked Cecile if she had a laundry basket. Cecile gave it to her, and a few minutes later the woman returned with thirty-one live lobsters, covered with seaweed and salt water. It was a gift in return, she said, for my help to her family. Somewhat shocked, Cecile put the basket of large, lively creatures in the kitchen and locked the door.

Obviously, the son of the lobster fisherman had been released from the armed services to help support his family. Cecile and I invited all our friends at Harvard and M.I.T. to dinner. We also delivered some lobsters to Dr. Shen and his wife. Harold Kwart had to borrow a huge cauldron from the chemistry lab in order to cook them all. It was the biggest lobster feast any of us had ever had, and a fitting farewell to New England for Cecile and myself.

In April of 1950, Cecile and I had to decide where we were going to go. We considered the outskirts of Boston, but a Dr. Carmody of Wooster advised against it.

"You are welcome here," he said. "However, I must tell you that practicing near Boston is not an ideal situation. People from New England, and farther, are attracted to the big medical centers in Boston. We in the suburbs and outlying communities get only our local patients, and the total population is much lower."

"I see." His logic was sound, and I felt he was sincere.

"However, Boston is an excellent springboard. With your training there, you should be able to migrate anywhere, and the farther away, the better."

I thanked him for his advice, and crossed off Massachusetts.

Cecile, using her experience with the Army Map Service, then began to chart the number of neurosurgeons per 100,000 people in a number of cities that we would consider. With the results, and our own regional preferences, we narrowed the field to Washington, D.C., Cleveland, Kansas City, Denver, Albuquerque, and Salt Lake City. The lease on our apartment would run out at the end of June, so we had two months to decide where to go.

In late April, we set out in our old 1941 Ford for Washington. There we spoke to Dr. James Watts and Dr. Walter Freeman. Dr. Watts had been to Kansas City and recommended it as a beautiful midwestern city. Our friends in Boston, who had never been there, considered it a provincial cow town. Anyway, we knew Washington, so we went on to Cleveland.

We found that Cleveland did not appeal to us. The city looked old and perhaps larger than what we wanted. After two days, we left for Kansas City.

Cecile's college roommate, Peggy O'Neil, was now married and living in Kansas City. We contacted Jim and Peggy Hunt, who put us up for a few days. We arrived on a cool and rainy day in early May.

The Hunts showed us the city, and we were intrigued by it. It was well planned, and full of budding trees and flowers. However, we wanted to see Denver and Salt Lake City, as planned, before reaching a decision.

Denver, the mile-high city, lay clean and distinctive beneath the beautiful, snow-capped mountains. However, I found that in the medical field, a large gap existed between gown and town — the physicians in academia were not on good terms with those in private practice. We decided against Denver.

Our old Ford was nine years old by this time, but we had added a new engine and a set of tires. Even so, we gave it its greatest challenge in crossing first the Rockies and then the desert on the way to Salt Lake City. Cecile was familiar with the car. Before entering the Army, I had sold it to her for one dollar in a formal transaction so she could use it. Knowing its quirks helped us. The car met the challenge, climbing the old mountain roads and passing newer and bigger cars that had pulled off to the side to cool their radiators. We watched our water level carefully, and also drove through the desert safely, even in the early summer heat.

Our Ford was probably one of the oldest cars on the road, but even going up the steep grades, we left Cadillacs and Lincolns behind. One particular Lincoln, driven by a middle-aged couple, did keep up with us. We stopped at the same gas station at about the same time on a number of occasions one day. Finally, the driver came over to me.

"I've been very curious about your buggy," he said. "It's good advertising for the Ford Motor Company. How have you managed to keep up with us, in our brand new Lincoln?"

"Well, we did put a new engine in it," I admitted. I was tempted not to tell him, but wanted to be honest.

"I see. Well, good luck."

Salt Lake City had majestic mountains on the north, east, and south, with the Great Salt Lake on the west. We visited a few hospitals and met some Chinese interns and residents. After a short time, we felt quite at home. In addition, Dr. Price, Dean of the Medical School at the University of Utah, told me that he had taught in China and he offered me a position at the University until I could establish my own practice. This was tempting, but we decided against moving here. While we knew little about the Mormon religion one way or another, Cecile felt that we should not become a minority within another minority. With some reluctance, we returned to Kansas City.

In Kansas City, I began to arrange a private practice. First, I had to get my Missouri State License, which I obtained through the state's reciprocity with Massachusetts. Then I contacted all the hospitals large enough to handle neurosurgical practice. At every hospital I visited, I was told that they had enough neurosurgeons on their staffs, and that they did not see many patients requiring that specialty. The last hospital, St. Mary's, was the only exception. The first person I met there was Dr. Arthur Altringer, a large, pleasant man. He asked if he could help, and took me to see the Sister Superior, administrator of the hospital.

The Sister Superior was cordial, but explained that she did not make staff appointments. She introduced me to Dr. James O'Neil, president of the staff. He did give me an application, which I filled out in his office. It was not much of a breakthrough, but it was all I had.

Cecile and I drove back to Boston dejected, with all our hopes on that one application. On May 15, I still had no word on it, and we had to find a place to live after the month of June. I sent a telegram to Dr. O'Neil, asking him to expedite my application and give me an answer.

Finally a letter arrived from Dr. O'Neil informing me that I had been accepted as a courtesy member of the staff. From that joyous moment, Cecile and I had one week to pack and hire a moving van to transport our basic belongings to the middle of the country. We hurried to start a new life in Kansas City, arriving in August of 1950.

Peggy and Jim Hunt kindly put us up while we looked for an apartment. It took us several months. I also could not find office space right away, until I was able to rent one in the heart of Kansas City in the Argyle Building.

Meanwhile, I applied for membership in the Jackson County Medical Society. My regular appointment at the hospital required this membership, though interns and residents did not need it. To save overhead, Cecile began working as my secretary.

Day after day, we had no patients. In the mornings, I would go to St. Mary's and try to get acquainted with physicians looking for a consultation. Most of them spent little time in the lounge because they were seeing patients. The surgeons would hurry in, perform surgery, and leave again. All were cordial, but few bothered to introduce themselves or ask who I was. After six weeks without patients, I began to get worried.

Occasionally, Cecile or I would say, "Let's sell the furniture and go back to Boston." Sometimes it was a joke, and sometimes not.

Cecile was already pregnant when we moved to Kansas City. However, we only learned of it after moving, from T.K. Lin, a Chinese American intern at St. Luke's Hospital. We were elated. Her condition had been considered unlikely because of her myasthenia, especially after her thymectomy.

Yet her symptoms actually improved during her pregnancy to the point where she required only minimal doses of her medication.

She acted much more like she had before becoming ill. During the last trimester, she hardly took any prostigmine. Later, we learned that pregnancy often puts myasthenia into remission, but only for the course of the pregnancy.

I asked my colleagues for a referral to the best obstetricians in town. We went to Dr. Harold Gainey. He told us that he had never treated a woman with myasthenia before, but did not expect difficulty, especially because she seemed so well now. However, he did confer with a pediatrician he often worked with, Dr. Herbert Davis. I told him I had read that babies born to myasthenic mothers sometimes had temporary symptoms of the disease and we wanted to be ready if that happened to our baby.

Cecile was still in the first trimester while I tried to get more work in the fall of 1950. One evening, as we walked out of the Argyle Building, an orthopedist named Dr. Drisko came up and greeted us. He put his arm around my shoulders and said, "Don't look so downcast, Bill. I know how you feel. I started only a year ago, and had the same slow start and gloomy outlook. In fact, I had to see a doctor to calm my nerves." He assured me that matters would improve.

More time passed. Cecile and I tried to find out if any Michigan alumni were in town, and managed to contact Dr. Alvin Baer, an ophthalmologist. Two days later, he called to tell me that he had made an appointment for me with Dr. Littauer, the administrator of Menorah Hospital. I was grateful, but hesitant. I had tried to get an appointment with Dr. Littauer once and had failed to get past his assistant.

This time I saw Dr. Littauer, who was very strict but kind. After our brief meeting, he said, "It will take time to process your application, so I'll introduce you to the admitting office personnel." He did, saying, "Dr. Wu is joining our staff as a neurosurgeon. As of now, if he has patients sent in, admit them." Before we parted, he said, "If you run into any difficulties, just let me know."

I later learned that he had been a colonel in the service, and still conducted himself in the same military manner.

The next day, I had my first referral. A patient with a glioma was referred by Dr. Paul Moss. As it happened, the patient's general status was poor. I was planning diagnostic studies when the family told me they had decided against having anything done for personal reasons. Though I did not really treat this patient, I had had my first case.

I continued to receive referrals from the Menorah staff, which was very generous of them. Most of the referrals were diagnostic problems, but I came across a few surgical cases. As I made my rounds, and met various staff members, more and more of them would say, "Oh, you're the new neurosurgeon here. By the way, I have a patient for you to see at your convenience."

I felt that I had finally arrived. Cecile became excited, as calls came into the office for appointments. One of the first patients I saw at the office was a baby, nine months of age, who had a cervical meningocele without neurological involvement. By transillumination of the sac, I was able to tell that no neural elements were in it. The baby, who had been brought to me on a referral from a pediatrician at St. Mary's, did well. I had a good feeling of accomplishment, though it had been a simple case, and we cried for joy at receiving a paying case.

About this time, I got a phone call from Lawrence Louis, a fraternity brother who was now on the medical faculty at Michigan. Paul Kwan was dying. I boarded a plane the next day and flew up to see him.

Paul greeted me when I first came into the room. We shook hands and then embraced. He yelled from pain, though, and I jumped back. After a few moments with him, I realized that he was intermittently confused and disoriented. We would communicate for a few minutes, and then he would drift away again. I could do nothing to help. All I could do was say farewell.

Dr. Bob Bartlett, one of Paul's classmates, found a cemetery plot for him. I thanked Dr. Coller for his kindness toward his former student. Paul had known suffering throughout all his life, but his final months had been relatively comfortable.

I returned home. He died several days later.

During the fourteen months he had been in the U.S., I had corresponded with his wife Anna. She had no way to come to this country, even for his funeral. I could only reassure her that a friend had found a final resting place for Paul. I did not hear from her again, though I wished I could have met this selfless and courageous woman.

By this time, Cecile and I had run out of money. We had used up our wartime savings during her illness. I was unable to get a bank loan in Kansas City, since I was a newcomer without any collateral.

Fortunately, we were able to resort to some close friends. Jim King, the difficult fellow I had first met at Camp White, Oregon, loaned me five thousand dollars. Still a bachelor, he now was a commander in the navy. He assured me that I could take my time repaying the loan. Steady referrals came in, and by the end of 1950, I had made some progress financially.

However, over three months had passed since I had applied for membership in the Jackson County Medical Society. My answer was not coming through, and I began to worry. One day at St. Mary's, Dr. Max Goldman stopped me and introduced himself.

"Dr. Wu, I'm President of the Medical Society. I am very much aware of your application, but there is a by-law in the Society stating that only qualified white physicians can be admitted. I want that by-law changed, and you are the perfect test case."

"Oh?" This was not exactly good news. I had not been aware of the by-law.

He listed my credentials in chronological order. "You have training as a general surgeon, wartime experience overseas in the U.S. Army, a Bronze Star, training as a neurosurgeon with some of the world's leaders in the field — it's a perfect resumé. Your chances are very good."

I thanked him for the compliments, but I was still worried. Kansas City's General Hospitals were racially segregated. I had not realized that this problem extended to my application to the local medical society.

In fact, I later learned that I was the first Chinese American professional to live in Kansas City. Chinese Americans had lived there continuously since the 1870s, originally having settled there after working railroad construction in Colorado, Texas, and Kansas. They

221

had gone into familiar businesses such as laundries, restaurants, and curio shops, three of which were side-by-side on Twelfth Street at one time. It might have become the center of a small Chinatown, but that never developed, probably because of the federal laws limiting Chinese immigration. Even in the 1950s, immigration laws allowed much less immigration from China than from European countries. I had entered a ground-breaking position without realizing it.

"Let's sell the furniture and go back to Boston," Cecile kept saying.

Finally, in January of 1951, the medical society notified me of my admittance. That was the last hurdle to my becoming a member of the Kansas City medical profession and with the referrals I was getting, my private practice now fully got underway. Obviously, Dr. Goldman had ended the by-law. In a short time, other non-white doctors joined, as well.

In early March, Cecile went into labor. I got her to St. Mary's Hospital. After a few hours, her contractions stopped, then started again. This sequence continued for over forty-eight hours.

I did not want to offend Dr. Gainey, and refrained from interfering as long as I could. After she had spent almost three days in labor, he considered a Caesarean section. At that point, I suggested that we give her some prostigmine first, which would make her stronger; during her third trimester, she had hardly needed any. He accepted my argument, and gave her a tablet.

On the following morning, strong uterine contractions started. As she was being wheeled into the delivery room, I asked if I could be present during the delivery.

"You are welcome at any of my deliveries except this one!"

He did allow me to stand at the door of the delivery room, and in the morning of March 13, 1951, a normal delivery took place. Dr. Gainey had remained outwardly calm to this point, but he announced, "You have a healthy Wu by the name of a boy!"

We got the message, anyway.

Cecile was fine, too. Now I could see on Dr. Gainey's face that he was relieved about both of them. I had a short glance at the baby when a nurse took him to the nursery where Dr. Davis waited.

222

I was overjoyed. Happiness is always hard to measure when a new life is brought into the world to loving parents and our case was even more extreme, with a mother whose lasting illness had endangered her life on many occasions and raised serious doubts about her ability to have a child. We felt we had experienced a miracle.

After the delivery, I went to Cecile's room and waited while she recovered from her anesthetic. Dr. Davis reported that the baby was fine, without symptoms of myasthenia. However, he did advise against breast-feeding, since Cecile had resumed her normal dosage of prostigmine and it would harm the baby if it was passed to him. We hugged and kissed happily, hardly able to believe that we were the parents of a healthy baby boy. I leaned down close to Cecile and said, "This is the happiest day of my life."

In Chinese culture, a boy is considered especially desirable. We sent telegrams to my parents, informing them of the new family heir.

My parents remained in China, but we were able to get the news to them. My father immediately wrote back with the Chinese name for the baby. It was Jiaqiu, a play on words which meant both "Gem of the family" and also "At home around the world," referring to both China and the U.S. He added his fatherly advice, telling us to treat our son with love and care. That way, he would grow up to be a fine young man to carry on the family tradition of intellectual pursuits and to bring glory to the family and to the Wu Clan in general.

My father also wrote that reasoning with love was better than resorting to spanking for discipline. As I read his letters, I remembered only one occasion when I was spanked. I had ignored his admonition not to watch a certain lion dance during New Year's when two feuding clans were using the situation to provoke a real fight. I didn't understand the situation and all my friends were going to see it. He later explained, as my mother held me.

Cecile and I agreed with his principles. "Our Billy," as she named him in English, "will have our love. No doubt, we'll spoil him also. What are babies for, if not for loving and spoiling?"

Right after the birth, Cecile and the baby remained at St. Mary's, so I visited them several times a day when I had a free moment. When friends came to visit, we insisted that they stay to see the baby. The glow of happiness lingered long after mother and child came home, about a week after the birth.

We hired a student from the Kansas City Bible College to help out. Shirley was a nice and gentle young woman who enjoyed caring for the baby as much as we did. Raising a baby meant loss of sleep for us, daily baths for him, the frequent diaper changes, and worries at every yell or cry. We accepted them all gladly, and life gradually became settled at home.

My practice was still picking up, but the baby required more expenditures. My income had been meeting our expenses, but we could not save any money for emergencies, and now the baby's expenses were a problem. Again, we wrote to a friend for help.

We had known I-Mien Tsiang, a Ph.D. in political science from Johns Hopkins, for many years. Now he was working with the Trusteeship Department of the U.N. At the time we wrote to him, he was about to return to his home in Jakarta. He had been born in Indonesia of Chinese parents and had come to the U.S. for his higher education; now he was joining a commission on its way to Indonesia.

I-Mien wrote back to say that since he was leaving the country for awhile, he would not need his salary. It was being deposited in Washington, D.C. He was kind enough to send us two thousand dollars.

The money came just in time. Kansas City had been built at the junction of the Kaw and Missouri Rivers, and in the spring of 1951, they flooded. The water supply became unsafe, so we had to boil it for drinking, especially for the baby. The city conducted salvage work for weeks, and the economic activity in the city slowed down greatly. My practice suffered as well.

We managed to get through the spring, however. Summer came, and the baby grew more cute each day. I could hardly wait to get home each day to my wife and child. One day, Cecile dressed him up in a little Chinese outfit because he was going to play the part of Confucius as a baby in a church skit. When I came home, he crawled out the apartment door and down the hall to meet me.

I was very touched, and could only scoop him up and give him an endearing squeeze.

Chapter Twenty-Eight

My practice still grew slowly. Up to this time, it had been mostly trauma cases, patients with head and back injuries referred from emergency rooms. Occasionally, an orthopedist would refer a case of a ruptured intervertebral disc, but he would have the ulterior motive of learning the surgical procedure as he assisted me during the operation. Such referrals ceased after a few occasions.

Eventually, I got a referral from an internist at Menorah. However, though I had confidence in my ability to handle the case, both the patient and the doctor demanded the presence of a more experienced neurosurgeon. I suggested Bill Williamson, Chief of Neurosurgery at the University of Kansas Medical Center. He was a gentleman, and expressed a regard for my ability. After agreeing to come over, he added privately that he would not interfere with my case, but would simply fulfill the patient's request for his presence.

I took care of this case, and all went well. Apparently, partly as a result of this case, the staff began to spread approving opinions of my work throughout the hospital. Another case at the time that contributed to my confidence and reputation involved an elderly woman who had fallen.

This patient had fallen and struck her head on the right fronto-temporal region, against the front steps of the house. She had been unconscious briefly, but had regained all of her faculties. I operated on her the following day and elevated the depressed fragments of her skull to prevent further damage to the brain and the formation of a scar that might cause focal seizure. She recovered and suffered no neurologic residual defect.

In July, Marilyn Sager called to ask if we would like to go on vacation with them. We had not considered a vacation before, but we realized that we had experienced some trying times without a break. We decided to join them in Washington, D.C.

This was not a rational decision. Our bank account was extremely low, but we felt we had to use the money we had for a vacation. I recalled the words of Robert Louis Stevenson: "Decisive actions are often taken within a moment without any conscious deliverance from the rational parts of man."

A week later, we were on our way, driving our small but new Studebaker. We had been forced to replace the old Ford a few months earlier. The baby stayed in his portable crib in the back seat during the several days we spent on the road.

From Washington, we and the Sagers drove along the Sky Line Highway across the mountains to Hungry Mother Park in Virginia. There, we rented cabins located at the edge of a beautiful spring-fed lake. We forgot Kansas City for a time and fished, swam, and did some amateur painting. The Sagers listened to our difficulties and we relaxed. Soon enough, of course, the vacation ended and we were on our way home.

As we approached Kansas City, we began to worry more about how to pay for the car and the rent. At least we had a home waiting for us this time. We arrived back at the apartment just before nine P.M. one night, exhausted from the trip, and put the baby to bed.

We were making some tea when someone knocked on the door. I answered it, and found a pleasant man in his thirties.

"Is this Dr. Wu's residence?" he asked.

"Yes. I'm Dr. Wu."

"I've been waiting all week for you to get home. You operated on my mother for a skull fracture and now she's well enough to come home with me to Oklahoma. I want to settle up with you before I leave town." He paid me three hundred and fifty dollars and left.

As soon as he had gone, Cecile and I embraced excitedly and congratulated each other for our luck. As we relaxed and drank our tea, we agreed that providence must be taking good care of us now. We decided that we didn't have to worry about money any more, and slept well that night.

When we woke up the next morning, we felt that we had been given a new future once again. The baby woke up cheerful and did not even cry that morning when he was hungry. We fed him, ate breakfast ourselves, and I went confidently off to work.

Now that Cecile would be staying home with the baby, I needed a new secretary. First I hired another student from the Bible College. As a rule, I made hospital rounds in the morning, and saw patients at the office in the afternoon. This student worked only in the afternoons, and I had my answering service accept calls in the mornings. However, I needed someone who could take calls all day.

I next hired a middle-aged woman named Reynolds. She did a small amount of bookkeeping and took appointments over the phone. When she started, she requested that she leave work every day at four-thirty instead of five P.M. That was all right with me. Then several weeks later she volunteered that she was also a private detective, hired at that time to follow a man after he left work every day. She carried a gun. I felt uneasy with this situation, and her bookkeeping was not satisfactory, anyway.

Finally, through friends, I located Doris, my first real secretary. She was a good typist, a fair bookkeeper, beautiful, and friendly. Patients enjoyed talking to her, and in fact my practice picked up after I hired her.

Shortly after Doris joined me, Bill Williamson called to ask if I would be interested in a consultation out of town. I accepted, and found myself driving that night to the town of Lexington, Missouri, about twenty-five miles from Kansas City. An automobile accident had occurred there earlier in the day.

Even in my new Studebaker, I took a long time getting there. The autumn night was foggy and rainy, and one of my headlights was out. I finally found my way to the hospital and went inside.

The night supervisor explained the situation. "The patient is an elderly lady in her early seventies. Her daughter, who hasn't seen her in nine years, is her only heir. She's here, and is difficult — sometimes downright mean."

The daughter was obviously displeased when I was led into the unconscious patient's room, and even more so when I asked her to leave the room while I conducted an examination. She left reluctantly. After I determined that the patient had an epidural hematoma, I informed the daughter that an immediate operation was necessary.

"Who's going to do it?" she demanded.

"I am."

"Don't you dare!" She hurried away to call Dr. Williamson, long distance.

Bill Williamson assured her that I was capable, and reiterated that the operation was necessary without delay.

"He said you'll do," she said to me doubtfully.

The procedure itself was not too difficult, but the age of the patient made the situation precarious. The operation succeeded, but I was concerned about the patient's postoperative course, so I stayed in the hospital throughout the night. Her condition stabilized, but she remained unconscious. During the week that followed, I continued to make daily visits out to Lexington to check on her.

The patient began running temperatures as high as one hundred and five degrees fahrenheit. I had to resort to placing her in wet sheets with fans blowing on her. Her daughter objected strenuously to this apparently primitive method, declaring that her mother would catch pneumonia "for sure." The patient did not, though, and returned to consciousness after a few days. She then began a slow but definite recovery. A month after her admission to the hospital, she was up and about.

During this time, I made daily trips of about fifty miles each to see her. On Sundays, I took my wife and baby along for the company. The patient's daughter gradually became more cordial.

Apparently, the word spread throughout this small community that a new neurosurgeon had performed a "miraculous" operation. The hospital staff asked if I would come out once a week to see their neurological and neurosurgical patients. I felt flattered by the invitation, and did this for about two years, until I could no longer afford the time.

The people of Lexington, Missouri, were honest and hardy, as well as friendly and considerate. The Chamber of Commerce once invited me to speak at a luncheon. Later, when I had to tell the local physicians that I could no longer make weekly trips, they either referred patients to my office or sent them to a hospital in Kansas City where I could see them.

I missed the weekly trips through rural Missouri, with its fresher air and sunshine, despite the occasional smell of fertilizer. The most startling sight, however, were the many signs along the Missouri River reading, "Fresh Fried Cats." My curiosity finally forced me to ask what they meant, and I learned that they served deep-fried catfish fresh out of the river.

By this time, I had joined the staffs of several private hospitals in addition to the Children's Mercy Hospital and the two Kansas City General Hospitals, which were racially segregated. At that time, General Hospital I was for white patients and General II was for blacks. I took six-month rotations at General I on the attending staff for charity patients. However, I was the only attending neurosurgeon for General II.

My own practice picked up steadily, but I still had time to attend indigent patients at the General Hospitals. I spent so much time there that some of the general surgeons thought I was the new resident. These hospitals did not have an established neurosurgical service. Instead, the residents in general surgery cared for neurosurgical cases under the supervision of the attending neurosurgical staff.

I received calls at these hospitals for a variety of injuries. Some were due to automobile accidents, falls, or dives into shallow water. Others were due to gunshots in fights, crimes, or accidents. I also saw a number of attempted suicides, with self-inflicted gunshot wounds to the head. Despite intense efforts to treat them, most of the last group became fatalities. I believe the reason is that such patients lacked the will to live.

One patient who had attempted suicide had shot himself in the frontal tip of the right cortex. Under the proper treatment, he recovered without difficulty. A year later, he shot himself in the right frontal lobe, more deeply and more to the posterior. In fact, he had given himself a pre-frontal lobotomy. We treated him successfully, and he recovered again. We teased him, suggesting that if he was going to shoot himself again, he should do it right, so that we wouldn't have to deal with him again. He laughed, and did not make any more suicide attempts. In fact, he changed significantly. He became a useful citizen, working for his mother as a produce truck driver. We saw him at the clinic from time to time for minor injuries or illnesses. I wondered if this change had resulted from his unintentional pre-frontal lobotomy.

As my practice grew, I found myself spending more and more time driving from one hospital to the next every day. I wanted to spend more time with my wife and growing boy, but my obligation to my patients prevented this. In addition to the Independence Sanitarium and Hospital, which I had to visit several times a week, I stopped at four hospitals in Kansas City every day. Cecile was very understanding, but I began to feel guilty.

In 1954, my income had improved to the point where we were able to buy a house. We moved to Prairie Village, a suburb of Kansas City just across the state line in Kansas. Also in that year, when Billy was four, we joined the Kansas City Cooperative Preschool for him.

Cecile had resumed her creative writing, and had sold her first short story to the New Yorker. She became more interested in poetry, however, and sold a poem entitled "Heredity" to Good Housekeeping. This was translated and published in Italian, and was reprinted many years later as a frontispiece piece in the textbook Genetics, by Robert King of Northwestern University. The scientific journal Perspectives in Biology and Medicine also used, one of Cecile's poems called "Recapitulation."

She began publishing many poems in the Kansas City Star. Then she joined the Diversifiers, a group of successful women poets. They met once a month to read and criticize each other's poems, which were presented to the group anonymously.

Billy took after his mother in this area. Even before he was able to read and write, he made up very brief stories which his mother wrote down for him. He would then illustrate them, and his mother made a little book out of the pages. As he grew older, he continued writing stories and sometimes poetry.

In the spring of 1957, a couple we knew went to the Jackson County, Missouri, adoption agency in the hope of adopting a baby. In the course of the conversation, they learned that the agency was hoping to find a home for a baby whose ancestry was Chinese, or perhaps half Chinese. Our friends notified us, and we became very interested.

Since I was at work, Cecile called the social worker in charge every twenty minutes for much of the day. She finally got through and made an appointment for us the next morning. The appointment went well; we explained that we wanted another child, described Cecile's mysasthenia gravis, and reported my income. They gave us forms to fill out. Cecile was so happy that she later said it reminded her of the moment in 1950 when she had been told she was pregnant.

At that time, potential adoptive parents were usually visited by a social worker over a period of a year or two. Since the baby now in question was due to be born at the end of the summer, we had only the summer in which to pass the agency's inspection. On top of that, we were interviewed by five different social workers.

We also considered the question of the baby's exact ancestry. Obviously, the mother was of Chinese descent, but the agency had not told us the father's race. If the baby was of mixed Chinese and white parentage, we felt it might be best if it turned out to be a girl. That way, the baby could grow up to identify with Cecile and her mixed parentage. In fact, we knew one mixed couple whose son was blond. Cecile had black hair, so if the baby did turn out to be blond, it would still stand out. If the baby was completely Chinese, we hoped it would be a boy who could then identify with me. Since Billy appeared fully Chinese, despite his single white grandparent, a younger brother could identify with him, as well. Of course, this was all just speculation, since no one had any control over the baby's sex anyway.

This matter of family identification also arose when Cecile introduced the idea of adoption to Billy, who was six years old. She explained that one family down the street whom we knew had adopted their son and daughter, and another family in the neighborhood had adopted a daughter he knew. He thought about this, but did not react with enthusiasm.

Finally, he asked her to start at the beginning and explain what she was talking about. When she told him that we had become interested because the baby was Chinese, he sighed with relief. "You didn't tell me they had that kind of babies," he said.

One of the social workers came to interview Billy while I was at work. He had not been shy at all until the age of three, but he had been quite reserved around strangers since then. When the social worker arrived, he was nicely dressed, fed, and in a good mood, but he crawled under the dining room table with a sign he had made. It said "yes" on one side and "no" on the other, attached to a stick.

As the social worker asked him if he liked children, would like a younger brother or sister, and if he was happy, he stuck the sign out from under the table with his answer on it. While this discussion continued, Cecile sat quietly on the couch, smiling but very worried about the impression it was making.

The fifth and final social worker came next. She was very supportive, though Cecile still made a point of not discussing our concerns about whether the appearance of a mixed-race baby would be difficult for it while growing up with us. We knew from friends that one wrong comment could eliminate a couple from consideration by the agency.

On September 7, 1957, this social worker called Cecile at home and said, "Your baby has been born." However, she did not know what sex it was.

Cecile called an obstetrician friend of ours, Dr. Bob Lamar. He made a few rounds and called back, saying, "I found him — a beautiful boy!"

We still had to go before a Jackson County judge and declare that we wanted to adopt the baby. In addition, we had to wait a customary six weeks before bringing him home, while the authorities made sure he was healthy. Finally the day came when we would go pick him up.

I usually drove Billy to school each day. However, that morning, Cecile looked out our second-floor bedroom window and saw him walking down the driveway. She called to him and asked where he was going.

"To school," he said.

"Dad always takes you," she said, puzzled.

"Well, I thought if you were getting a new baby, you wouldn't care about me any more."

Cecile told him to wait and hurried downstairs and outside. She told him that when we picked up the baby, we would bring him to the school so Billy could see him. In the meantime, of course, I drove him to school as usual.

At mid-morning, we picked up the baby and drove to Billy's elementary school. He was in the first grade, with a pleasant, experienced teacher. When we arrived, he came bouncing out and said, "Mrs. Brown says I can bring him in for show and tell."

In fact, she suggested that he introduce the baby to the class and explain the adoption process.

Startled, Cecile asked me if it was safe to expose the baby to the germs of so many people. I told her that he would have natural immunity from his mother for the first few months of his life, so this was a safe time to do it. We agreed it would be a good education for the class and a chance for Billy to participate in the adoption.

We had Billy sit in a chair in front of the class, and his mother gave him the baby. He held his new brother on his lap and explained the adoption, as we had explained it to him. Then the startled first-graders began asking many questions, which Cecile and I answered. When the questions ended, Mrs. Brown thanked us and we took the baby home.

That night, I baby-sat while Cecile attended a routine mothers' meeting at the school. She found all the mothers of Billy's class-mates converging on her to find out what we had done. Apparently, the explanation of adoption had not been clear to the kids, because they had told their mothers a multitude of stories. One reported that we had just been walking along the sidewalk and found the baby. Another, whose mother had seen Cecile in the supermarket the day before, clearly not about to give birth, had claimed she had just given birth this morning. Of course, Cecile set the record straight and left them to explain the adoption process to their own children all over again.

Soon after that, a number of women in the neighborhood gave Cecile a baby shower.

We named the baby Christopher, in honor of Christina Helm. My father approved, and gave him the Chinese name Jialan, meaning "Family Orchid." He was a happy and lovable baby.

Chris was a big baby with a healthy appetite and he grew quickly, remaining big for his age. However, we noticed that his legs were bowed. When he was six months old, we consulted an orthopedist at the Dickson-Diveley Clinic, who recommended leg braces. These heavy steel braces were placed on his legs and he had to wear them for two years, day and night. Cecile and I felt sorry for him because they were obviously uncomfortable and difficult to move. However, he learned to walk with them at a normal age and even climbed stairs in them. They did their work, and his legs were straight by the time they were taken off.

Surgeons generally have no reason for a house call, but I made one during this time as a favor to Dr. Sidney Pakula, dean of Kansas City pediatricians, who also took care of our two kids.

This child had had his tonsils removed by a well-qualified otolaryngologist, under anesthesia by a well-trained anesthesiologist. Yet after the operation, the child did not regain consciousness, day after day. All tests relevant to the situation were performed, but turned up no information. The child remained somnolent with vital signs well within normal limits. I was not consulted until after the child had been brought home. My only judgment was that the child might have viral encephalitis. This had no specific treatment, only supportive therapy. I told his parents that I was optimistic that the child would awaken and grow up with minimal brain damage, but I never saw him again.

My private practice developed during these years. I worked long hours, usually seven days a week, and gradually such habits paid off. For the first time, we had some financial security.

In 1959, we spent three weeks in Honolulu. We took Cecile's niece, Marilyn Ann Franking, who was a teenager, to help watch the boys. It was a true vacation for the rest of my family, but I spent the trip learning a controversial new procedure for anterior cervical discectomy and interbody fusion of the cervical spine — basically, a surgical procedure involving the spine accomplished by entering the front of the neck. This procedure had been developed by Dr. Ralph

Cloward of Honolulu, with whom I had arranged to work for two weeks.

Each morning, I went to Queen's Hospital before 7:00 A.M. and prepared to scrub with him. He had an operation scheduled for every morning, and sometimes had two. They were not all anterior cervical fusions; I assisted him in intracranial and lumbar disc operations also. He had always been a master surgeon, and I learned from him at every surgical procedure.

Dr. Cloward was very considerate, not only to me, but to everyone, especially his patients. He and I would finish around 2:00 P.M. and he would say, "Go join your family for a swim at the beach." He did not have lunch when I was with him, and I noticed that he never invited me to join him for lunch either. On my last day with him, he surprised me by turning over the operation on anterior cervical fusion to me, while he assisted. Fortunately, all went well.

"Bill, you'll do well," he said when it was over. "You have the touch."

Dr. Cloward then drove me to his office to give me copies of some articles he had written. On the way, he pulled a sandwich from a brown bag and offered to share it with me. I declined, but at least understood why he gave the appearance of working all day without eating.

When we had first arrived in Hawaii, we had moved into a high-rise hotel. However, the lanai, or balcony, had a railing that left substantial open space just above the lanai floor. Chris, who was two years old, crawled out onto the lanai and his legs slid through the open space. When we noticed him, only the bulge of his diapers was preventing him from falling many stories to the ground. He was oblivious to the problem, since he was facing inside and had not actually fallen. When I picked him up, he was still smiling and happy.

We moved into the Halekulani, a hotel constituted entirely of individual bungalows on the ground. It also offered a feel of Hawaiian ambience that the high rise lacked, though our taxi driver told us it was known for either "newlywed or nearly dead" guests. Best of all, it lay near the beach.

Chris was equally fearless at the beach. He enjoyed jumping

into the waves and letting them wash him back up on the sand. We constantly watched him, afraid that he would be pulled out to sea instead. He was fine, however.

In contrast, Billy did not like the water much. He was nine, and spent the time at the beach making sand castles. Cecile enjoyed swimming. Her myasthenia still caused her to tire easily, of course, but the support of the water made this physical activity better for her than most forms of exercise.

We stayed in Honolulu another week after I had finished my stint with Dr. Cloward. For me, this stretch finally became a real vacation, but it ended too soon. Shortly before we left, Cecile and I took Dr. Cloward and his wife out to dinner at Lou Yu Chai, a famous Chinese restaurant. We had a fine evening together and they both enjoyed the Chinese cuisine. It was a small token of appreciation for all his help. Two days later, we were aboard the propeller plane for the nine-hour flight back to Los Angeles. Commercial jetliners were not introduced until the following year.

The trip was very enjoyable, and we arrived home pleasantly exhausted. We were greeted with bad news, however. My father had passed away in Hong Kong.

Chapter Twenty-Nine

The Communist Revolution in China had achieved victory in 1949 and the Communists had entered Guangdong Province without resistance. My father, in his first letter after they arrived, wrote that the new regime was efficient and dedicated to its principles. After the corruption and inefficiency of the Guomindang under Chiang Kaishek, he likened their coming to a new wind blowing across the Pearl River.

The good feeling did not last long. The Communists considered him one of the elite of the old society, as a scholar, and therefore an enemy of the revolution. My family lost their house and all their property. Three of my four younger brothers fled to Hong Kong.

Later, those three brothers and some friends helped my father escape to Hong Kong. However, my mother was not able to go immediately. She was imprisoned and subjected to ridicule and harassment. Eventually, she was released and went to live with my fourth brother and his new bride, who had chosen to remain in China. She and my father were separated for nine years during the 1950s, until my four brothers among them arranged for her, too, to reach Hong Kong. At that time, she told her story, emphasizing that most of her suffering had been due to a few vindictive people jealous of my father's position as a scholar. Unfortunately, she and my father had only been reunited for a year when he passed away at the age of seventy-four in 1959.

I was sorry that neither Cecile nor our children had been able to meet him. According to Chinese custom, he had given our sons their Chinese names as their grandfather. I remembered him as a gentleman whose dignified mien commanded respect wherever he appeared.

Many people had admired and revered him because of his scholarship and his willingness to champion peasants in their dealings with the local and provincial governments. Especially among the Wu Clansmen, he had been considered a lawyer, teacher, and general arbiter. In Hong Kong, he had continued to live in the company of other refugees from the Chinese Communist Revolution, with whom he had values in common.

When I was growing up, my father was strict with us, but we always knew that he loved us. We loved him, but of course we were timid around him when we had acted improperly. He usually sensed this and showed us affection in order to dispel our fears. Though he encouraged my siblings and myself to read and recite stories back to him, he also wanted us to play outdoors. "Someday you boys may have to sail out in the four seas to make your mark in life," he said. "You must be active, outgoing, and healthy."

When we had heard that my mother had reached Hong Kong safely, we had thought this particular storm in their lives had passed. However, even at my father's age, his death was a shock because his health had remained outwardly good. Not only our family, but all the Wu Clansmen, had known him as a pillar of support.

Since my father had become a Buddhist in his later years, he had left word that he wanted to be buried with Buddhist rites. My brothers and other relatives in Hong Kong carried out these wishes and my mother acquiesced. However, several days after the funeral, my mother also had my brothers arrange a memorial service in the Taoist tradition.

My father had been a Taoist most of his life, and my mother felt that this would cover all exigencies. According to this tradition, my family and close relatives were required to spend a month in mourning. As a Christian, I did not participate, but my thoughts were with them often.

When I returned from Hawaii, I wanted to try my skill at the new procedure I had just learned. About two weeks later, I had a patient whose symptoms and signs indicated that he was a candidate for this procedure. He was an architect who, according to X-rays and myelography, had a nerve pinched by a degenerated intervertebral disc and also spurring between the vertebral bodies between the cervical sixth and seventh vertebrae. These problems caused pain in his lower neck, radiating down his right arm. The basic cause of the problem was removed in the operation.

The postoperative course for this patient was characteristically uneventful. He was able to get out of bed by the second day after surgery. The healing process for the bony structures took six weeks, during which the patient was able to sit up and do paperwork and similar activities. At the end of six weeks, he resumed his normal work. I was gratified by his success.

Dr. Cloward endured a great deal of criticism for developing this procedure, for unsound reasons. It came from jealous colleagues. At a business meeting of the American Association of Neurological Surgeons, I happened to be sitting next to him when the association announced its evaluation of his operation by an ad hoc committee on neurosurgical procedures. "The Cloward procedure has benefited more patients and neurological surgeons during the past twenty years than any other," the statement concluded. Dr. Cloward said nothing, but held his head high and began jabbing me in the ribs.

During these years, Chris was a husky, rambunctious toddler; Billy was in the upper grades of elementary school. We attended PTA meetings, Cub Scout meetings, school plays, and field days. For vacations, we usually drove to the Lake of the Ozarks in Missouri, where we fished and swam. On another occasion, we went to Chicago to see Cecile's brother Al and his wife, Phyllis. We also took the train to visit friends in Houston several times.

When Chris was three years old, he developed a case of rubella. Complications from this led to encephalitis, and for a temporary time, he became hyperactive. Still big for his age, his mother found him especially difficult to handle with her mysasthenia. However, she discovered that he enjoyed bowling. He had in fact made his first strike at the age of three, by putting a light ball between his feet and rolling it forward with both hands. When he became hyperactive, she took him bowling often to work off his extra energy. Even after he became well again, he continued to bowl whenever he could.

In 1963, when Billy was in the sixth grade and President of the Student Council, and Chris was in kindergarten, we decided that they were old enough to travel overseas. I also felt that it was time for Cecile to meet her mother-in-law and my other relatives in Hong Kong. My father's death was still on my mind, and I wanted to take my family to see my mother as soon as we could. Cecile agreed, and we began to make plans for a trip to East Asia. We arranged to take both boys out of school on the grounds that this was a special occasion, and departed in April, 1963.

On jetliners this trip, we flew much faster than on our trip to Hawaii. We stopped in Los Angeles the first night and checked into a small Hyatt House near the airport. The woman behind the counter looked at my confirmation of our reservations and whispered to herself, "Dr. Wu ... Kansas City ...."

I looked at her, curious.

"Now I remember!" she exclaimed. "You're the doctor who saw our baby at our house when he was very ill. Dr. Pakula brought you. No one else gave us any hope. We've been grateful for your optimism and the ray of hope you gave us. I wish you could see our Joey now — he's fine! We could bring him here in the morning."

I remembered her boy, probably because I had seen him in that rare house call. He was the child who had not awakened after having his tonsils removed. "I'm glad he's all right. I'm sorry I can't see him, but we're leaving in the morning. We have an early flight to Tokyo."

In Los Angeles, we joined a tour group of doctors and their wives. We flew by Japan Air Lines. The first leg was a five-hour flight to Honolulu for an overnight stop. The next day, we took a seven-hour leg to Tokyo.

This trip across the Pacific compared strikingly to my earlier journeys by steamship. In the 1920s and '30s, the voyage by sea had demonstrated to me just how wide the Pacific Ocean was, and metaphorically how great the cultural gap that lay between Asia and America. Our boys had no way of knowing how that felt. At the same time, of course, they did not suffer the many weeks of seasickness I had experienced on my first childhood trip. If not as romantic as a sea voyage, certainly jet travel was much more efficient.

Of course, Japan had changed greatly since the 1930s. In Tokyo, we were met by Japanese guides and taken to the Imperial Hotel. I was startled at Haneda Airport by the crowds of Japanese waiting to meet friends and relatives. They vividly represented the phrase "population explosion." Yet the Japanese also remained orderly and unfailingly polite. They managed to conduct their affairs smoothly despite their numbers.

Tokyo had the appearance of the other large, modern cities we had seen. The Imperial Hotel's older section had been designed by Frank Lloyd Wright to survive earthquakes up to a certain degree. We stayed in a newer wing, but visited the original area.

While we were in Tokyo, every day seemed to be a holiday. The crowds of people were everywhere. The department stores, in particular, caught my attention. They were large, modern buildings with people in western-style uniforms who stood outside the elevators at each floor to call out the merchandise available there. Some of the larger stores had rooftop gardens with playgrounds for the children. The busiest location was the Tokyo railroad station.

While Cecile and the boys took tours of Tokyo, I visited hospitals and medical schools. I was surprised to learn that at one medical school, the medical library had been donated by the China Medical Board. The Japanese neurosurgeons were very good in presenting their papers at meetings and seminars.

From Tokyo, we took the "bullet train" to Kyoto. It was a fast, smooth ride and we were served Kobe steak on the way. The countryside was green, with budding trees, and we happened to get a rare glimpse of Mount Fuji because the clouds that usually surround its peak had cleared that particular day. In Kyoto, we stayed at the International Hotel, a more westernized establishment.

Our group held scientific sessions at the hotel and also at the University of Kyoto. I had the opportunity of scrubbing with one of the Japanese orthopedic surgeons in an operation for a ruptured intervertebral disc. His approach was different from mine, but not very much. Other members of our visiting group preferred just to observe.

We took the China Air Transport airline to Taiwan. Most of our group either remained longer in Japan or went on to Hong Kong where the rest of us would join them later. In Taiwan, we stayed at the Grand Hotel.

The Grand Hotel was in Taipei, built on Yuan Shan, a hill where the Japanese had previously built a temple when they had controlled the island prior to World War II. It was very ornate, designed in the style of traditional Chinese architecture. They quartered us in the new wing, called "Qilin Ting," or "Unicorn Wing." The red lacquered columns and long, level walkways reminded me of Chinese temples, theaters, and other buildings from many years earlier. I also had the first opportunity in a long time to speak Chinese directly to the clerks and room attendants. Our rooms opened on an exterior balcony overlooking the city of Taipei below and the river winding through it.

The day we checked into the hotel, the boys went out to find a place where they could change some U.S. money to local currency. While they were gone, a stranger called to invite us to dinner. He was Dr. S.K. Wang, a neurosurgeon at the National Defense Medical Center here in the Republic of China. Dr. Wang explained, in a warm and courteous manner, that he was conveying the invitation from Dr. Loo Chiteh, Director of the Medical Center and Superintendent of the Veteran's Hospital, which was the teaching hospital for the medical school. Dr. Wang told us that a car would arrive to pick us up at seven that evening, and we were honored to accept his invitation. However, we had no idea how they had known we were coming, nor why they wished to entertain us.

The island of Taiwan, and a few neighboring islands, were of course the only parts of China that remained under the control of the Nationalist Chinese government, or the Republic of China. Jiang Jieshi (Chiang Kaishek) and his followers had taken their final refuge from the Chinese Communists there in 1949, and subsequently had struggled to develop and maintain the independence and quality of life on Taiwan. However, it remained a dictatorship and a police state.

During the dinner that evening, Dr. Loo explained that we had a mutual friend and colleague in Dr. Leslie Cheng. Dr. Cheng, a graduate of PUMC, had been invited some years earlier by Drs. William and Carl Meninger to join their clinic in Topeka, Kansas. About a month earlier, I had casually mentioned to Dr. Cheng that I would be traveling to Taiwan, and that remark had led to our invitation.

Dr. Loo introduced us to most of the department heads of the National Defense Medical Center, and we gradually became friends with them in succeeding years. They were all dedicated professionals who wanted to rebuild PUMC, in a sense; at least, they wished to create a new facility in Taiwan that would carry on the same high standards as the center they had left behind in Beijing. I felt they had succeeded.

All the department heads had received some or all of their postgraduate training in Europe or America, so their medical knowledge was up to date. While they received minimal salaries compared to those in the U.S., their fringe benefits were substantial. The director of the hospital and the dean of the medical school received large houses, servants, cars, chauffeurs, and basic household needs. Department heads received a house, a servant, and household expenses. A small bus transported them to and from work each day.

Even with these fringe benefits, they did not receive enough cash to maintain a regular living. So they had proposed to the Ministry of Health that they open a private clinic to supplement their income. The government had allowed this, but ironically placed a ceiling on their income, much as a Communist government might do. All income over the ceiling went to the government. I admired their dedication, but I was glad I was not in this situation.

After a few days in Taiwan, we prepared to leave for Hong Kong. The flight took only an hour from Taipei. There, for the first time, my wife and children would meet my mother, my brothers, and their families. I would see them for the first time since 1935, almost three decades earlier.

Chapter Thirty

We arrived in late morning, Hong Kong time. A huge crowd jammed the airport waiting for various arriving flights, across a barrier inside the airport from customs and immigration. Cecile and I warned the boys to stay close to us, since they could not speak Chinese and might get lost very easily. Even worse, as we left customs and immigration, the shouts from the crowd to their friends and relatives created a deafening roar. I looked through the crowd anxiously, not sure what to do if I couldn't recognize anyone.

Finally I saw some people jumping up and down and calling my Chinese name. Just to their right, more hands were waving. I recognized two of my brothers, who pointed which way we should go to reach the exit. Then they all moved down to meet us.

My three brothers in Hong Kong had met us with their entire families. Even in the immense crowd at the airport, they made a large welcoming committee. I recognized them immediately, in spite of the years of separation, and they knew me. Many of us shed tears at this clumsy reunion in the mobbed airport, but in the confusion we did not even try to get everyone introduced properly. However, they received Cecile and our boys, strangers to them who spoke no Cantonese, very warmly.

From Kai-tak Airport, we boarded taxicabs and two private cars, one of which belonged to a cousin, Dr. S.K. Kwan, a surgeon educated in England. The entire entourage drove to the Ambassador Hotel. At that time, it overlooked Hong Kong Bay from the Kowloon side, though since then other buildings have obscured the view.

In the hotel, we had two comfortable connecting rooms that faced the harbor. We could see ocean liners, naval ships from various countries, small motor boats, sailboats, and even sampans. Across the water, we had a view of bustling Hong Kong Island, with Victoria Peak rising in the distance. All the children, whose ages ranged from three to twelve, gathered at the windows to look. Though the hotel was air conditioned, the crowd in the room warmed it, and we ordered Cokes and Seven Up for everyone.

In Chinese tradition, sons remain a part of their parents' clan, while daughters join the families of their husbands. For this reason, our branch of the Wu Clan now consisted of my mother as matriarch, myself and my family, my three brothers in Hong Kong and their families, and finally my brother remaining in Guangzhou and his family. Traditionally, my brothers and I were referred to by our order in the family; as the eldest brother, I was the first brother, the next oldest, Kwok Git, was the second brother, and so on.

As we all sat down and relaxed, we completed introductions. I met two of my sisters-in-law for the first time; a third had stayed home with my mother. At first, the conversation remained stilted because I had been gone so long and my wife and children could not speak directly to any of our relatives. However, Cecile greeted everyone with a hug and I shook hands with everyone except some of the shyest of my nieces and nephews.

We introduced the children to each other last. After a few minutes, they went into the other room and gradually began playing among themselves, even though a language barrier existed between our boys and their cousins. However, the eldest son of my second brother had learned some English in school and was only a year older than Billy. He had taken the English name Alfred and the two of them were able to communicate some.

Since I was the eldest son, my brothers and their wives were politely reserved in their manners. We talked briefly about the weather in Hong Kong and the short supply of drinking water at that time. Then I asked my brothers about our mother, who was living with Kwot Git's family in a fourth floor flat on Hong Kong Island. The only son of our fourth brother in Guangzhou also lived there; he had come out of China with his grandmother.

Kwok Git suggested we phone our mother. He called her and put me on. As soon as she heard my voice, she mumbled my name and began to cry. I had to hold back tears, too, in order to speak, but we did not get much of a conversation going. She did tell me that everyone had planned dinner together at Kwok Git's apartment that night, so we would see each other then.

My family needed to relax and unwind for a while. Our relatives left in the early afternoon, allowing us to unpack and become familiar with the hotel. We had already had an exciting day.

In the evening, Kwok Git arrived to escort us to his home. While many taxis were available, the boys wanted the novelty of taking the rickshaws they had seen waiting outside the hotel. All of the rickshaw had been painted bright red, and the men pulling them wore expensive watches and revealed several gold teeth when they smiled. Since the Star Ferry terminal lay only a few blocks from the hotel, we hired them for the short trip.

Kwok Git took the first one, since he would recognize the way. Billy took the second, while Cecile and Chris rode the next one together. I took the last one. On the way, we passed a group of well-dressed white tourists, who aimed cameras at us and began clicking away quickly.

"Don't get excited!" Cecile yelled. "We're from Kansas City!"

From the terminal, we rode the Star Ferry across Hong Kong Bay to Hong Kong Island. In the evening, the lights of the elaborate skyline on all sides created a magnificent view. Cecile and I began to feel more anxious about meeting my mother as we rode the slow, steady ferry to the other side.

From the terminal, we took two taxis through the crowded streets. Cecile and I held hands; while trying to appear calm and nonchalant, my heart started pounding as we approached our destination. Finally we arrived at the dirty, concrete apartment building.

The building had no elevators. Once we had climbed up four floors, I was surprised to see the apartment door already open. Several of the kids were waiting out in the hall already.

Kwok Git led us in, where my mother was sitting calmly in a chair just outside her tiny bedroom. She had been slightly over five feet tall in her prime, but now was wrinkled and shrunken with age. When she saw us, she started to rise, but I told her to stay seated. I hugged her gently, as did Cecile; then we introduced the boys to her.

While Mother began to speak Chinese as though all of us understood her, other relatives pushed chairs next to her. She took Cecile and me by the hand and pulled us to seats on each side of her. Cecile gave her a big hug and a kiss. My mother held our hands tightly as she talked to us.

In the meantime, our nieces and nephews watched and milled around the small apartment, while my sisters-in-law brought steaming tea to everyone. They served it in glasses because they did not have enough teacups for everyone. I interpreted for my mother and Cecile, though they really seemed to understand each other's warmth just fine without me.

As all of our relatives watched in the jammed little apartment, my mother next gestured for my sons to sit down on each side of her. Cecile and I stood up to give them our seats. She held their hands and spoke to them. The boys felt her love without understanding a single word that was said to them. Meanwhile, more relatives had arrived, and some were forced to stand out in the hall, for lack of room.

After a while, Billy joined Alfred and they continued to get acquainted. Chris, who became restless and uncomfortable in the strange surroundings, stayed close to Cecile as she continued to visit with my mother. None of their cousins his age could speak any English.

My mother arranged to have a variety of dishes cooked, with the help of all her daughters-in-law present, but especially Kwok Git's wife. When the dishes were ready, my mother had pork, chicken, and fish on a table placed in front of the little ancestral altar set high into one wall. Three teacups, each with a set of chopsticks to the left, were placed at the front of the table. My father's picture already stood on a shelf in the family altar, with his name written in Chinese on a red tablet beneath it.

According to Chinese tradition, each male in the family was expected to make a gesture of reverence. This meant standing before the table on which the food had been placed and bowing three times with hands clasped and raised over one's head at each bow. Then he would pour a small cup of wine across the floor at the foot of the table. These were gestures of respect and remembrance.

Since we would perform this ceremony in the order of my father's sons first, according to age, and then their sons, I was first in line. My mother, knowing that we were Christians, was alert enough to realize that I might not wish to do this. However, I did it without hesitation. I had done this before and felt that Jesus himself would not object to this gesture of reverence. My mother was obviously pleased.

I invited Billy to take part but he declined out of shyness; in fact, he had never seen or heard of this before and knew nothing about it. I did not pressure him. Chris was too young to understand it. We watched while our other male relatives participated, my brothers Kwok Git, Kwok Yiu, and Kwok Poon, and Ging Kwan, the eldest son of my fourth brother, representing his father.

To follow the ceremony, my brothers had arranged a banquet at a nearby restaurant. This was called a "xi chen" dinner in Mandarin, meaning literally to "wash dust" away after traveling. It was a custom passed down through the centuries.

We took a taxi, though most of our relatives walked. In the restaurant, we all sat around a large, round table. As the banquet began, Chris became restless and uncomfortable in the strange surroundings, where most of the people spoke only Chinese, and he announced that he was "going home." Though only in kindergarten, he was very big for his age and started to leave on his own. His mother had to swat him twice to convince him to stay. He ate very little at dinner.

My mother was concerned and Cecile felt self-conscious about spanking him in front of his relatives. However, no one objected, and my mother expressed her understanding of his discomfort. He eventually fell asleep in my arms. Billy was probably uncomfortable, too, but he tolerated the situation quietly.

In fact, many of the dishes were new to Cecile and the boys. Billy discovered shark's fin soup, which he has liked ever since. Other dishes included chicken, duck, roast pork, fish, abalone, sea slugs, and various vegetables, rice, and noodles. The adults drank tea, while the children had Cokes or Seven Up.

During the evening, I learned more details about my family's experiences during and after the Communist Revolution. My second brother, a graduate of the Guangzhou Police Academy, escaped to Hong Kong next, but had to leave his wife and son behind. He had arranged to get them to Hong Kong some years later. My father had been smuggled out of China as a common laborer by some of his students, in a small boat at night.

My third brother, a graduate of the National Military Academy at Du Shan, in Guizhou Province, had been fighting the Communists in Manchuria when he had been wounded. He had been sent home to recover, and during that time the Nationalists collapsed. Since he had fought for the losing side, he promptly left for Hong Kong. He had been the first of the family to go.

My fourth brother had just gotten married in Guangzhou at that time, and his father-in-law suggested that he and his bride not be swept up in mass flight. His father-in-law felt that the momentum of the Communist Revolution might sweep through Hong Kong as well, and that they would be safer remaining home in that event. He was wrong, of course, but my fourth brother and his wife had remained in China. My fifth brother also reached Hong Kong, and once my father and brothers had established themselves financially, they had all arranged for their families to join them.

Before my mother had escaped, she had been forced to endure the indignities of kangaroo courts, because she was the wife of a scholar. She had to kneel on broken glass during these "trials," and suffered other physical torture before she was imprisoned for a year. When she was released, relatives and friends helped her reach my fourth brother in Guangzhou, with whom she lived for a number of years. They nursed her back to health and she took their son out to Hong Kong with her when she was able to go. My fourth brother also had two daughters, who remained behind with their parents.

At the end of dinner, we had Sunkist oranges for dessert, with the brand name stamped on them. We departed about eleven P.M. and took a taxi back to the ferry terminal. Kwok Poon and his family lived on the Kowloon side of Hong Kong Bay, so they accompanied us back on the ferry. On the way, speaking English to each other, Cecile and I decided we could afford to help my mother and my second brother's family get a larger flat for their family, my mother, and my fourth brother's son. We were later able to arrange it.

As we took the ferry back across the bay at night, the ocean

250

breeze was cool, and the lights of both Hong Kong and Kowloon created a magnificent view. Lights from various ships in the harbor sparkled across the Bay, while the lights on Victoria Peak shone above the rest of the cosmopolitan city on both sides. Colorful neon signs advertised Rolex watches, Coca Cola, the Japanese department store Dai Maru, and many other brand names. The clock tower of the Guangzhou-Kowloon railroad station was lit, and reminded me of the Aloha Tower in Honolulu. Exhausted but happy, we walked back to the hotel.

❖

The next morning, I joined the medical members of our tour group again. We went to the University of Hong Kong's Queen Mary Hospital, located above the main business and financial sections of Hong Kong. The staff included both British Physicians and Chinese physicians trained in Britain. In a briefing session, the dean of the medical school proudly announced that Dr. Sun Yatsen had been one of their first two graduates.

We found the surgical departments and medical services up to American standards. I was surprised, though, by Dr. John Hunter, an Australian who was head of the Department of Neurological Surgery. He informed me that he was treating patients from Guangzhou because at that time Guangzhou lacked the facilities to take care of these patients. When they had recovered, they returned to China. This quiet cooperation between China and Hong Kong in the early 1960's was unknown to the world in general.

I also visited Dr. Li Shufun, a well-known thoracic surgeon, at the clinic and hospital he ran. I had first met him in 1948 when he had visited the Lahey Clinic and Massachusetts General Hospital. He also told me that he had been the official physician for the Chinese delegation when the U.N. was formed in San Francisco in 1945. At that time, he had seen my marriage proposal to Cecile when it appeared on the communications screens of all the delegations.

In the meantime, Cecile and the boys first stayed in the hotel and later went out shopping with some of our relatives. Chris became more comfortable with his surroundings, especially when more of their cousins came to visit. She assured me that they would manage without me for the day.

Late in the day, I returned to visit my mother alone, as I had promised the night before. Now we were able to catch up on the passing years in more detail. She recalled my childhood, recounting stories with delight, and then told me about my father and his last year living in Hong Kong, after they had finally been reunited. Her sadness over his passing was intermingled with joy in these memories.

My mother also expressed bitterness over her suffering during the early years of Communist rule. At the same time, she was generous in forgiving those who had subjected her to torture. I felt terrible for the pain and suffering she had experienced, but I admired the fact that my mother, who was very petite, had endured so much physical and mental abuse without losing her strength or her big heart.

We also talked about my brothers and their families and especially my sisters, all of whom were still in China with their own families. At that time, the political situation made contact with them impossible. I finally had to return to the hotel, but I told her I would come back for more such visits.

During our remaining days in Hong Kong, I stopped to talk with my mother as often as I could. In addition, Cecile and I looked up old friends from the University of Michigan who were now in Hong Kong. Mr. Ko Wingyu, a close friend in our student days, told us to let him know when we wanted to go shopping. He said, "With your American bow tie and crew cut, any shopkeeper in Hong Kong can see you're an American. The prices will go up automatically in most stores."

We took his advice. He and his wife accompanied us on our shopping trips and saved us a great deal of money with their knowledge of buying and haggling in Hong Kong. On subsequent trips, they continued to do this for us.

My brothers' children frequently came to the hotel to spend time with our sons. Though the language barrier was substantial, it did not prevent all the cousins from playing cards together and going to movies. Alfred and Billy took the younger kids along with them. They saw a number of movies; Billy particularly liked the "sword movies," cheaply produced Chinese historical films made popular by the Shaw Brothers. Every day, the kids rode the Star Ferry across the Bay to Hong Kong and back to Kowloon again. Chris had to make do with gestures toward his cousins, though of course he could always speak to his older brother. In both cases, however, they were able to establish a rapport with the cousins who were closest to them in age.

At that time, U.S. citizens were not allowed to travel in China itself. Our tour group did take a trip through the New Territories, the most northern section of the Hong Kong Crown Colony. The New Territories bordered on China and because we were a group of physicians, we were granted special permission to get as close a view as possible.

We were escorted to one of the British guard stations on a hilltop overlooking the Sumchun River and the small city of the same name beyond it. The river represented the boundary between the British colony and China. I could see several Chinese guards walking along the far river bank. One of them kicked dirt in front of him idly as he patrolled the border.

Three large boats sailed down the river. The British guards told us that they carried water daily from China to Hong Kong to help supply the colony's needs. A few years later, a pipeline was built to carry water directly along this route.

From this vantage point, I could almost imagine that I had returned to China. The hills and mountains, the villages, and the rice paddies lay almost within reach. Though my mother and most of my family were now in Hong Kong, my home village in Toisan remained out of reach. No one knew how long the "Bamboo Curtain" would remain closed.

On our last evening in Hong Kong, my second brother and his children came to the hotel to escort us back to their home again. By now, the trip across the bay had become familiar. This time, my mother would host our farewell dinner.

My mother met us at the door again. I had seen her several times since we had first visited, but this was our farewell, and it became another emotional scene. We performed another ceremony before the altar in honor of my father. This time, Billy chose to participate.

After another big dinner, late in the evening, my mother pulled both Billy and Chris next to her and spoke to them as she patted their hands and faces. The boys smiled and nodded as she told them to be good, diligent in school, and obedient to their parents and teachers. Later, when I translated for them, they laughed and complained that they had not known what they were agreeing to.

Finally, we said farewell to my mother. She was too frail to make the trip to the airport the next day.

In the morning, my second brother and his children came to the hotel. They escorted us to the airport, where the other families were waiting to see us off. Our farewell was sad, and my sisters-in-law all cried. The visit had been memorable for all of us, and we did not know how long we would have to wait before another reunion would be possible.

Cecile had finally met her in-laws, and the boys had seen something of their heritage. I had been very glad to see my mother and brothers again. However, I still wished to see China itself once more. I also felt that Taiwan and Hong Kong, while interesting, were poor substitutes, and I wanted Cecile and the boys to visit China someday. During the 1960's, though, that remained impossible.

Our visit to Hong Kong in 1963 brought us the first reunion I had had with my family in twenty-eight years. It still lacked my father, who had passed away, and my fourth brother and his family in Guangzhou and my three sisters in Toisan. However, our family identity remained strong and my brothers in Hong Kong had maintained a regular correspondence with our relatives in China which helped keep our ties close. All of us, in fact, had survived many of life's monsoons over the years.

Epilogue

Beginning several years later, we were able to return to Hong Kong during some of the summers in the 1960s and '70s. My mother, in fact, lived into her nineties, so I was finally able to see her more often in these years than any time since I had first left home as a child. Our boys truly made friends with their cousins as they all grew older. These family reunions over the years added a new dimension to our lives. My wife and children became part of a larger family, as we formed a bond that crossed the Pacific.

During these trips, Cecile and I learned that the population pressure in Hong Kong had created severe competition among high school graduates for limited college openings in the colony. We decided to make an offer to my brothers. If the eldest child of each brother could receive acceptance into an American college or university, we would sponsor their coming. Since their ages were staggered, we were ultimately able to help some of their younger siblings, too; as a result, as they reached college age, seven of my nephews and two nieces, and also the grandson of one of my sisters, came either through our direct sponsorship or partial assistance; some were able to earn scholarships on their merit and obtain summer jobs.

In the same period, I had a successful career in Kansas City because of the recognition from my colleagues and the public. The segregation of the local medical society was long over, of course, and many doctors of Asian and African descent followed me into careers locally. In fact, most did not know the recent history that had preceded them.

While Kansas City General Hospitals I and II remained segregated, I donated voluntary work to them three months of the year. When these outmoded hospitals were replaced by Truman Medical Center, I served there and in the early '80s, I ended my private practice to work there full time. Over the years, I also became a Professor

255

of Surgery at the University of Missouri at Kansas City Medical Center and remained so until my retirement in 1991.

Our family joined St. Andrew's Episcopal Church in Kansas City, Missouri, where both our sons were baptized. While they were young, Cecile taught Sunday school. Billy participated as an acolyte through his teenage years, but Chris did not.

During the years of the civil rights movement, I served on the church's Committee of Community Concern. Our congregation was nearly all white. A similar group from a church in the black community challenged us to meet and participate in mutual visits and joint church attendance to promote greater understanding and communication between the two congregations and institutions. Being of Asian origin, I felt caught in the crossfire between the blacks and whites, but the experience was illuminating.

I never really lost the desire to return to China and help with medical care, as I had intended just before the Communist Revolution ended my chance to work at Yale-in-China. However, during the sixties and seventies, I was able to take additional trips to Taiwan and Hong Kong, always bringing the entire family. On these trips, we always saw my mother and my brother's families. Also, I led seminars and gave lectures at various medical institutions. In this way, I maintained cultural contact with my origins and made a medical contribution as well. I focused on improving medical care, rather than on politics because I always felt that the profession of medicine transcended politics. Everyone deserved sound medical treatment.

In the seventies, Billy attended the University of Michigan for both undergraduate and graduate school. Chris went to Shimer College in Illinois as an undergraduate and graduated from the University of Michigan Law School, so both our sons continued our family tradition at Michigan. Since Cecile's parents had both been students there as well, they represented the third generation of the family to study in Ann Arbor.

In 1975, Cecile and I had an unexpected opportunity to join a group of American physicians organized in New England to visit China. We met with Chinese doctors and toured medical facilities. It was a thrilling trip that also allowed us to visit my fourth brother and his family in Guangzhou. I had not seen him since he had been a child in the 1930s.

In May of 1978, I received a call from my youngest brother in Hong Kong, reporting that my mother had passed away. She had been living with his family for the past few years. The call was a shock, even though she was ninety-three years old; we had visited her again only eight months before and she had been lively and talkative. In fact, my brother told me that she had been walking around the apartment chatting with a neighbor only the day before, her mind still sharp. After dinner, she had gone to bed; the next morning, her heart simply stopped.

In Chinese tradition, my mother had been a matriarch of our branch of the Wu family, though she had too kind a heart to exercise authority abusively. On one occasion in the early nineteen-seventies, Kwok Git's wife had expressed concern over her son Alfred's long hair when he returned from college in the U.S. to visit. My mother had reminded her that my father had once worn a queue down the middle of his back. Alfred was a remarkably good student and my mother had seen that his hair length was simply irrelevant.

My mother was a model of strength and character, demonstrating wisdom, a good memory, and a subtle sense of humor during our visits over the years. After spending much of my life without her, I had finally been able to re-establish a closeness with her. We often reminisced about my early childhood, and I remembered that I had thought she was partial to me because I was the eldest son. Later, I realized that she had been "partial" to each of her children; in that sense, she was a real mother.

I felt a great void when she passed away, but I was glad that she had lived a long, full life and had remained active to the end. My brothers assured me that they would take care of the funeral arrangements. Cecile and I paid our respects on our next trip back to Hong Kong.

After diplomatic normalization occurred between the two countries in 1979, more opportunities to visit China developed. Cecile

257

and I became active first in the U.S. - China People's Friendship Association, an organization of ordinary citizens seeking to make cultural and professional contacts between the two countries without political involvement. We later joined the Edgar Snow Memorial Fund, Inc., dedicated to scholarly exchanges. Usually together, but not always, we made another seventeen trips to China, Hong Kong, and Taiwan, always including visits to relatives. Cecile was even able to visit Xiamen, the home of her father whom she had never really known, and she met some relatives on his side of her family.

In 1980, I took our elder son, now calling himself Bill, back to the village in Toisan where I was born. By this time, he had a Ph.D. in American Culture and was a published author, having continued writing all his life. A few years later, I took Chris back as well; he had become a lawyer in California and Director of Legal Services for Children — and also bowled professionally, having remained devoted to the sport. One of my sisters still lived in the village, and another lived in a neighboring village. They had pictures of our family from the Kansas City area that I had sent to Hong Kong as far back as the sixties. My brothers there had passed them on, so when I arrived with my sons, their cousins recognized them.

I thought of my father when we were back in the village. As an Imperial Scholar, he had been a learned individual who commanded respect and admiration from his peers, the clan, and family. As a child in the village, I had wanted to emulate him; I was frequently teased as the "Prince of the Wu Dynasty." He gave me much advice along the way, even by correspondence after I had moved to the U.S. Perhaps by traditional custom and maybe because I had left home as a child, I felt a closeness yet an invisible distance. I loved him no less, but I had felt closer to my mother. In the end, after leaving so young, I had not been able to form a new father-son relationship in adulthood as I had with my mother, because he had died before I could see him in Hong Kong. Yet my feeling for him endures.

During these years, I was able to maintain professional contacts and friendships in Taiwan and Hong Kong as well as form new ones in China. Professional diplomats and my medical colleagues understood that our purpose was medical and not political. Some ordinary citizens objected to our participation with China because the government remained Communist.

Professionally, the most satisfying visit took place in the middle '80s, when Professor Henri Walder of the Netherlands was president of the International Society of Neurological Surgeons. In 1984, we met with officials of the Chinese Medical Association asking them to permit Chinese neurosurgeons to participate in the organization. They refused, because Taiwan was a member. The next year, Dr. Alan R. Hudson hosted the Society's annual conference in Toronto. He extended an official invitation to the Chinese Medical Association but did not receive a reply. On my next trip to China, I talked to officers of the association, suggesting that they respond. The association did not give in, but ultimately individual Chinese neurosurgeons were authorized by their own institutions to attend specialized conferences outside China, ignoring the stand of the Chinese Medical Association. I was pleased that the result was greater exchanges of medical knowledge internationally.

I also wanted to inform the public in Kansas City about these efforts. Beginning in the middle seventies, I wrote many letters to the Kansas City Times and Kansas City Star, most of which were published, about the efforts of many people to promote cultural exchanges based on the welfare of ordinary citizens. In addition, I gave talks both locally and elsewhere when I could. The response over the years has generally been favorable.

In 1990, I was honored by the Edgar Snow Memorial Fund, Inc., with a banquet to introduce the Dr. William Q. Wu Scholarship at the University of Missouri at Kansas City. Recipients of the fund would be either Chinese students coming to study at UMKC, or American students at that school who were studying China.

The following year, I was honored at the Metropolitan Medical Society's annual meeting. This organization had formerly been the Jackson County Medical Society that had not allowed non-white physicians to practice before my arrival in 1950. In 1990, they gave me their Merit Award for professional and educational contributions to local medicine.

These two honors were unexpected, and I greatly appreciated

them. However, the event I prized the most occurred the day after Thanksgiving in 1992. Our sons and all their cousins who were in the U.S., and their families, came back to Kansas City for a reunion.

The family banquet, hosted by their generation, was held in a local Chinese restaurant. Including spouses, fourteen members of our children's generation were present, some with children of their own, including Chris's wife Jenny and their son, Michael. Among the fourteen, Cecile and I counted seven Ph.D.'s, four master's degrees, two M.D.s, one law degree, and one bachelor's degree still in progress. As Cecile and I looked over them, we felt a mixture of humility and pride.

Cecile and I have had our struggles in life, but we finally emerged from each with a new sense of accomplishment and purpose. We have been especially blessed in the love that has bound our family together in ways that allowed each of those who followed to develop their own confidence and skills. They all took advantage of what we could provide to enhance their own lives.

A meaningful life is rewarded by the achievements of the generations that follow. When my grandfather first told me of America the night after the monsoon had cleared over our peasant village in Toisan, he was hoping that our family would take advantage of the opportunities in the U.S. to better ourselves. Our children and their cousins represent the third generation after his, and of course they never met him. Yet I think he would be pleased with the results.

William Q. Wu, M.D.

Dr. William Q. Wu, now a retired, internationally respected neurosurgeon in the Kansas City area, was born in a small peasant village in southern China. He came to the U.S. at the age of eleven without his family and grew up in the Chinatown of Philadelphia at an uncle's restaurant. With hard work and the help of a caring teacher, he attended the University of Michigan.

In 1942, as a surgical resident, he volunteered for the U.S. Army though immigrants from China were prevented by law from becoming naturalized U.S. citizens. Assigned to the 22nd Field Hospital in which about half of the men were Chinese Americans, he became a U.S. citizen after the law was changed. His unit was sent to the China-Burma-India Theater where he was awarded the Bronze Star.

His wife, Cecile, contracted a mysterious disease six months after their wedding in 1945 and he diagnosed it as myasthenia gravis when her doctors could not. While tending her, he trained to become a neurosurgeon in the late 1940s. They moved to Kansas City in 1950, where he became the first non-white doctor accepted into the local medical society. Now, after forty-six years in the Kansas City area, they have celebrated their fiftieth wedding anniversary and have remained active in many civic affairs, including the William Q. Wu Merit Scholarship Fund at the University of Missouri in Kansas City. They have two sons, William F. Wu and Christopher N. Wu.

Dr. William Q. Wu
Merit Scholarship Fund

The Dr. William Q. Wu Merit Scholarship Fund was established by Dr. Wu in 1990 for the purpose of assisting Chinese students studying at the University of Missouri in Kansas City or UMKC students studing China.

If your are interested in receiving further information pertaining to participation in the Dr. William Q. Wu Merit Scholarship Fund, please address inquiries to:

Dr. William Q. Wu Merit Scholarship Fund
UMKC
5100 Rockhill Road
Kansas City, MO
64110

Thank You

DO YOU KNOW SOMEONE
WHO WOULD LIKE THIS BOOK?

"*MONSOON SEASON* Makes A Great Gift!"

Yes, I would like to order *Monsoon Season* Please send me
____ copies at $10.00 plus $3.00 S&H. Allow 1 - 2 weeks
for delivery. Send check or money order now in U.S. funds,
payable to:

> **UniStar Publishing, Inc.**
> **P.O. Box 27740,**
> **Las Vegas, NV 89126**

Name ————————————————————————

Address————————————————————————

City, State & Zip————————————————————

Day time telephone ————————————————

Summary:——— copies @ 10.00 each   ——————

Add Shipping & Handling @ $3.00 per book   ——————

(*Nevada Residents add 7%* sales tax)   ——————

TOTAL . . . . ——————

If you would like to order in quantity, please write or call for
prices: Sales Department, UniStar Publishing. (801) 233-9319

UniStar BONUS #1
MONSOON SEASON

Order 2 or more Books and Save $1.00 per Book

- Refer to "UniStar BONUS #1".
- Deduct $1.00 from price of each book ordered.
- Offer valid while supply lasts.

(Coupon not redeemablefor cash)   4/96